I0793231

IMAGES
of America

POCONO AND JACKSON TOWNSHIPS

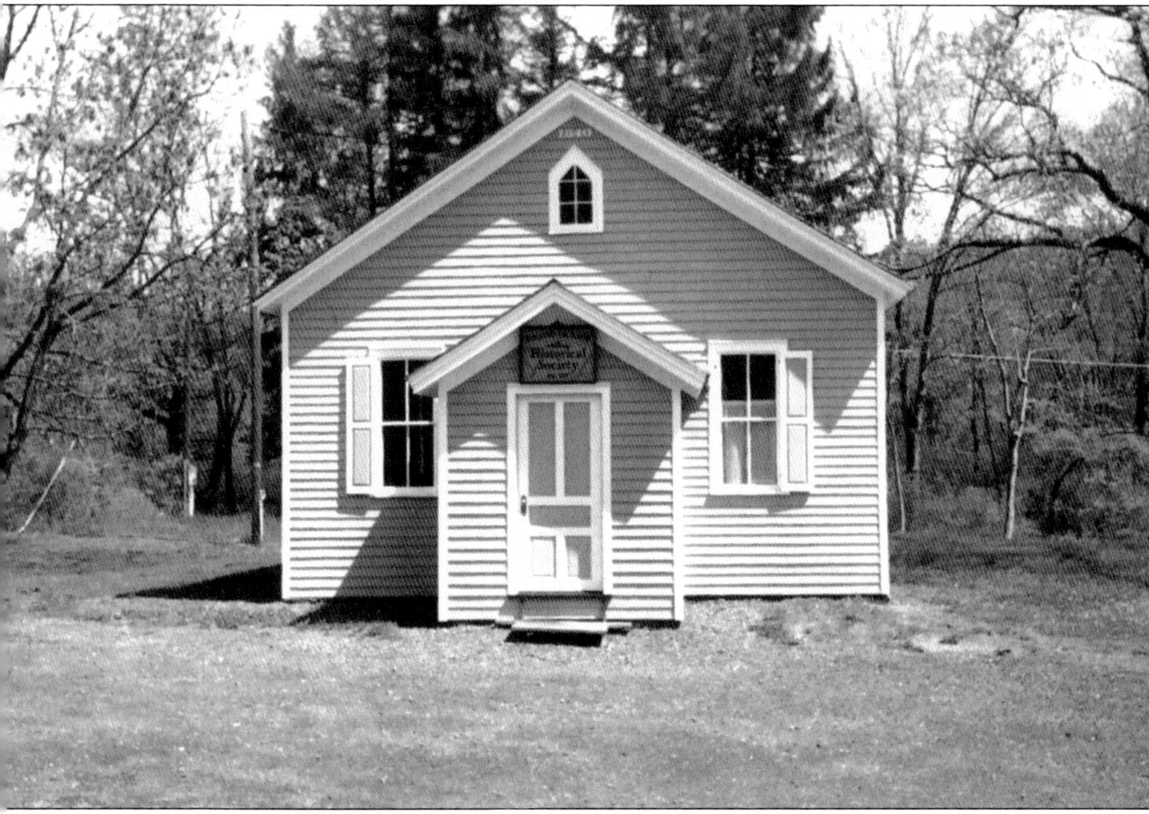

The original Appenzell School was built of logs, torn down in 1874, and replaced with a frame structure. This school was destroyed by an October 18, 1874, fire that was deliberately set. The present-day school was built in 1875, and restoration by the Pocono-Jackson Historical Society was completed in 2005. Notable teachers were John Frailey, Hannah Kresge Shupp, James A. Wallingford, John Ruehlman, Blanche Reimel, Romaine Reimel, Marion Hobbs, and Libby Small. (Courtesy of the Pocono-Jackson Historical Society.)

On the cover: This photograph from the late 1800s shows a covered freight wagon in front of the Learn and Waas store at the intersection of present-day Route 611 and Route 715N in Tannersville. (Courtesy of George Learn.)

IMAGES
of America

POCONO AND JACKSON TOWNSHIPS

Pocono-Jackson Historical Society

ARCADIA
PUBLISHING

ISBN 978-0-7385-7218-5

Published by Arcadia Publishing
Charleston SC, Chicago IL, Portsmouth NH, San Francisco CA

Printed in the United States of America

Library of Congress Control Number: 2009930318

For all general information contact Arcadia Publishing at:
Telephone 843-853-2070
Fax 843-853-0044
E-mail sales@arcadiapublishing.com
For customer service and orders:
Toll-Free 1-888-313-2665

Visit us on the Internet at www.arcadiapublishing.com

This book is dedicated to all the people, living and dead, who cared enough through the years to save the wonderful photographs presented in this book and in some manner provided information for the captions about the people and places.

Contents

ACKNOWLEDGMENTS

We wish to extend a sincere thank-you to those persons who provided so many wonderful photographs and memories. Without their assistance and support, this publication would not have been possible. One of those friends was Amy Leiser, executive director of the Monroe County Historical Association, who opened the association's boxes and files to us and gave so willingly of the many interesting and special photographs that added so much to this work.

A special thanks to George Prosser, president of the Pocono-Jackson Historical Society; book committee chairperson Marie Starner Guidry; and committee members Diane Davis Abeel, John Alleger, Robert Demarest, Olive Metzger Learn, James Price, Verdon Rustine, Clyde Wallingford, James Werkheiser, and Linford Werkheiser, who met week after week to give their time and talents to organize the photographs and provide captions. Thank you to Alice Cyphers, who originally suggested the project. Also we must thank those many members of the Pocono-Jackson Historical Society who came month after month with envelopes and albums full of photographs to share with the committee. We heard many stories of "remember when?" We would be remiss to leave out the generosity of the Appenzell St. Mark's Community Lutheran Church and the Bartonsville Masonic Hall, which opened their doors for our book meetings.

Also thank you to Erin Vosgien, editor at Arcadia Publishing, for her patience and assistance as we put the images on paper. As we go to press, thank you to each and every person who provided photographs and memories for what is truly a celebration of community spirit.

INTRODUCTION

When the older residents of Pocono and Jackson Townships get together at the church, fire hall, or any meeting place, they more often than not say "remember when?" And for those who have an interest in the history and people of the townships, they lean in close in an effort to add to mental photographs of the area and how it came to be.

In the years prior to the Revolutionary War, the area that later was named Pocono Township was made up of mostly uninhabited land. Early records indicate the first settler, John Learned, came to the area about 1740. Eighty years later, the population numbered less than 600 persons. Many of these early settlers came from Germany through Bucks County, which lies to the south.

Monroe County, which encompasses Pocono and Jackson Townships, was formed from Northampton County in 1836. Pocono was decreed a township in 1816 and subsequently divided in 1843 into what is present-day Pocono and Jackson Townships.

Through the years, the area that later was named Pocono Township was a base for farming and timbering where numerous early sawmills were built. Tanneries, for which the village of Tannersville is named, came on the scene in the 1830s, with hotels and stores soon following. The largest tannery located in Pocono Township burned in 1884 for the third time, and with it, the economy attached to this industry declined. Ice harvesting took place during cold winters on local lakes, with railroad spurs being built to transport the ice to distant markets.

Many one-room schools were built throughout the townships starting about 1818. However, beginning in the 1920s, these schools began to close in favor of a "consolidated and high school" in Tannersville for Pocono Township students. Jackson Township students had to pay tuition to be able to attend this school.

In the late 1800s, people began coming to the area by railroad, bus, and automobile from New York and Philadelphia to take in the cool mountain air. The area became part of what is now known as the Pocono Mountains of northeastern Pennsylvania, which attracted many tourists each year. Summer camps for children dotted the landscape, with names like Camp Akiba, Camp Cherith, Lindenmere, Massad, Pinemere Camp, and others. The pristine cold water creeks and wooded landscape provided ample fishing and hunting opportunities for sportsmen.

The resort industry experienced a decline beginning in the 1950s with the closing of many of the large resort hotels. However, a recent resurrection has occurred with the development of a year-round ski and water park and a major shopping outlet located nearby. These two attractions have generated a need for hotel and restaurant services to exist in the area.

Interstate 80 was built in the early 1960s and courses directly through Pocono and Jackson Townships. This road has provided easy access to the area from points east and west and has lead to the development of a bedroom community for New York and New Jersey commuters. The communities continue to draw people with many interests, including shopping, sports, and the area's natural beauty. Those who call it home take pride in Pocono and Jackson Townships and their unique history.

One

BUSINESSES, LARGE AND SMALL

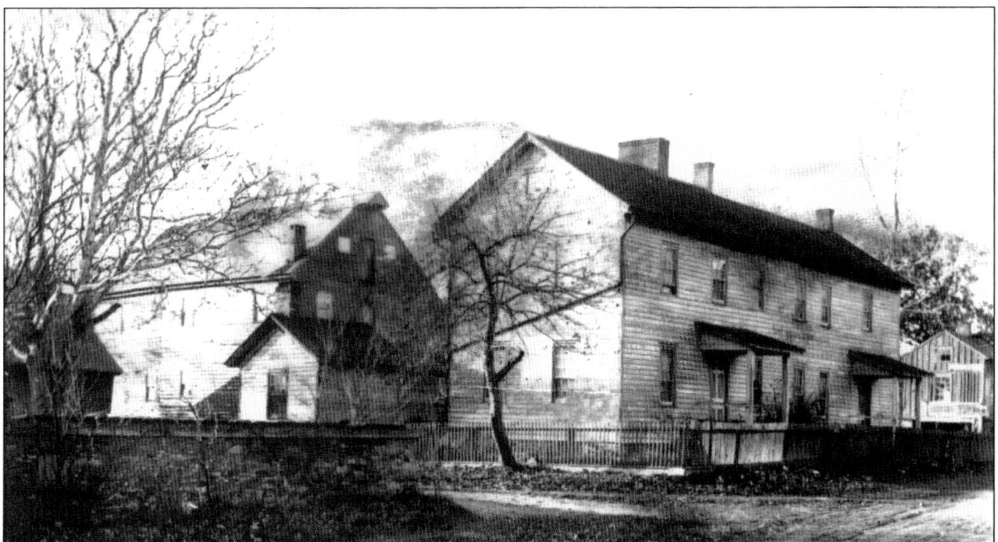

Kistler's Mill was located to the north of Glenwood Hall behind what appears to be a multifamily home. The mill was torn down when the Pocono Township Consolidated and High School was built in 1924 and 1925. (Courtesy of the Pocono-Jackson Historical Society.)

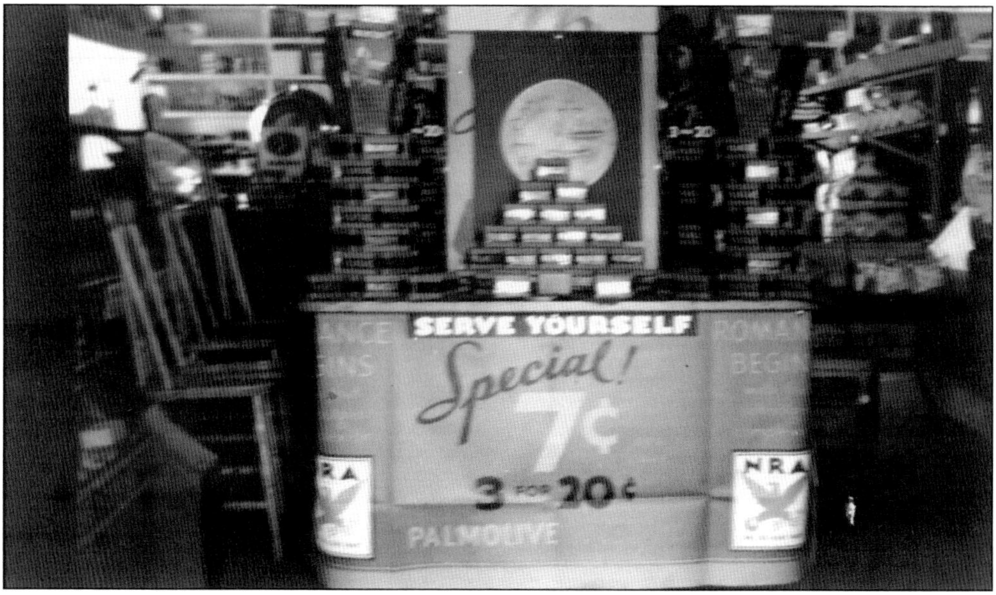

The Wallingford store interior features a sale on Palmolive soap during the early 1930s, as evidenced by the National Recovery Act sign common to the Depression years. (Courtesy of Robert Wallingford.)

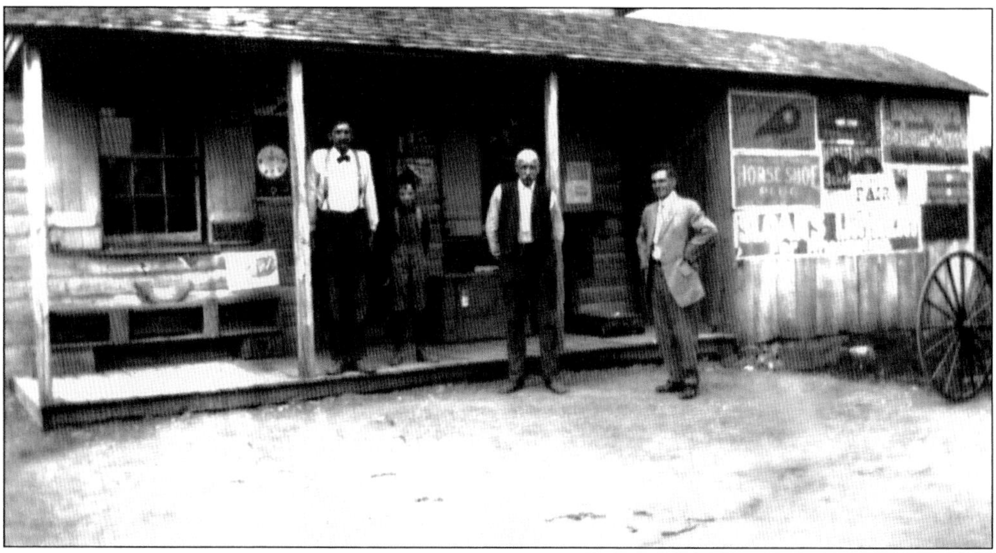

Records show that the first store in Jackson Corner, now known as Appenzell, was built by John Osterhack of New York. The first post office was located in the store, and W. H. Rhinehart was its first postmaster. Shown in the photograph are Aaron Smith, Amandas Possinger, Stanton Smith, and an unidentified boy. This photograph was taken prior to 1918, when the Wallingford family purchased the store. (Courtesy of Diane Davis Abeel.)

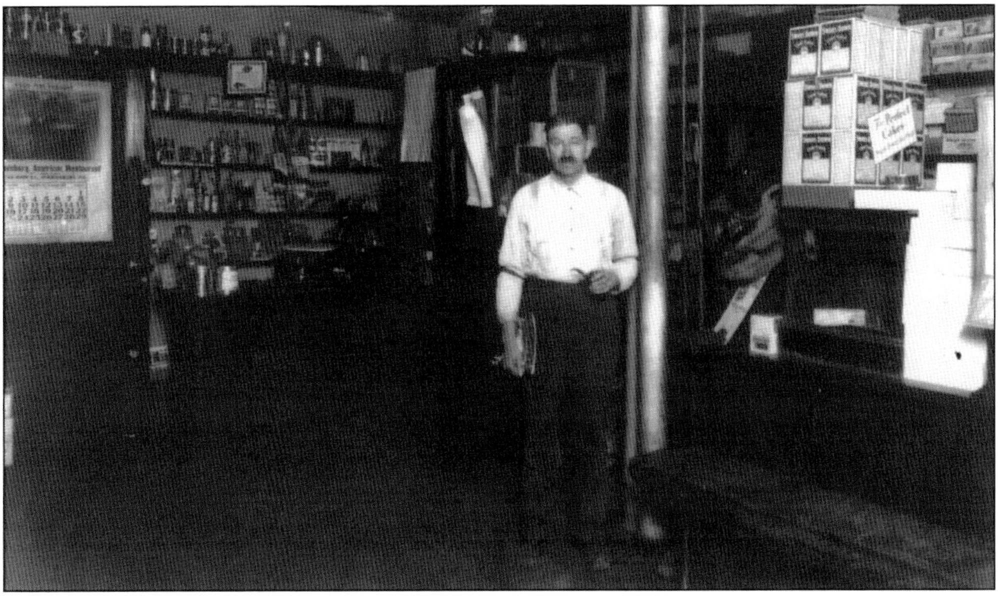

This 1930 photograph shows storekeeper and postmaster John Alleger Sr. (1876–1946) inside the Bartonsville general store that he owned along with his wife, Daisy (1883–1974). He served as postmaster from 1912 until his death in 1946. The Bartonsville Post Office remained in the Alleger home from 1912 until 1989, when it moved to its present location on Route 611 north of the village center. (Courtesy of John Alleger.)

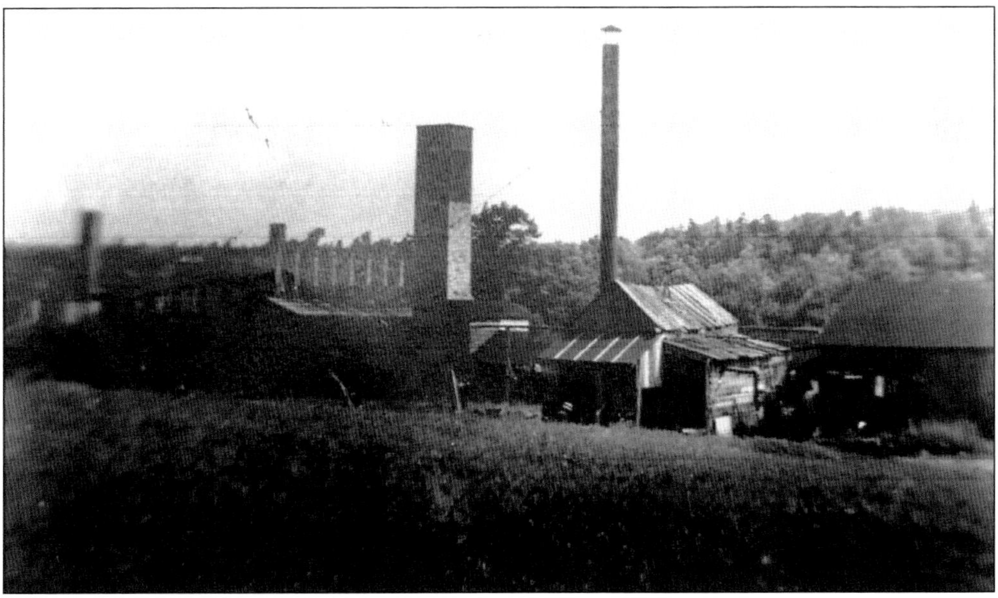

The Pocono Brick Company was located in White Oak Run along Sullivan Trail. The Wilkes-Barre and Eastern Railroad stopped here to pick up bricks. The property was eventually purchased by Daniel Wise and later became a housing development. (Courtesy of Patricia Widdoss Hennings Bonser.)

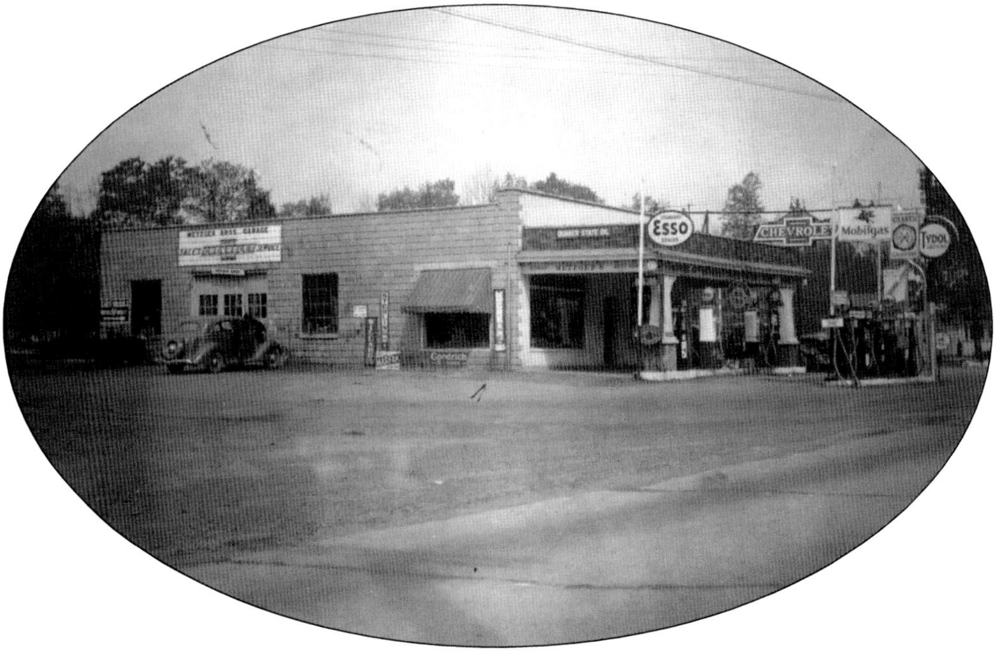

Edward and Thomas Metzger purchased this garage at the Tannersville intersection of Route 611 and Route 715S from Fred Scheller in 1929. This photograph shows at least four different brands of gasoline for sale. The business was also a Chevrolet dealership that was sold to Louis Gray in 1953. This building is now Citizens Bank. (Courtesy of Olive Metzger Learn.)

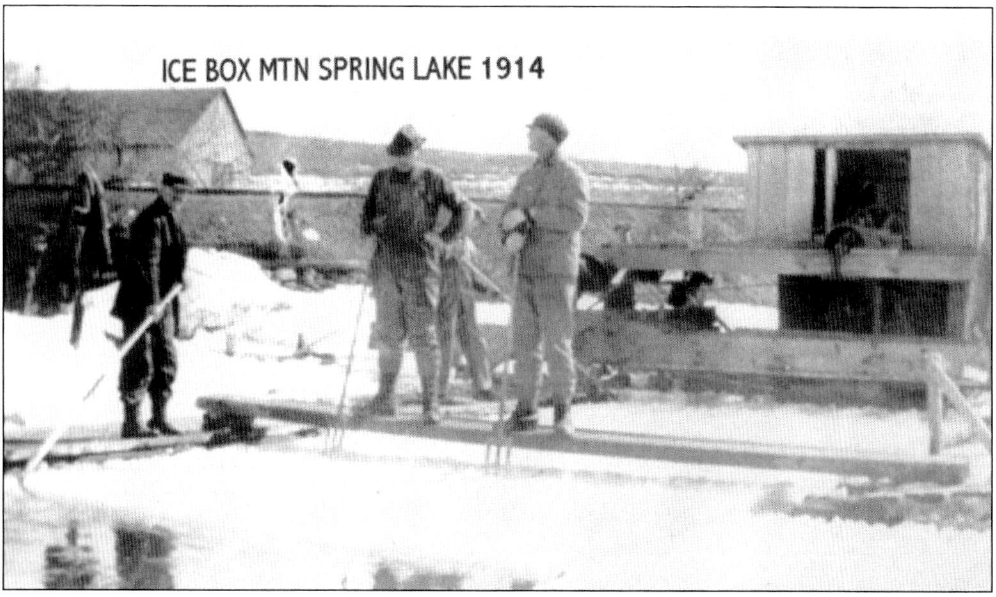

This photograph shows the water box used to float ice cakes during ice harvesting on Trout Lake. Ice blocks were cut and floated into the water box, where the ice was broken with spud bars along the score marks. (Courtesy of the Pocono-Jackson Historical Society.)

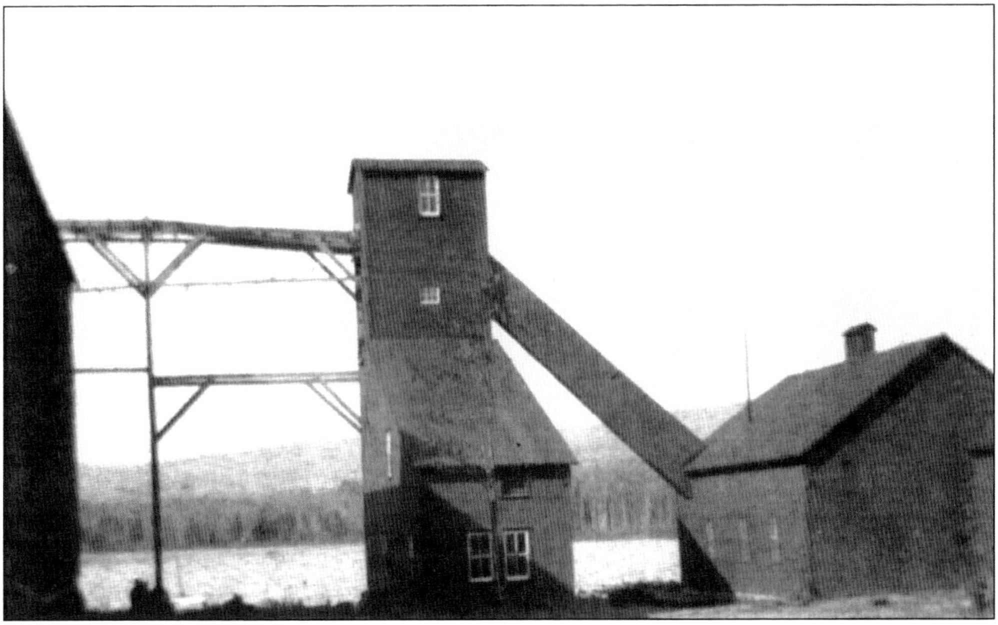

The ice blocks were then loaded onto a conveyor belt powered by steam to raise them for storage in the icehouses. (Courtesy of the Pocono-Jackson Historical Society.)

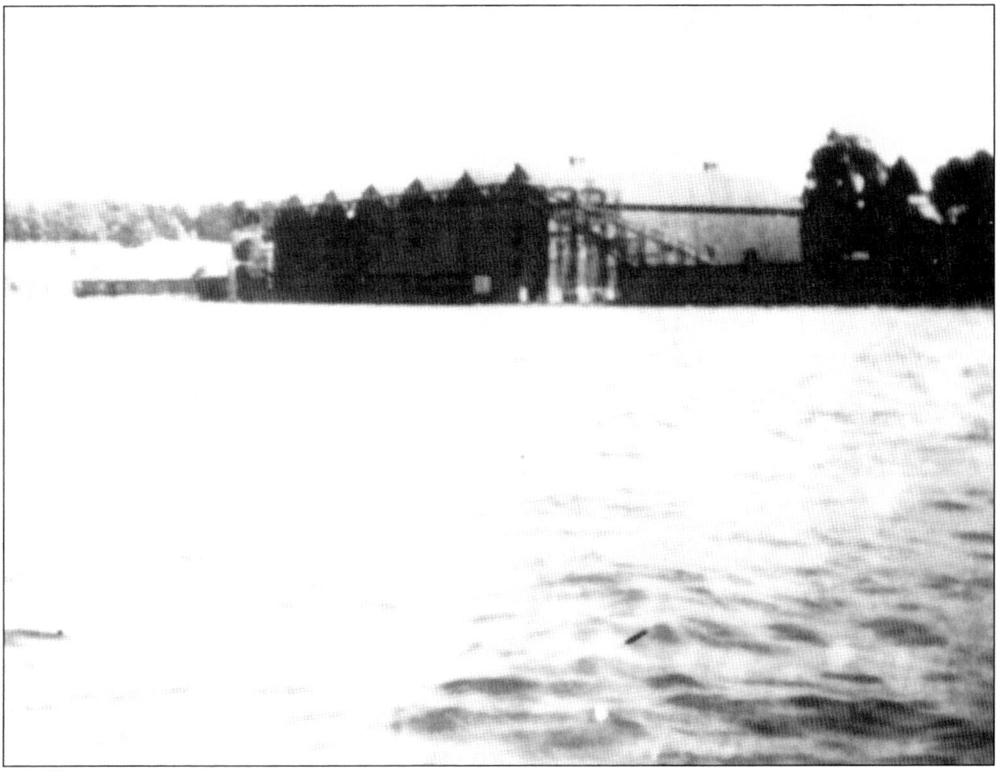

During the 1890s, Trout, Gruber, and Mountain Spring Lakes were constructed for the purposes of supplying ice to Philadelphia and points beyond. A railroad spur was laid to the icehouses. (Courtesy of the Pocono-Jackson Historical Society.)

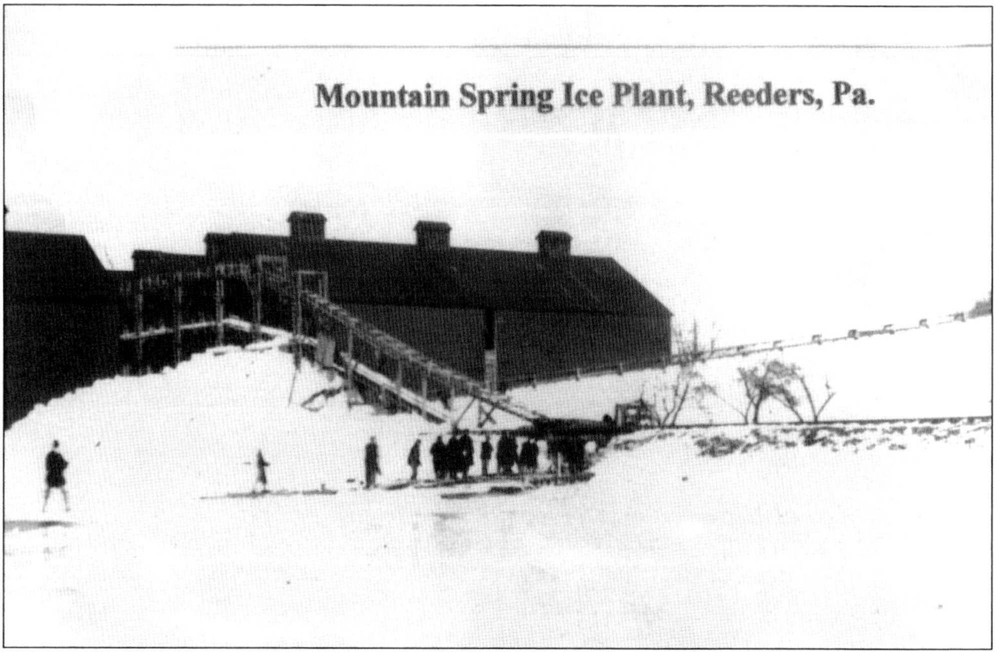

The icehouses were among the largest structures in existence at that time, with each compartment four stories high and 100 feet long. In this photograph, the Mountain Spring Lake icehouses dwarf the workers as they pull the ice blocks into the water box and place them on the conveyor belt to be lifted into the icehouses for storage. (Courtesy of the Pocono-Jackson Historical Society.)

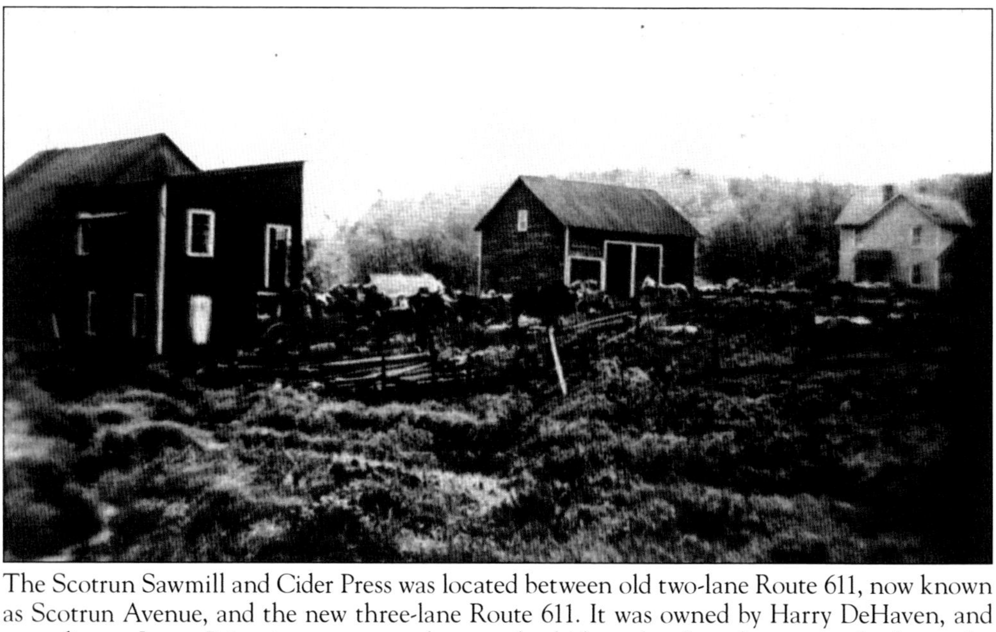

The Scotrun Sawmill and Cider Press was located between old two-lane Route 611, now known as Scotrun Avenue, and the new three-lane Route 611. It was owned by Harry DeHaven, and according to James Price, it was a great place to play hide-and-seek and get a sip of cider in the fall. This photograph was taken prior to 1918. (Courtesy of Verdon Rustine.)

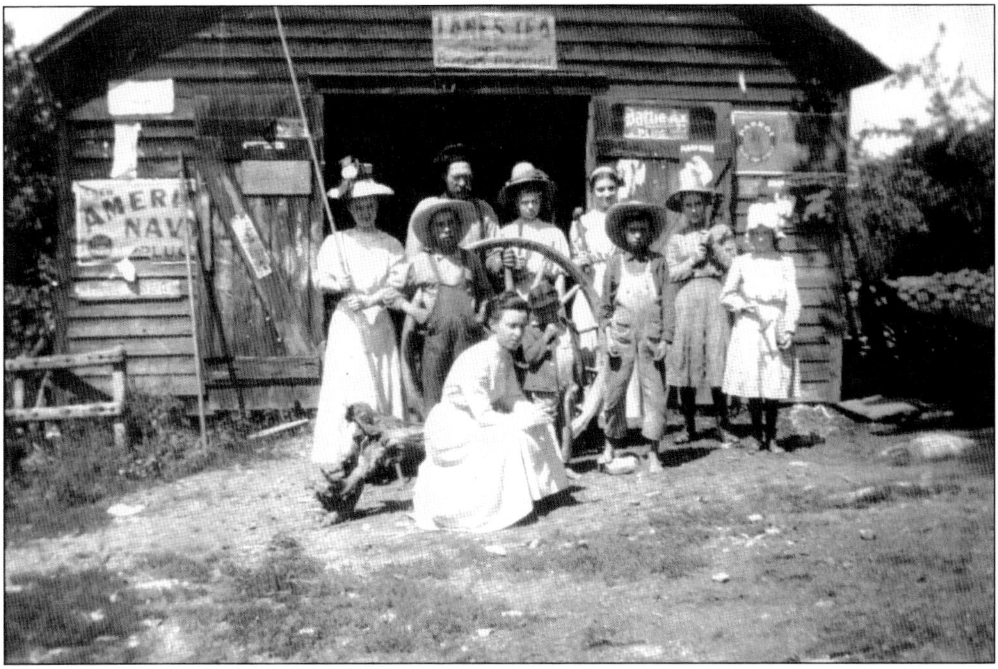

The blacksmith shop shown in this photograph was owned by Ulysses Everett and located in Appenzell directly across from the Wallingford store. The occasion for the women to pose for the photograph is unknown. (Courtesy of Robert Wallingford.)

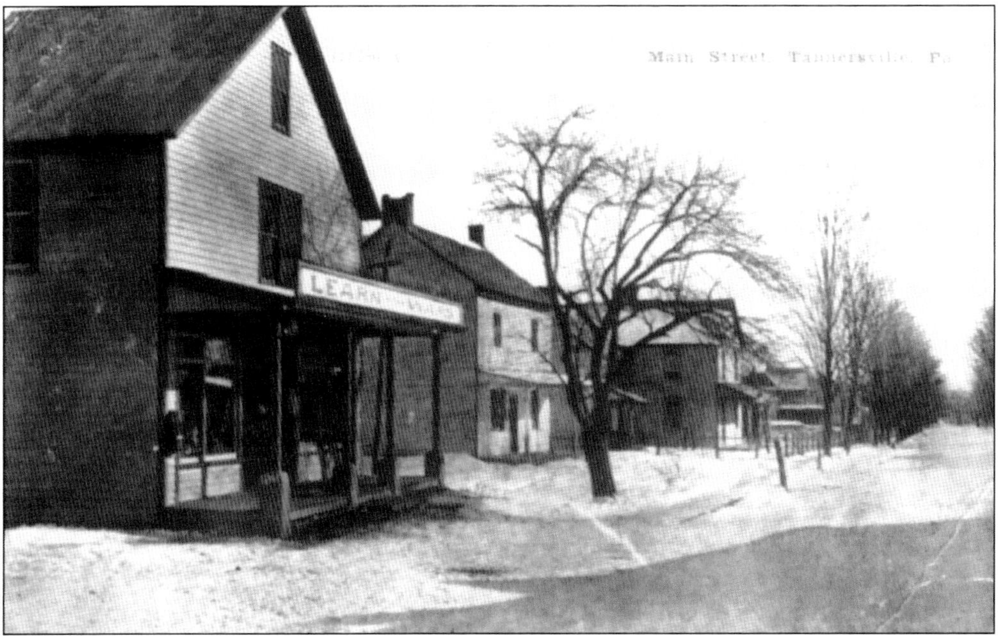

The Learn and Waas store was located at the intersection of present-day Route 611 and Route 715N. Charles Waas was Addison Learn's brother-in-law. The store went out of business in 1949. The site of the store is now a vacant lot. (Courtesy of George Learn.)

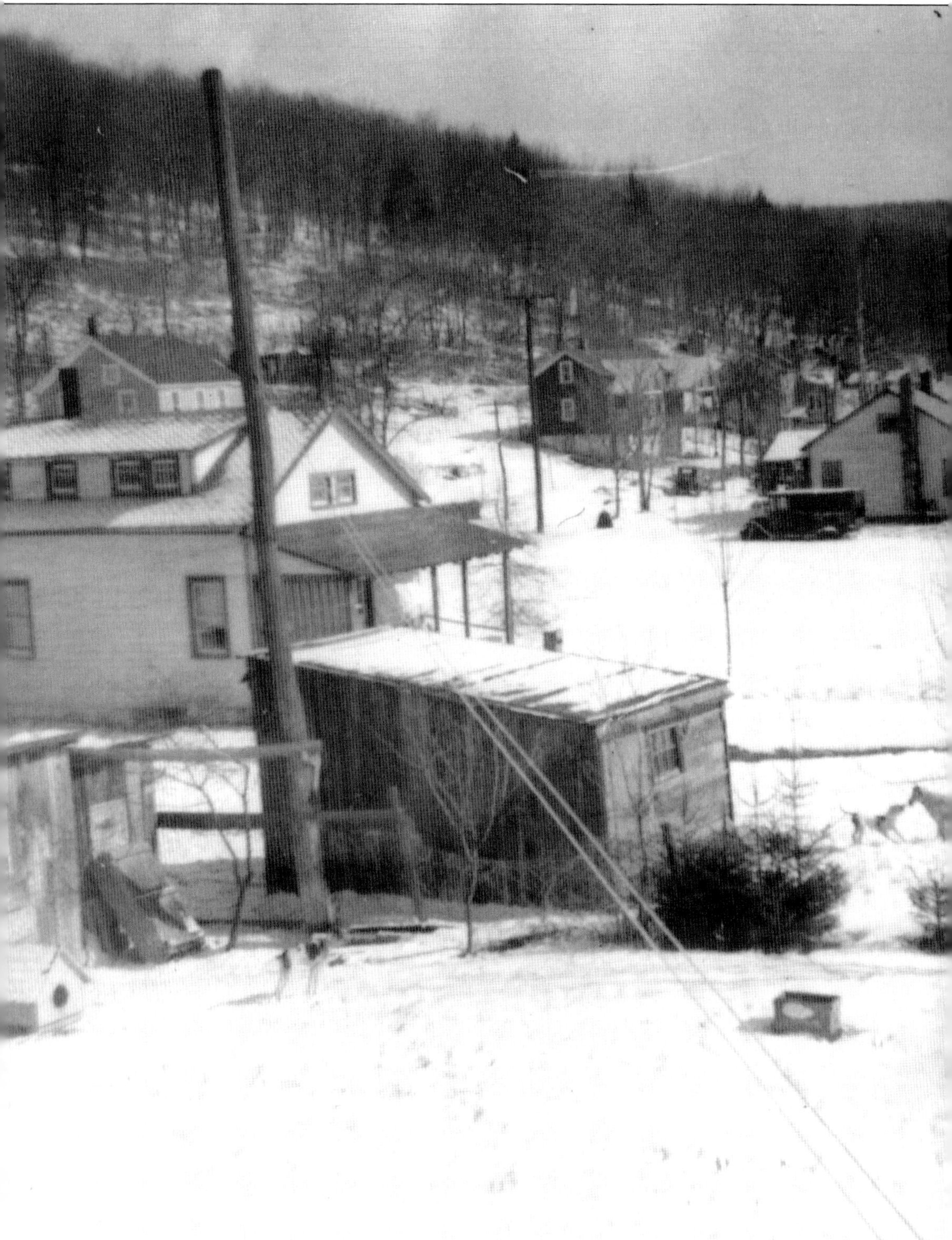

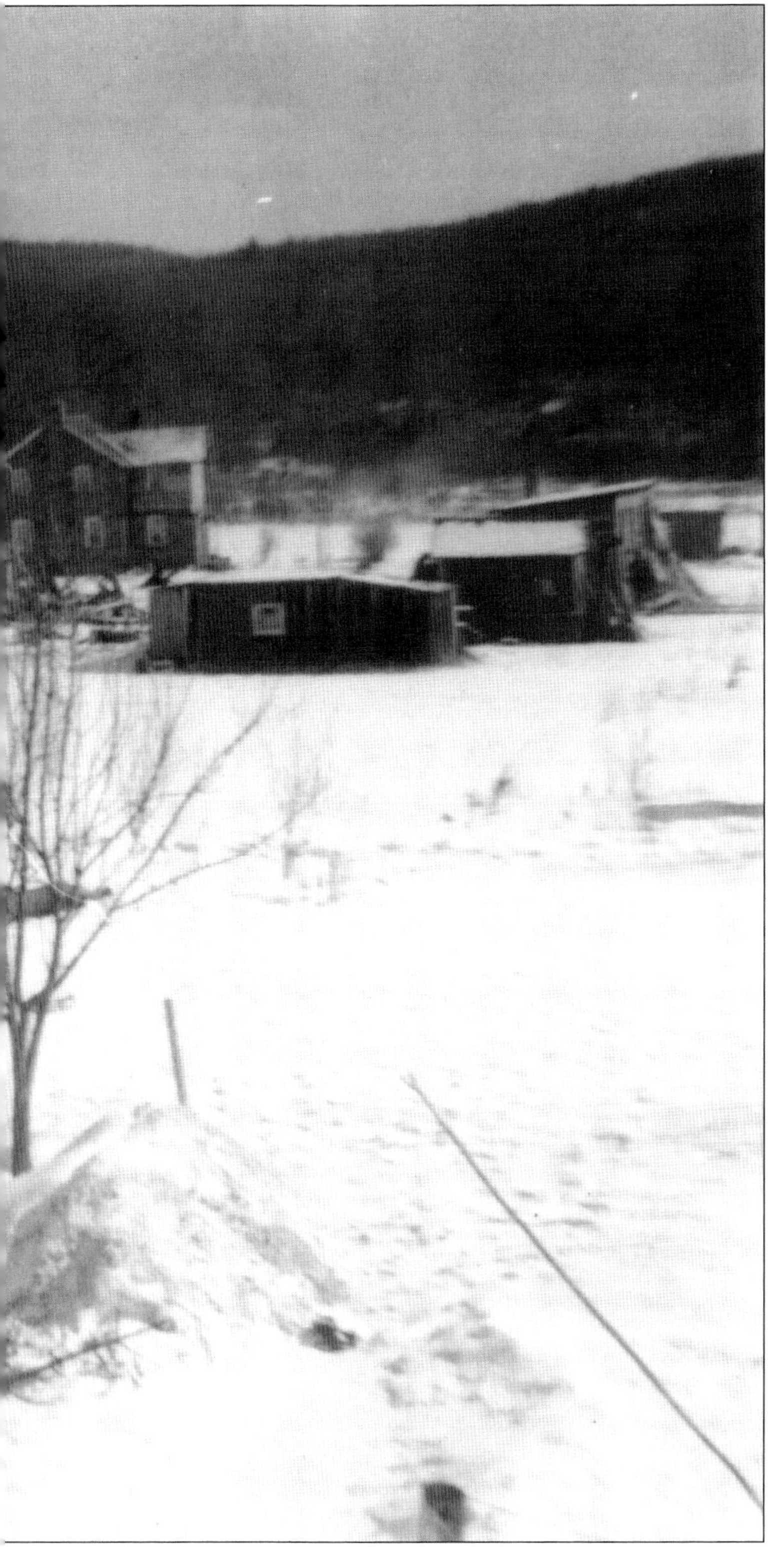

This Tannersville view looks northeast on present-day Route 715N near its intersection with Route 611. When the tannery was in operation, this area was lined with bark sheds used to store hemlock bark for tanning hides. The homes shown here on the hillside were company houses built for workers and their families. Pigs kept by tannery workers' families were fed scraps and scrapings from the hides being tanned. The pigs and their droppings caused this stretch of present-day Route 715N to become known locally as "Pig Turd Alley." At the time of this photograph, the wood-frame house on the extreme left was home to Edra Landis. The house at the center belonged to Bert Stitzer, while Earl Peechatka built and owned the stone house just behind. Interestingly, the building closest to the photographer is a CG-4 glider box, which was obtained from Tobyhanna Army Depot after World War II, with five boxes costing $75, including the glider. Outbuildings like this were common in Pocono and Jackson Townships due to the proximity to the depot. (Courtesy of John Alleger.)

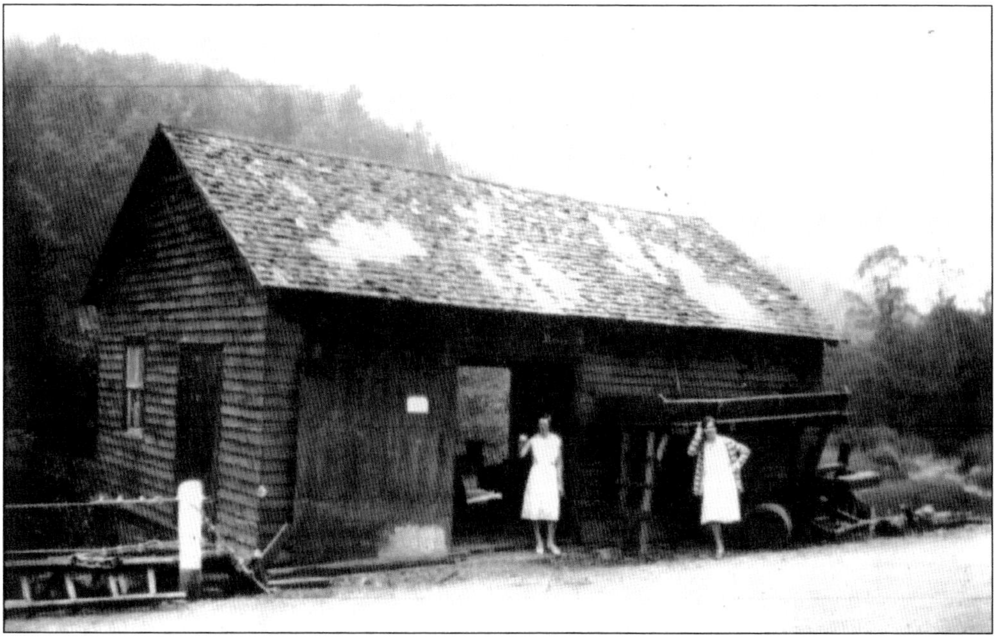

The original Appenzell cider mill was run by waterpower from the Pensyl Creek, which is now referred to as Appenzell Creek. A new cider mill known as Heller's Cider Mill was built across Neola Road. The old mill was recently demolished. (Courtesy of Clyde Wallingford.)

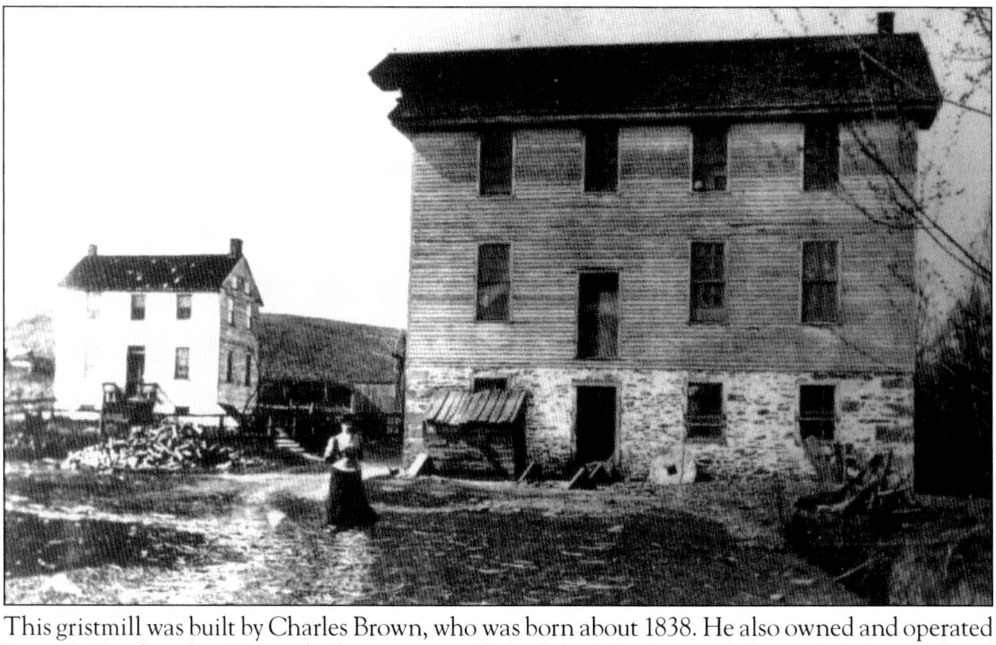

This gristmill was built by Charles Brown, who was born about 1838. He also owned and operated Brown's Hotel in the 1860s, which was originally built by John Learned about 1740. Learned and his family were killed by Native Americans in 1781. Gen. John Sullivan led troops from Easton up through the Wyoming Valley to settle the Native American uprising. The route taken in Pennsylvania is known as Sullivan Trail. (Courtesy Olive Metzger Learn.)

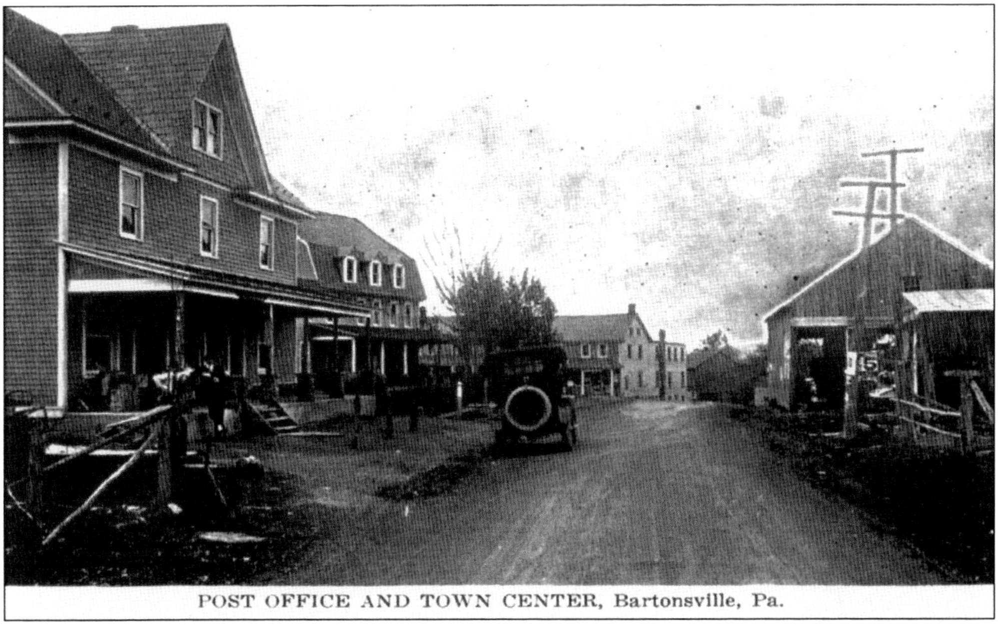

Looking south on present-day Bartonsville Avenue toward Route 611, the Alleger family home and general store are seen on the far left, with the Forest Inn slightly behind. The road to Stroudsburg makes a sharp left turn just beyond the Forest Inn. The road to Snydersville descends a slight hill before crossing the Bartonsville covered bridge and the tracks of the Wilkes-Barre and Eastern Railroad. (Courtesy of John Alleger.)

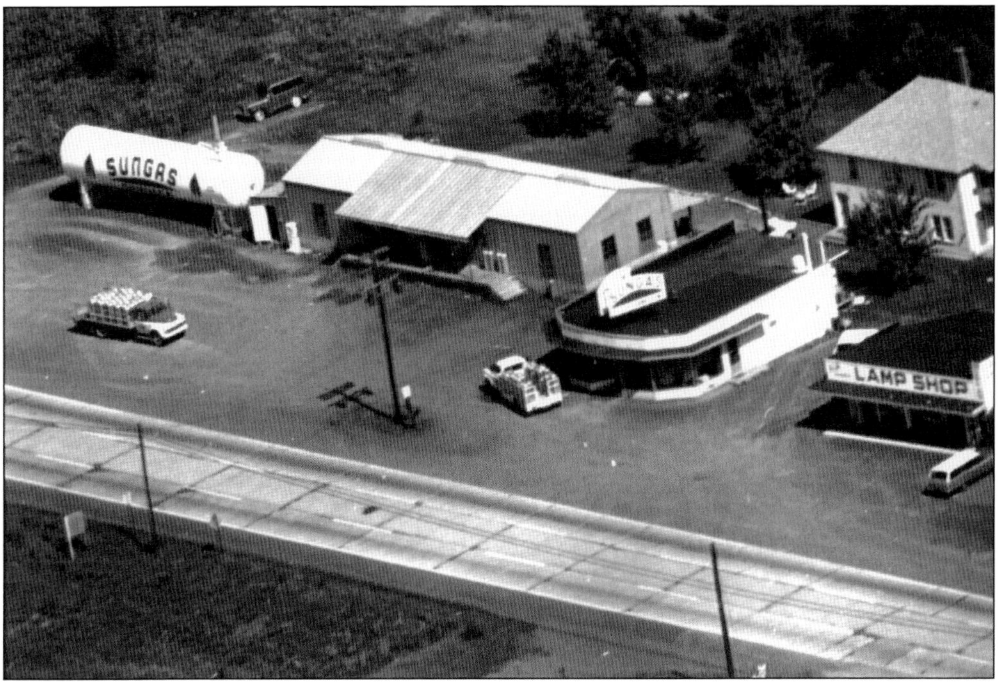

Sungas and Chic's Lamp Shop are shown in this aerial photograph taken during the 1950s. Harold Schmoyer was the manager of the Sungas propane business, and the lamp shop was built by Austin "Chic" Coco. (Courtesy of Harold Schmoyer.)

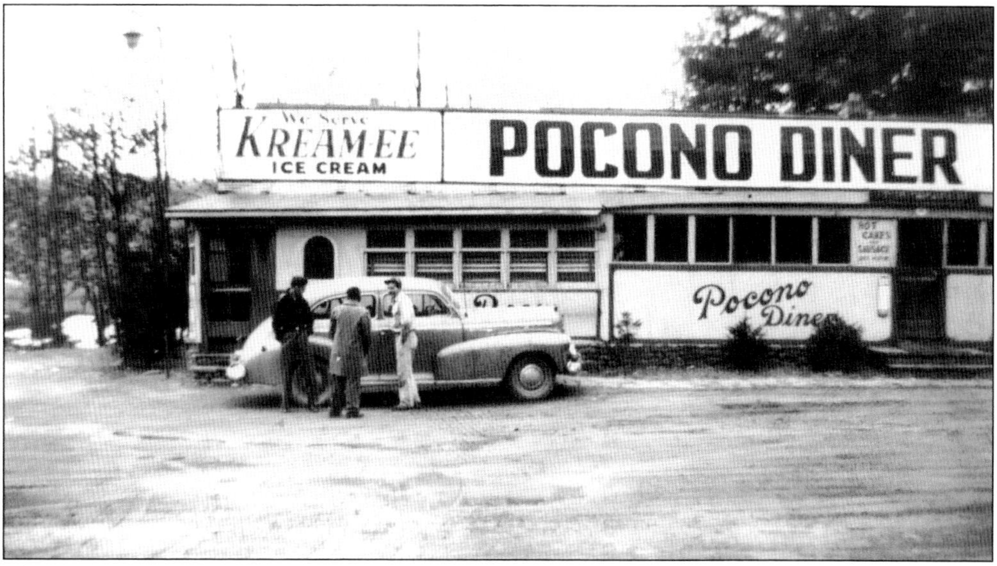

The Pocono Diner was purchased by Otis "Doc" Alger. It was run by Charles, James, and Clint Besecker. Pocono Antique and Pottery Shop was built next door, and Amos Johnson completed its stonework. (Courtesy of Dick Peechatka.)

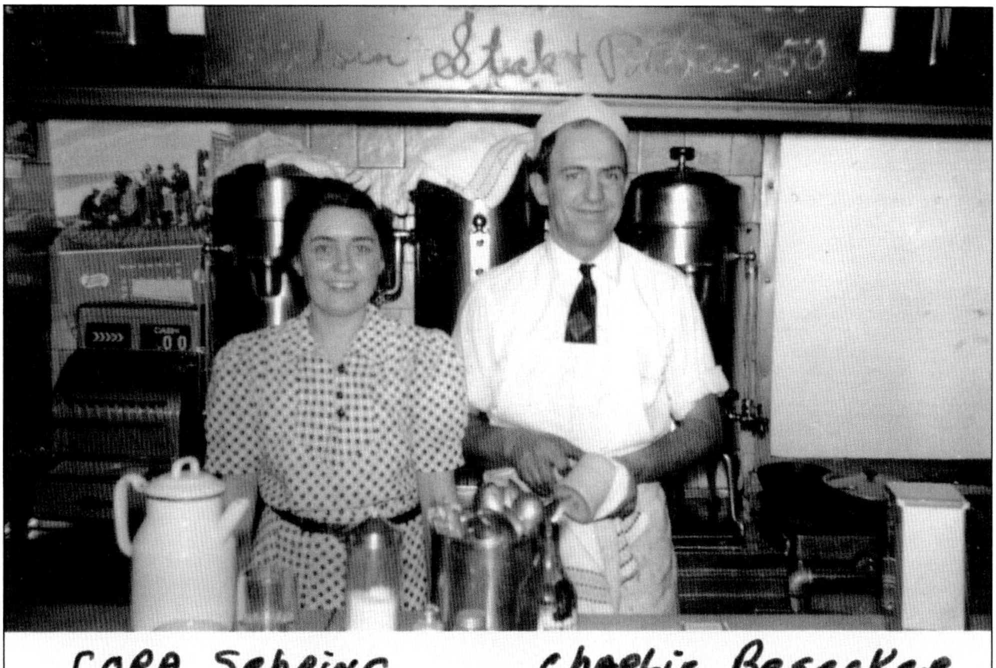

This interior shot of the Pocono Diner shows Cora Werkheiser Sebring and Charles Besecker taking a break from work behind the counter. The signboard above their heads lists steak and potatoes costing 50¢. (Courtesy of Dick Peechatka.)

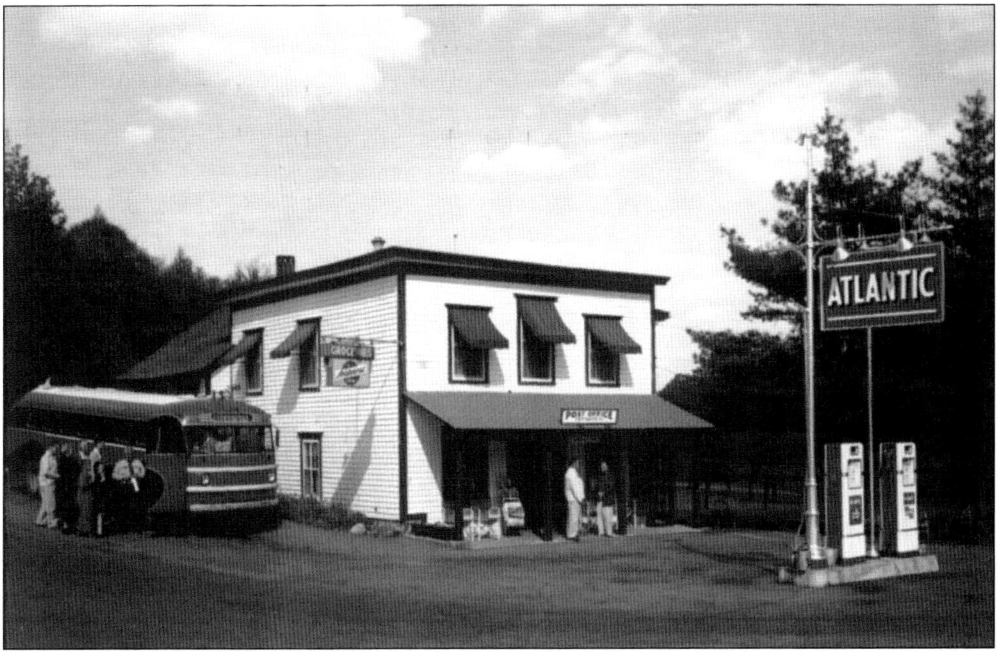

The Swiftwater Post Office also served as a store and bus stop. It was operated by Thomas and Cora McGuire, and their living quarters were upstairs. (Courtesy of Jack Hamblin.)

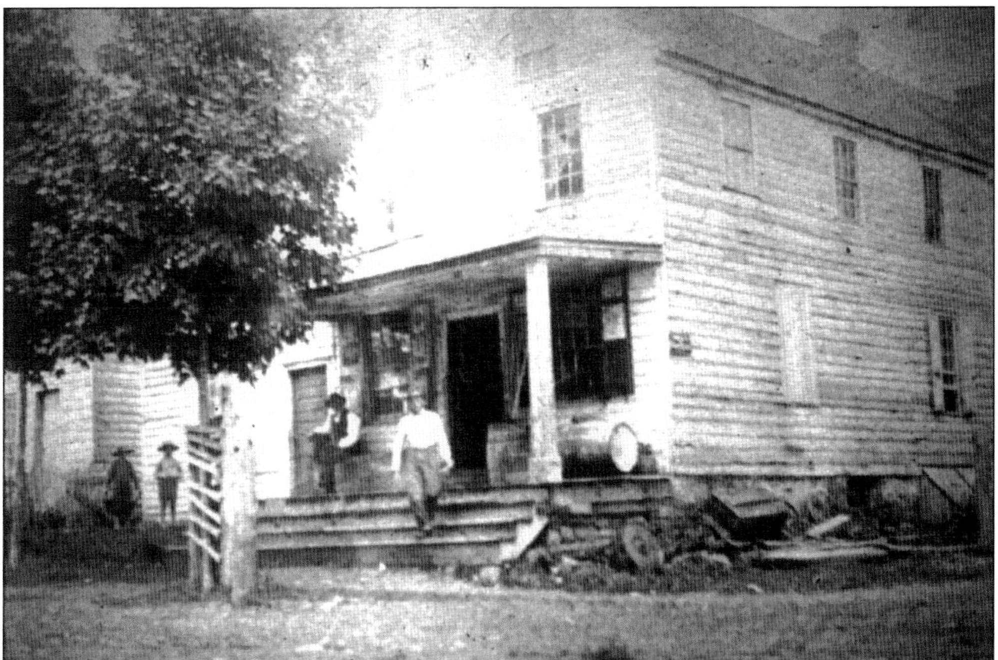

William Kresge owned and operated a store and the Tannersville Post Office directly across from the Pocono Hotel in Tannersville. He also rented upstairs apartments to area families, including John and Phyllis Gabel DeHaven, Dick and Jeanne Anglemyer Howell, and Gordon and Blanche Metzger Starner. (Courtesy of the Pocono-Jackson Historical Society.)

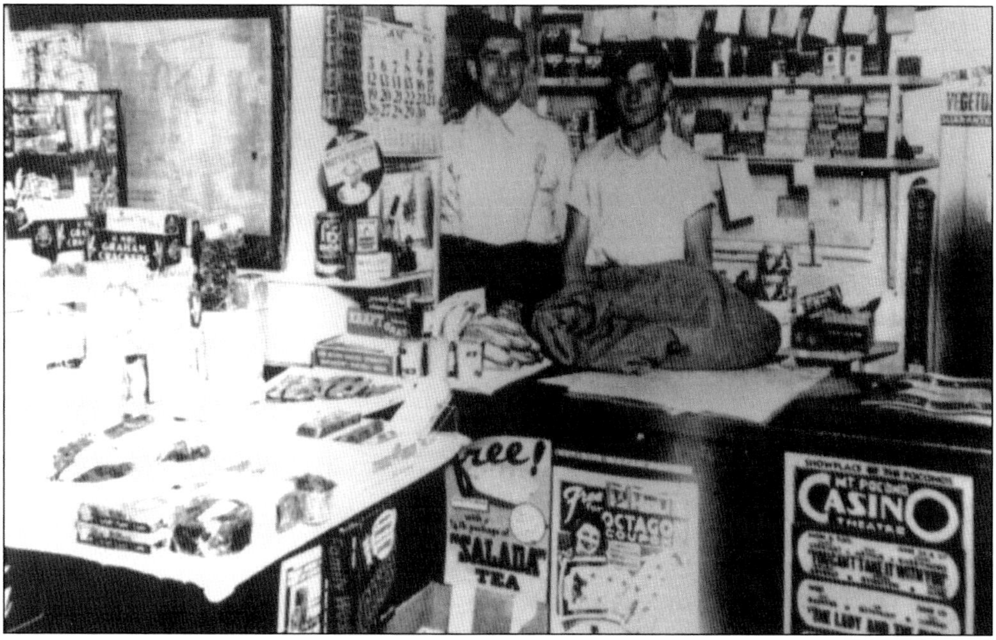

This interior photograph of the Niering store in Scotrun shows William Niering (left) and Edward Werkheiser smiling broadly for the camera. Later occupied and run by Clayton Kinsley, the store relocated to Tannersville in the 1960s. The building still stands in Scotrun. (Courtesy of James Price.)

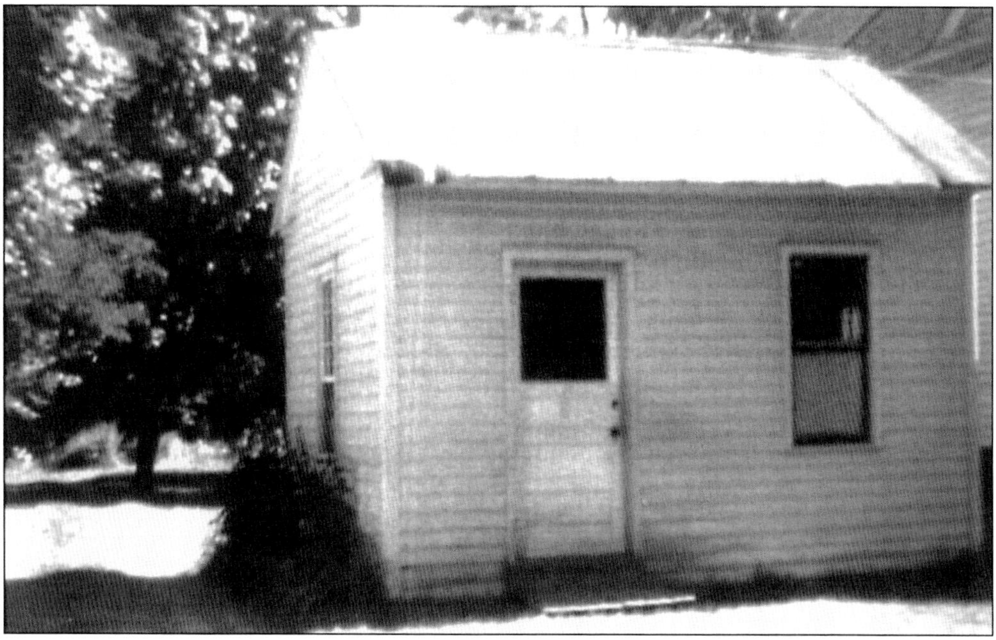

The workshop of Fred and Ethel Hill in Tannersville is pictured in this 1952 photograph. The Hills manufactured cotton swab mops used to apply varnish to hardwood floors or to wax them after they were finished. They also manufactured wet mops and dish mops. This small building was originally a barbershop operated by Harry Werkheiser Sr. The location of the shop is now the Turkey Hill Mini-mart. (Courtesy of the Pocono-Jackson Historical Society.)

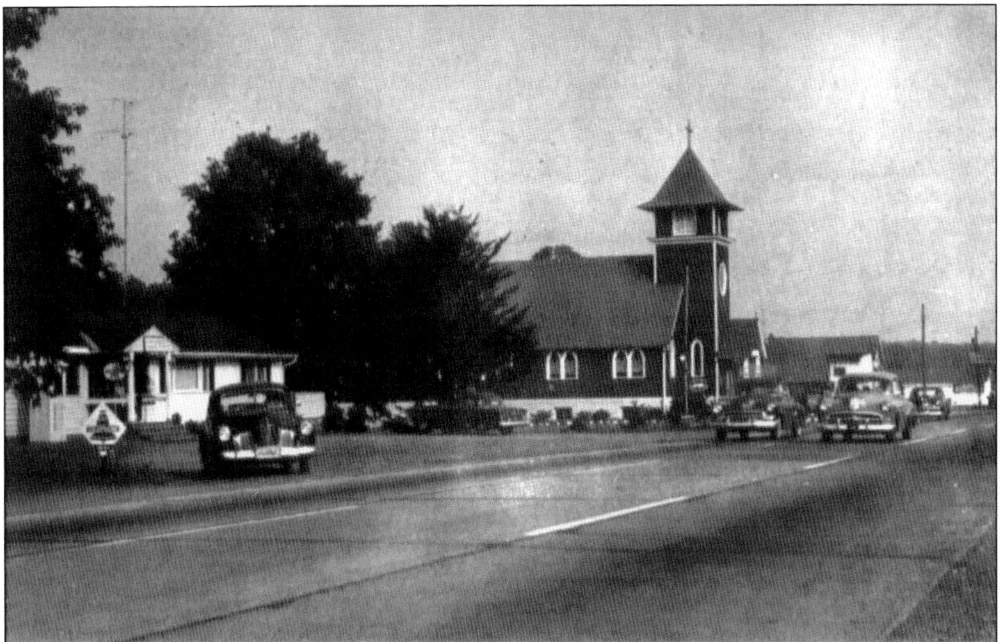

Post Office and Catholic Church, Tannersville, Pa.

Shown in this photograph is the Tannersville Post Office and Our Lady of Victory Catholic Church, a mission church built prior to 1950. The church was torn down in 2005 to make room for a bank. A new one was built on Cherry Lane about a mile from Tannersville. (Courtesy of John J. Riley.)

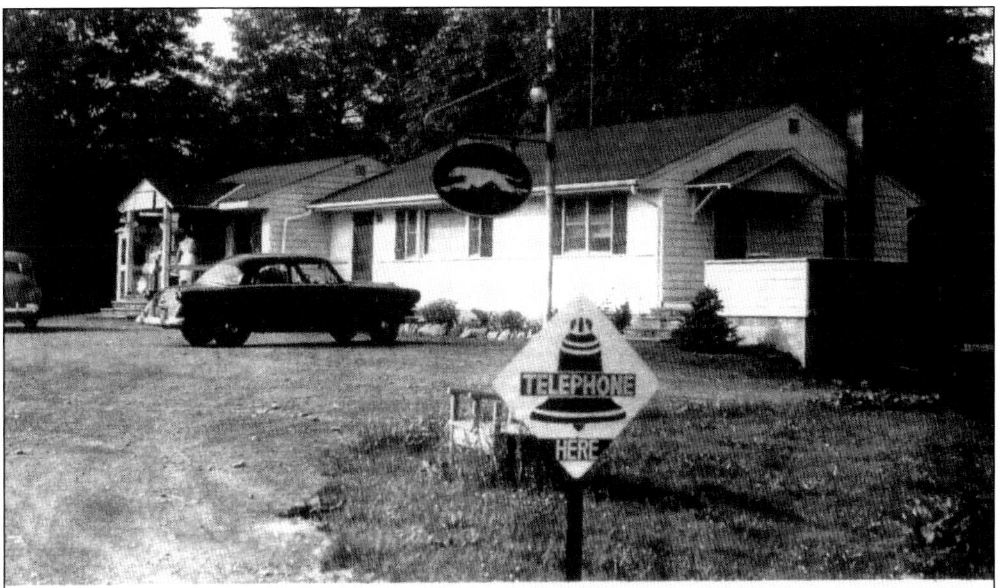

United States Post Office and Greyhound Stop, Tannersville, Pa.

The Tannersville Post Office was operated by postmaster Charles Brader and his wife, Betty. He took over the post office duties when former postmaster William Kresge passed away. The post office started out in a small addition to their house that expanded as the population in the area grew. (Courtesy of John J. Riley.)

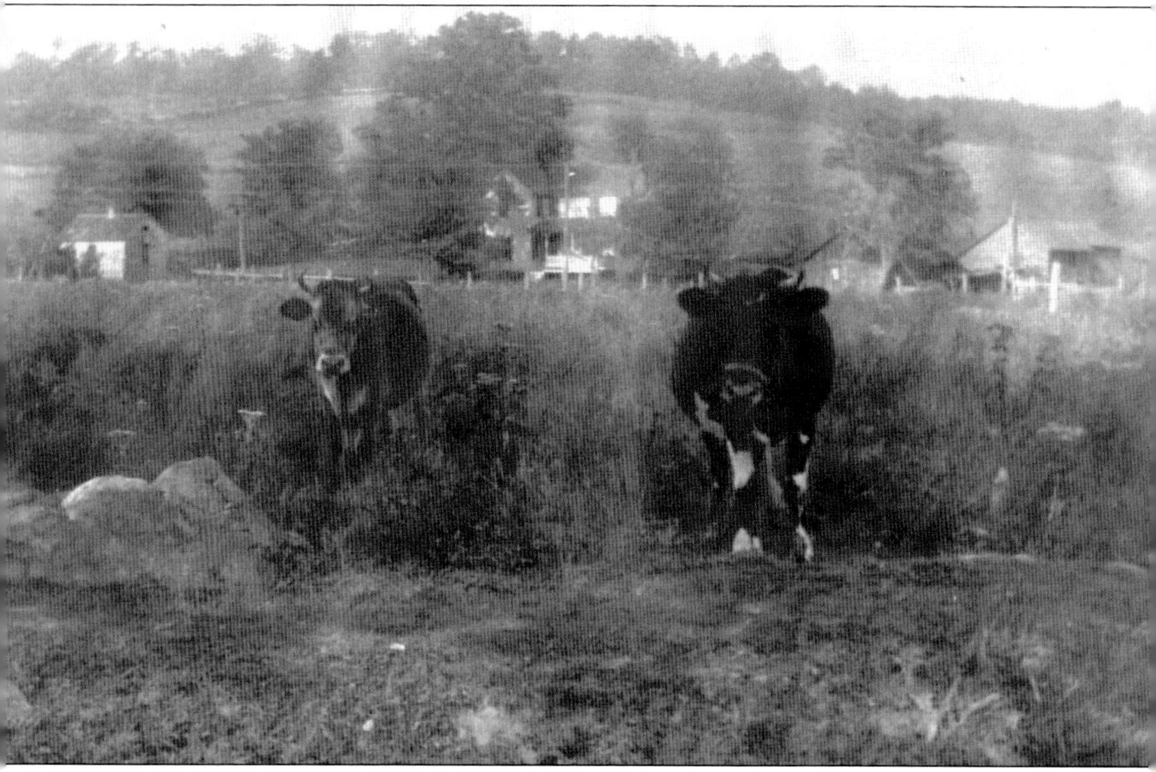

This view from around 1900 looks east from present-day Route 611 across a meadow toward Bartonsville Avenue. The small structure on the left was the Jacob Repsher Shoe Shop. At the center is the home of Samuel (1846–1921) and M. Anna Musselman (1850–1927). Samuel Musselman was a blacksmith in Bartonsville at this time. The blacksmith shop, its associated outbuildings, a pig pen, and a chicken coop are seen on the right. The Musselman home still stands and is currently a private residence. Another Bartonsville blacksmith, Steward Singer (1870–1892), lost his life during the dynamiting of a rock cut by construction workers on the Wilkes-Barre and Eastern Railroad. As workers detonated a charge, a 25-pound rock blasted free from the face of the cut and was thrown more than 1,000 feet from the work site through the roof of the blacksmith shop, killing Singer as he worked. (Courtesy of John Alleger.)

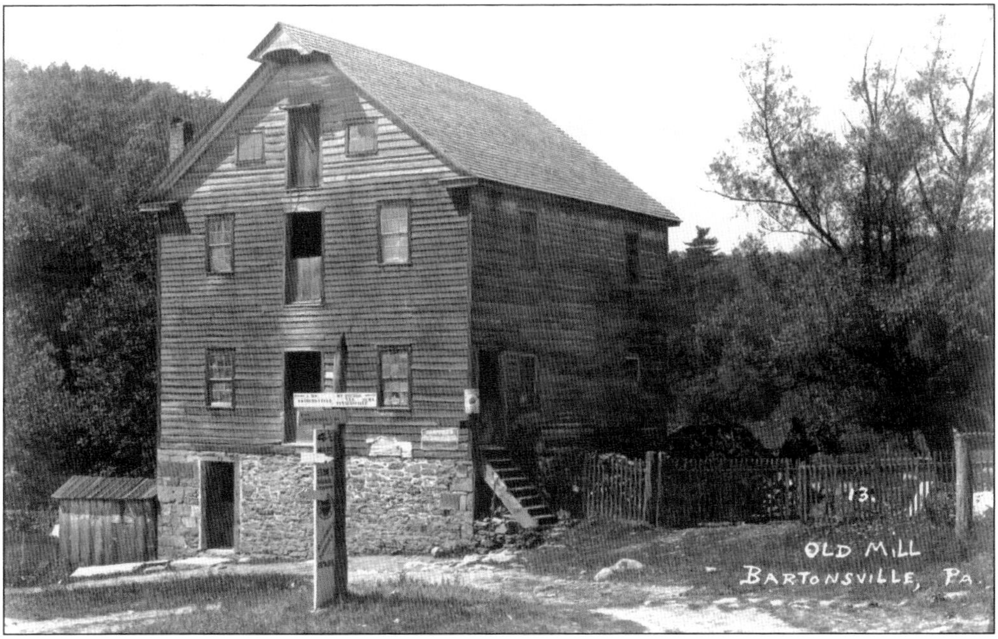

The Bartonsville gristmill once stood on the southwest corner of present-day Route 611 and Rimrock Road. A sawmill is situated to its right in this picture. Carved into the cornerstone are the initials R. H. M. and the date 1848. After standing at the location for more than a century, the mill was dismantled and moved to its present location in Millbrook Village, New Jersey. (Courtesy of John Alleger.)

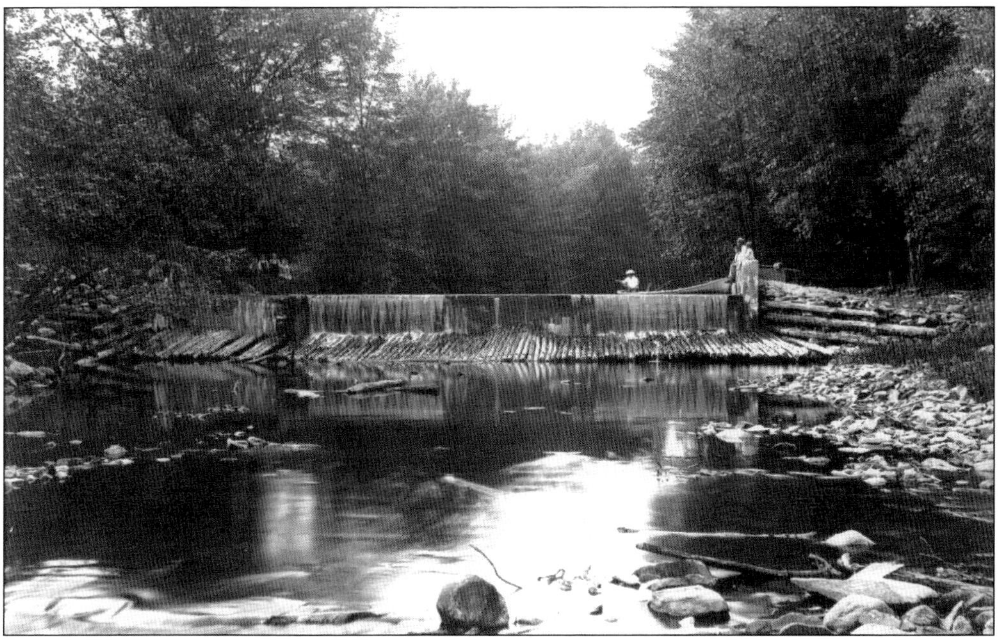

The milldam in Bartonsville was located on the Pocono Creek. Today remnants of the dam are still visible in the creek when looking north from the bridge adjacent to Knight's Inn. The millrace constructed from the dam to the Bartonsville gristmill on the corner of present-day Route 611 and Rimrock Road was nearly a quarter mile long. (Courtesy of John Alleger.)

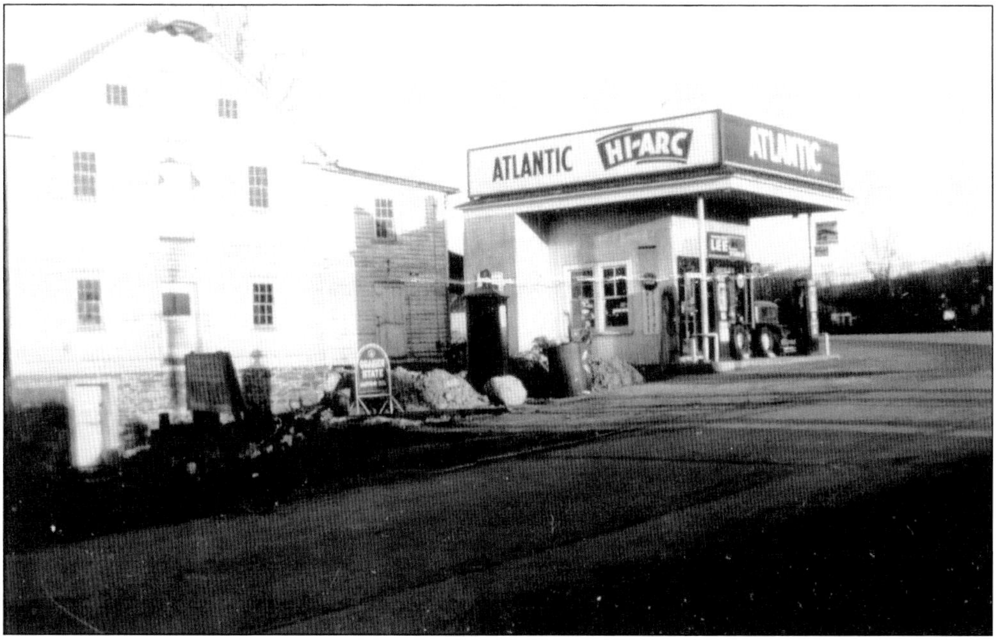

Canfield's Service Station served motorists traveling along the Lackawanna Trail and later Route 611. Of special note is the Bartonsville gristmill, seen in the rear of this photograph. Neither structure survives at this location; the service station was razed, and the mill was dismantled and reconstructed at Millbrook Village, New Jersey. The office of Pocono U-Lock-It storage facility occupies this site today. (Courtesy of Joan Franks.)

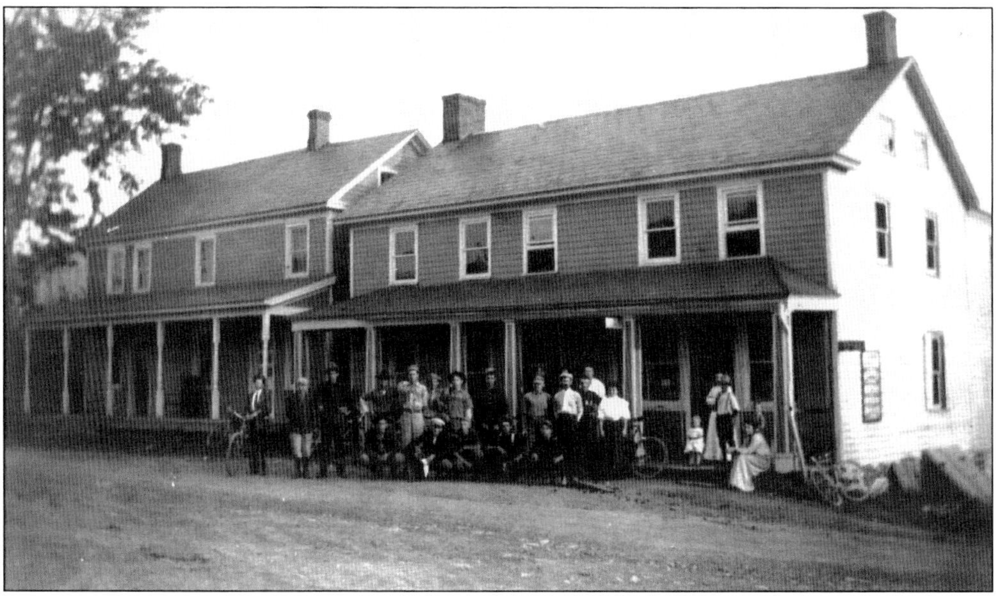

Standing side by side, these were two of the oldest structures in Bartonsville. They housed the post office and a general store operated over the years by a number of different individuals, including John Alleger Sr. The final business to occupy this structure was Francis Marvin's Marvinette Restaurant, which was destroyed by fire on Easter morning, April 17, 1933. The blaze leveled both structures. (Courtesy of John Alleger.)

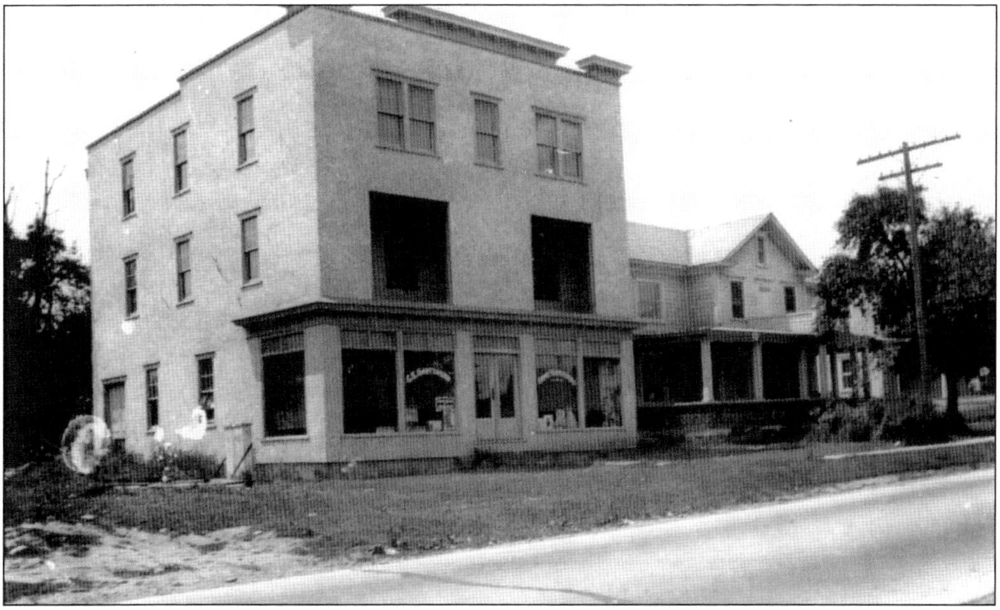

Clarence Gantzhorn married Carrie Warner, and they became one of Tannersville's most enterprising families. They operated not only Gantzhorn's Funeral Home, shown on the right, but also a furniture store, which is shown on the left. Many of the company houses that were built for tannery workers became the property of the Gantzhorns. (Courtesy of Emma Gantzhorn Arndt.)

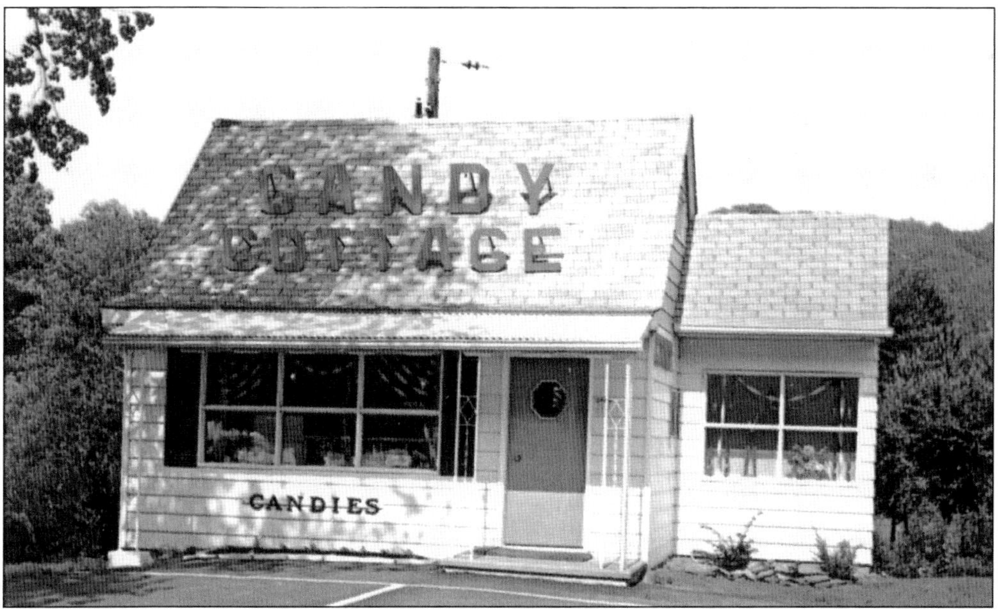

Candy Cottage, located along Route 611 in Scotrun next to the present-day Muldoon's Gas Station, was a small building used by Charles and Izella Kimmel as a sales office for their home construction business during the 1950s. It is currently a real estate office. (Courtesy of John J. Riley.)

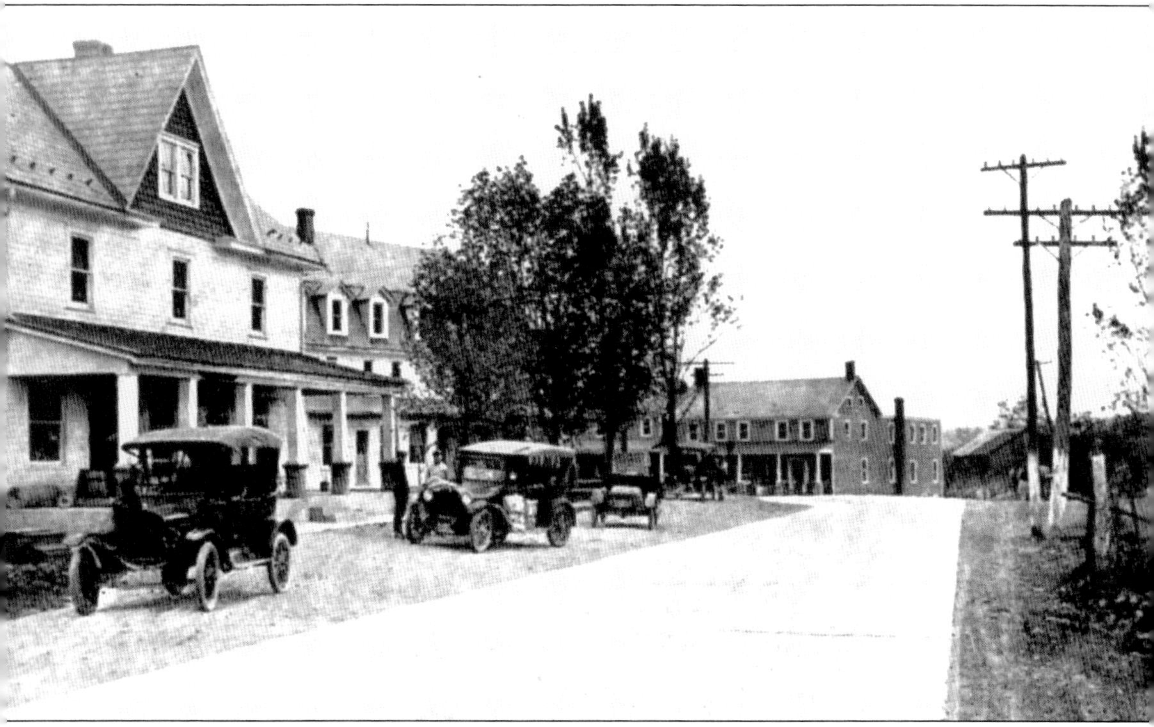

The newly concreted roadway of the Lackawanna Trail entered Pocono Township at Bartonsville and followed the course of present-day Bartonsville Avenue. Touted in travel literature of the 1920s and 1930s as a fine and modern highway, the trail also passed through the villages of Tannersville, Scotrun, and Swiftwater before exiting the township on its way north. (Courtesy of John Alleger.)

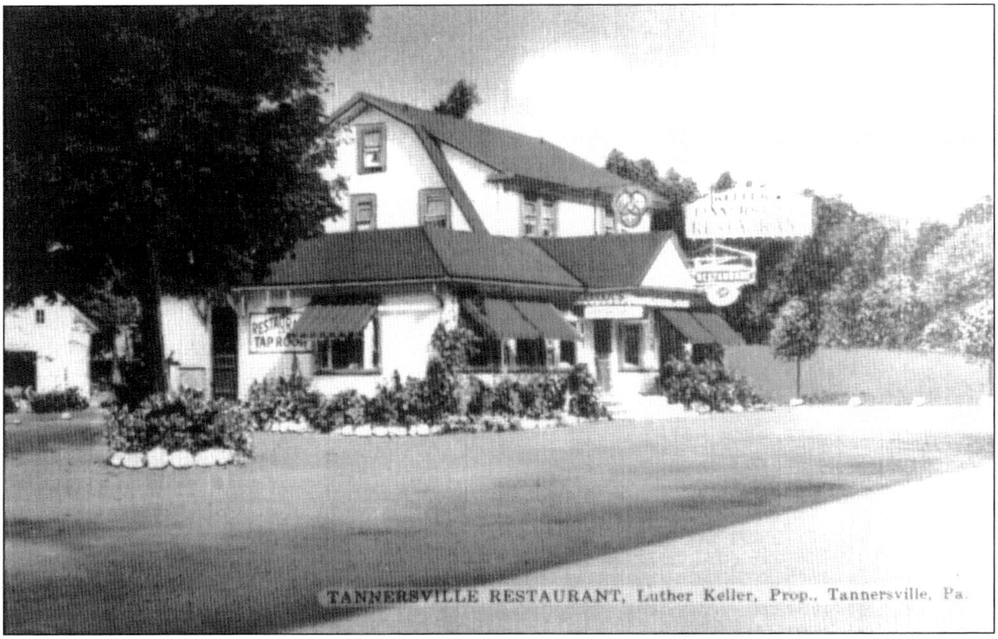

Tannersville Restaurant, located in Tannersville on Route 611, was built by Paul Edinger in 1934 and owned by Luther Keller, Paul Seager, Bill and Stella Gabel, and Oakie Smith. Later the building became a plumbing supply shop and currently houses Switzerland Olde World Gifts. (Courtesy of John J. Riley.)

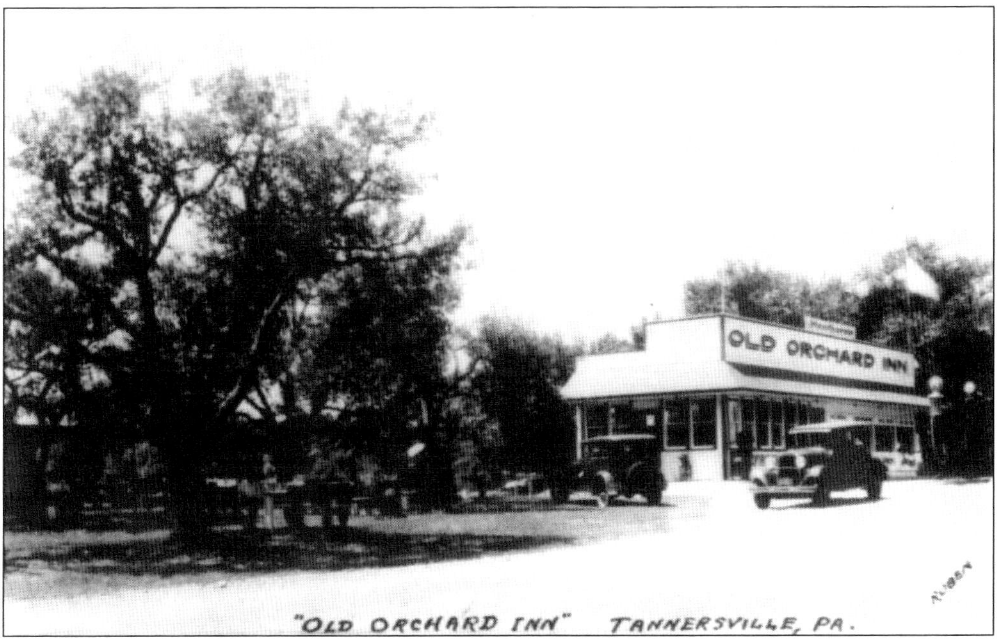

Old Orchard Inn was located near the Pocono Hotel in the center of Tannersville. It later became Cliff's Hof Brau, owned by Clifford Simpson. The building now houses a pest-control business. (Courtesy of the Pocono-Jackson Historical Society.)

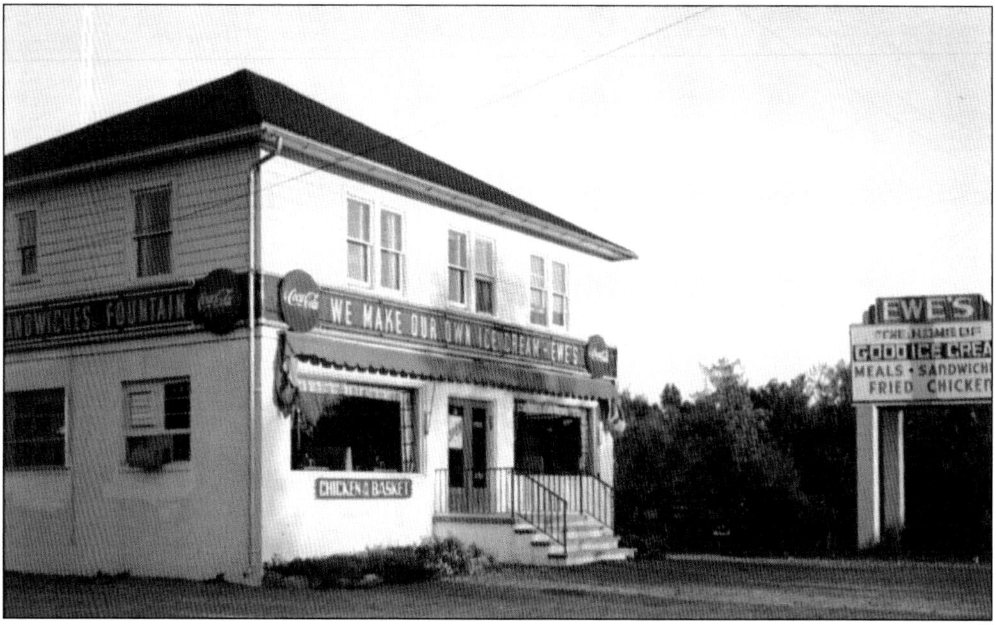

This postcard's caption reads, "Ewe's Home of good Ice Cream, rich in flavor, cream and fruits . . . That's the Ice Cream we produce. Excellent meals, sandwiches and delicious fried chicken. Hans and Katherine Ewe, Owners-Mgrs." The building is located in lower Tannersville along Route 611 and now houses a fitness center. (Courtesy of John J. Riley.)

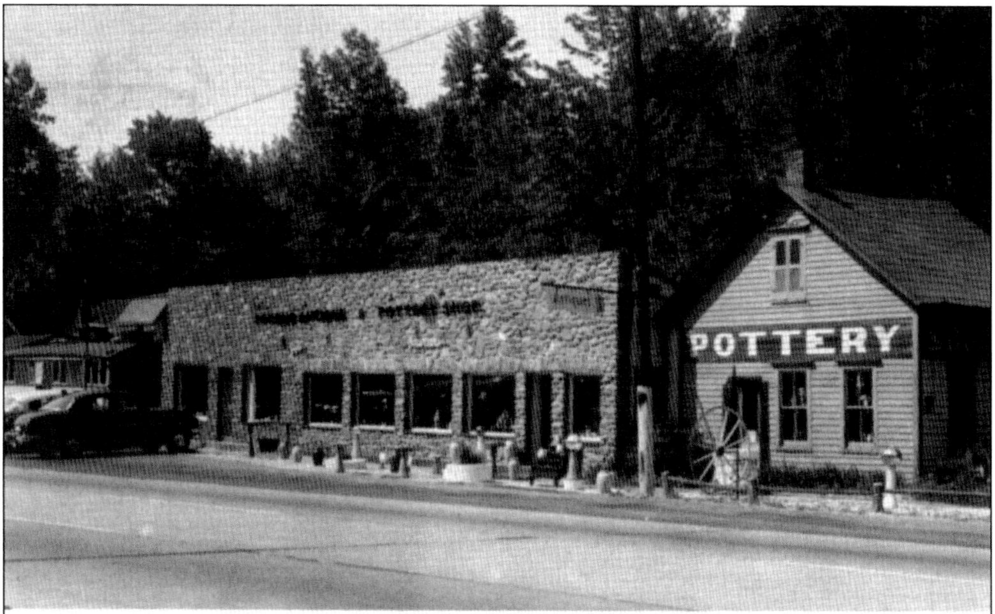

Pocono Antique and Pottery Shop was built by Otis "Doc" Alger, who purchased a diner that he placed next door. The pottery shop was purchased by Kasmir and Marian Mazur in 1950. During the 1955 flood, the Mazurs' house was washed away along with the frame portion of the shop; however, the stone portion still stands today just north of Tannersville along Route 611. (Courtesy of John J. Riley.)

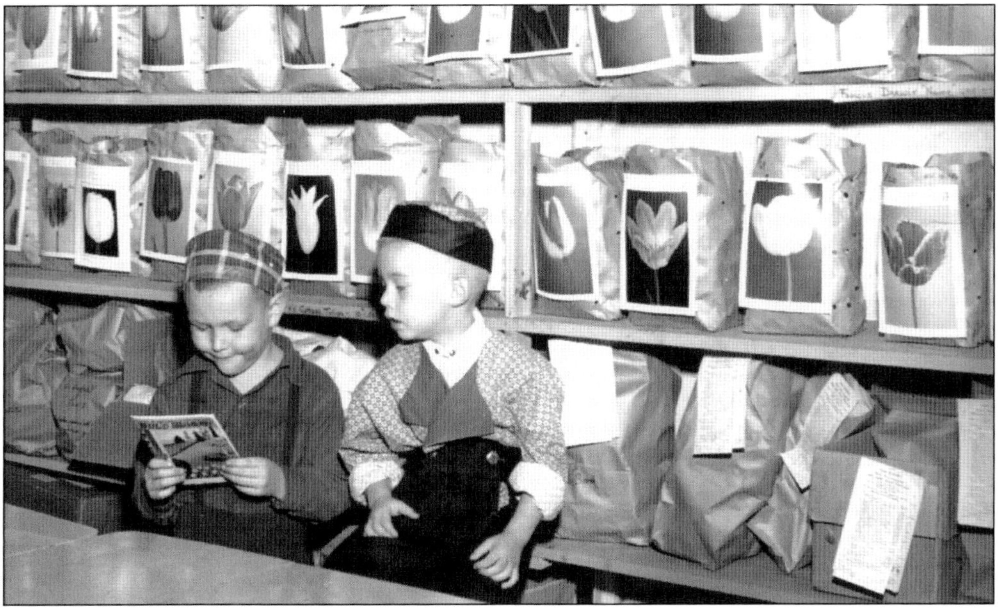

David (left) and Jonathan Van Sciver are shown during the 1950s sitting in front of the many boxes of bulbs for sale at Van Sciver's Dutch Gardens along Cherry Lane in Tannersville. Attesting to his father's sense of humor, David's middle name is Nedrag, which is *garden* spelled backward. (Courtesy of David Van Sciver.)

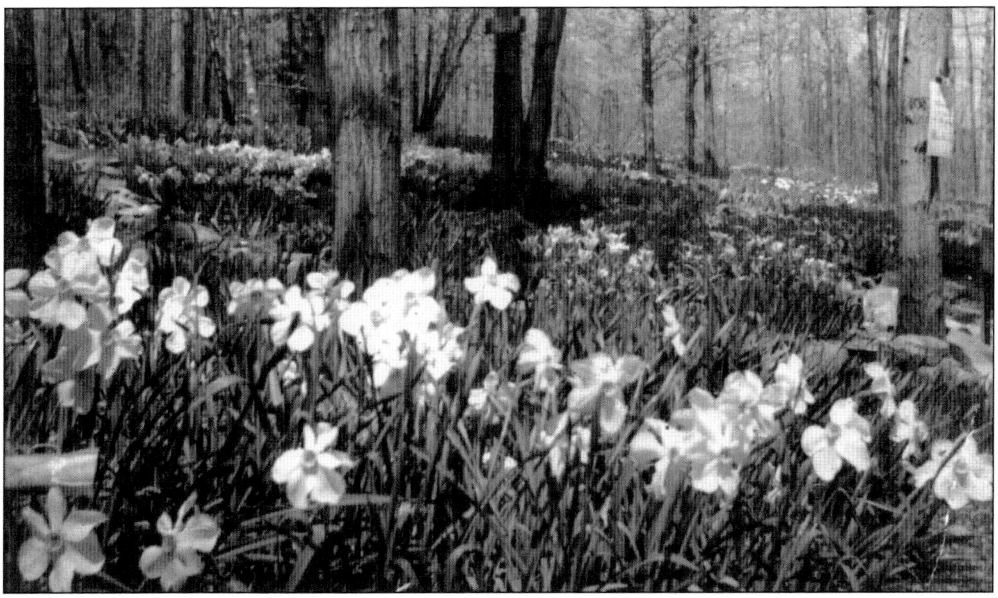

Van Sciver's Dutch Gardens in Tannersville was a beautiful sight during the spring, summer, and fall growing seasons. It sold hundreds of tulip and daffodil varieties imported directly from Holland in the store and through mail order. (Courtesy of David Van Sciver.)

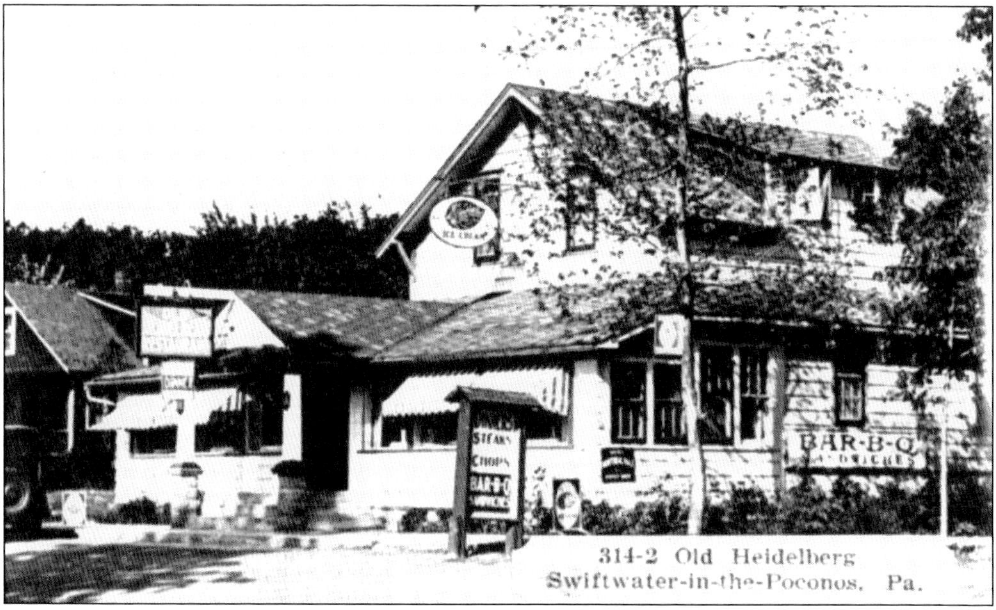

These two photographs show two restaurants located between Scotrun and Swiftwater along Route 611, where the Pocono Brewing Company now stands. The Old Heidelberg Inn is shown above. Small cabins to the rear awaited weary tourists. The photograph below shows its sister German restaurant, the Rhineland Inn, which stood to the north. (Courtesy of Jack Hamblin.)

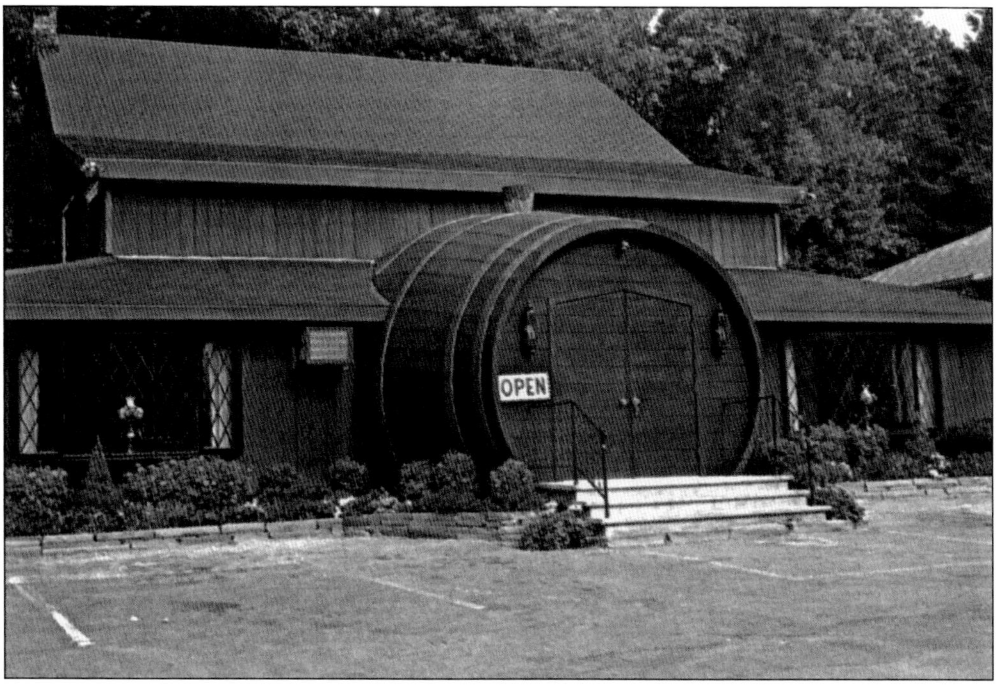

Two

Home Away from Home

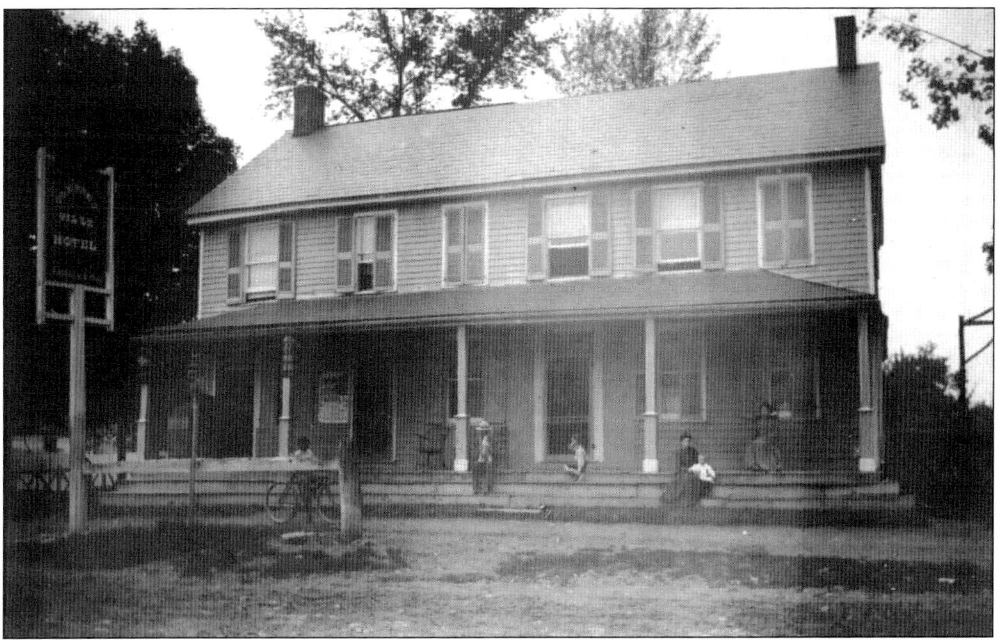

Tannersville Hotel is reputed to be the oldest hotel in the area still in use today. The hotel was built in 1825 and is now known as Tannersville Inn, a popular restaurant located along Route 611 in lower Tannersville. (Courtesy of Diane Davis Abeel.)

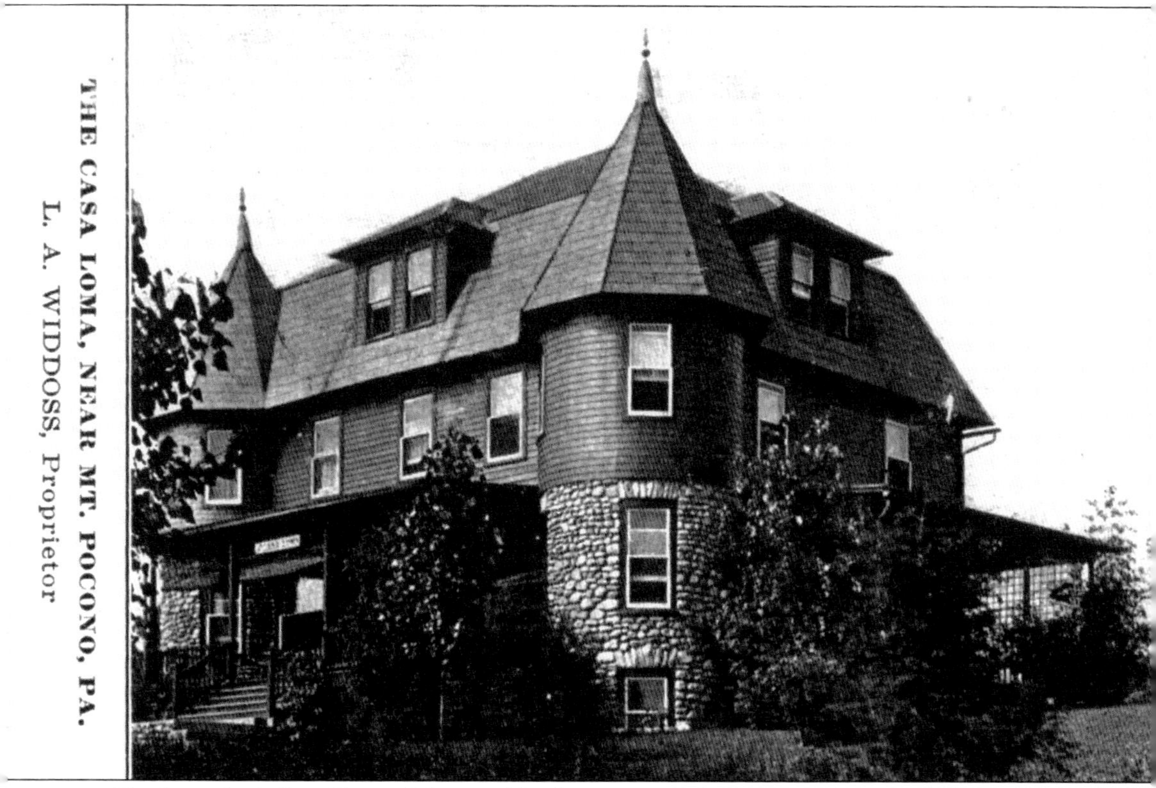

Climbing the hill on Route 611 out of Swiftwater toward Mount Pocono stood the Casa Loma Boarding House. Known for good food, clean mountain air, and good trout fishing nearby, the Casa Loma was typical of the many boardinghouses that catered to vacationers in the early 20th century. The Casa Loma still stands as a transient rental place. (Courtesy of Jack Hamblin.)

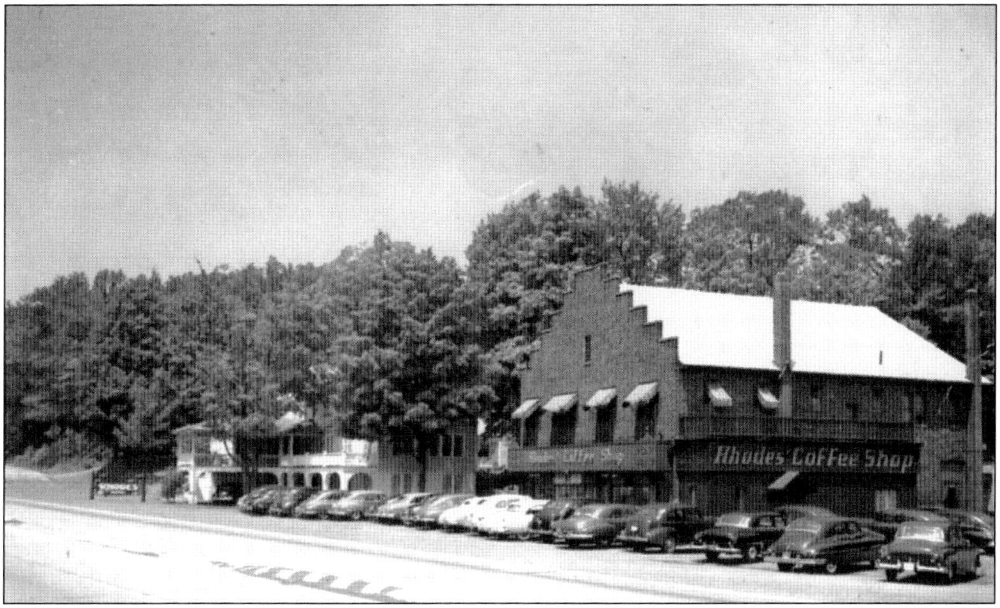

Rhodes' Coffee Shop (above) and Rhodes' Mountain Inn (below) stood on the hill passing from Scotrun north to Swiftwater. Rhodes' Coffee Shop was a successful restaurant in what was originally the automobile garage for the inn. Present-day Pangea Restaurant now occupies this building. Rhodes' Mountain Inn was destroyed by fire in the 1970s. (Courtesy of Jack Hamblin.)

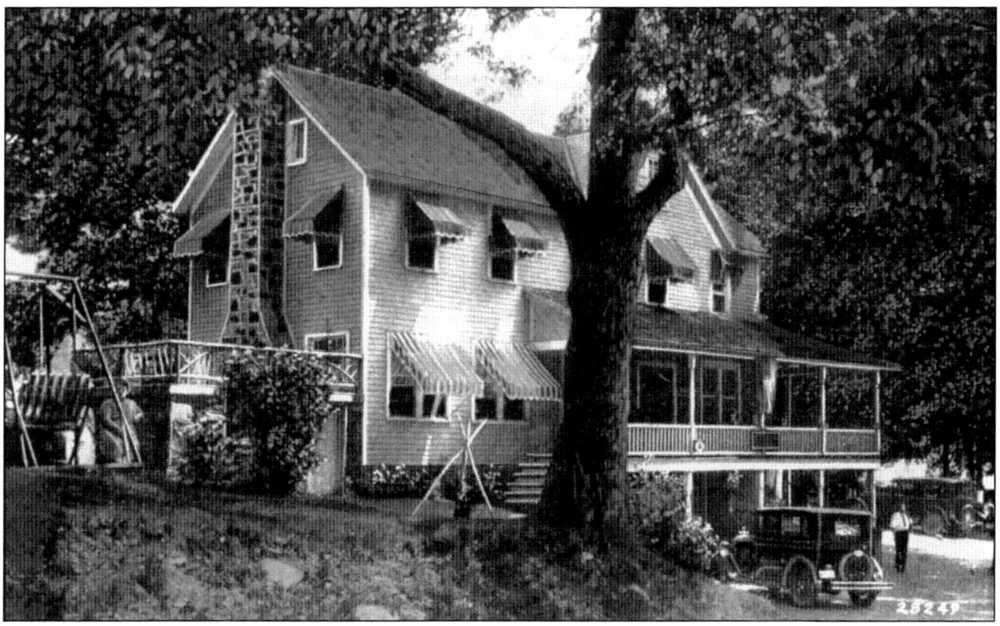

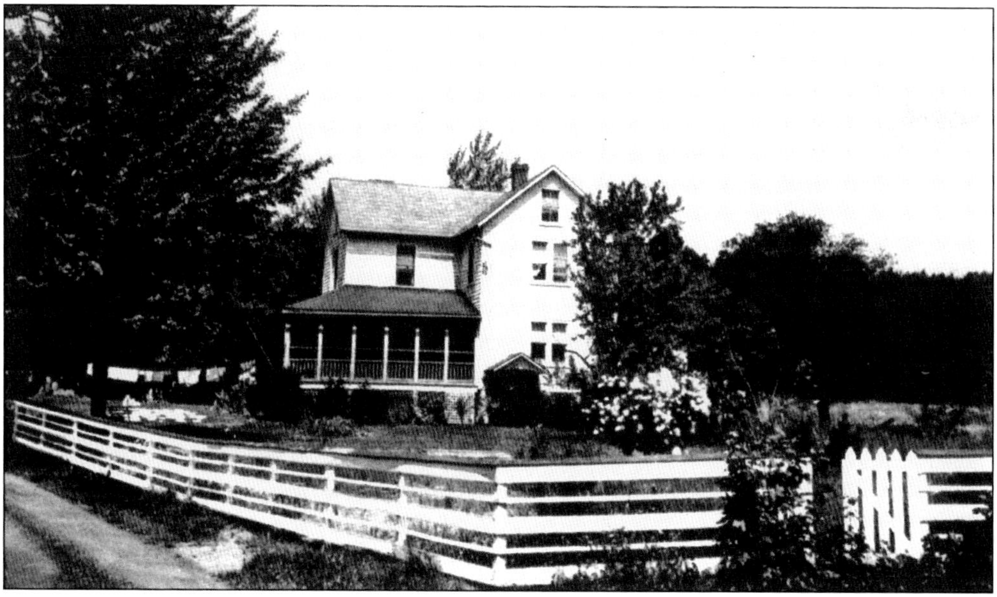

Abeel Farm Camp for Children, located on Abeel Road in Pocono Township, was founded by Essie Olive Smith Abeel, a native of Jackson Township. This camp was formally located in Minisink Hills as a summer extension of Abeel's private school in Hackensack, New Jersey. In the 1940s, the operation was moved to the old Frank Keltz farm where it flourished until the late 1960s. (Courtesy of Diane Davis Abeel.)

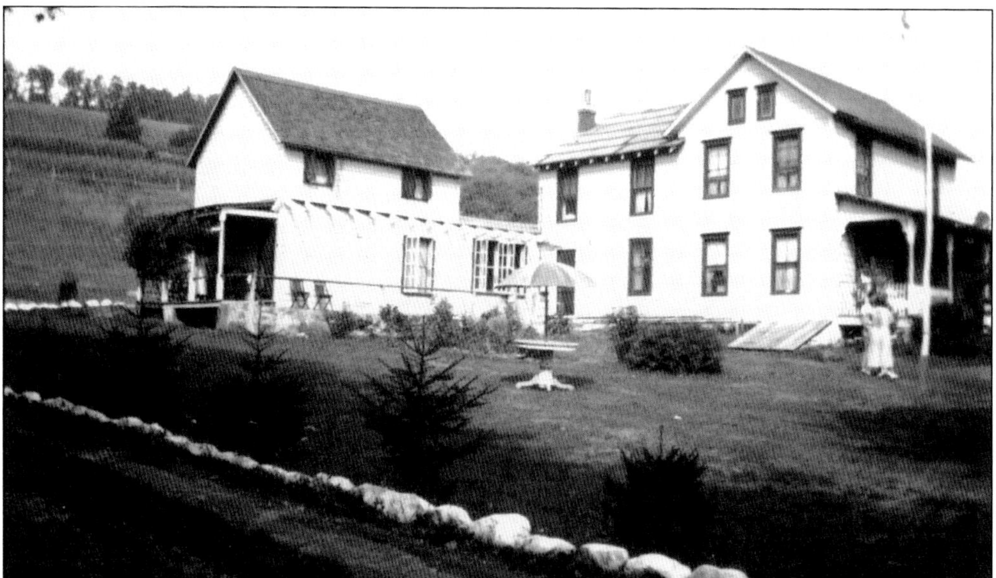

Munch's Boarding House was owned by Elmer and Olive Sebring Munch and located about one mile from Tannersville toward Henryville. Three meals a day were served to the guests. Located at the intersection of present-day Route 715N and Munch Drive, it was converted to apartments in the early 1970s. (Courtesy of Olive Munch.)

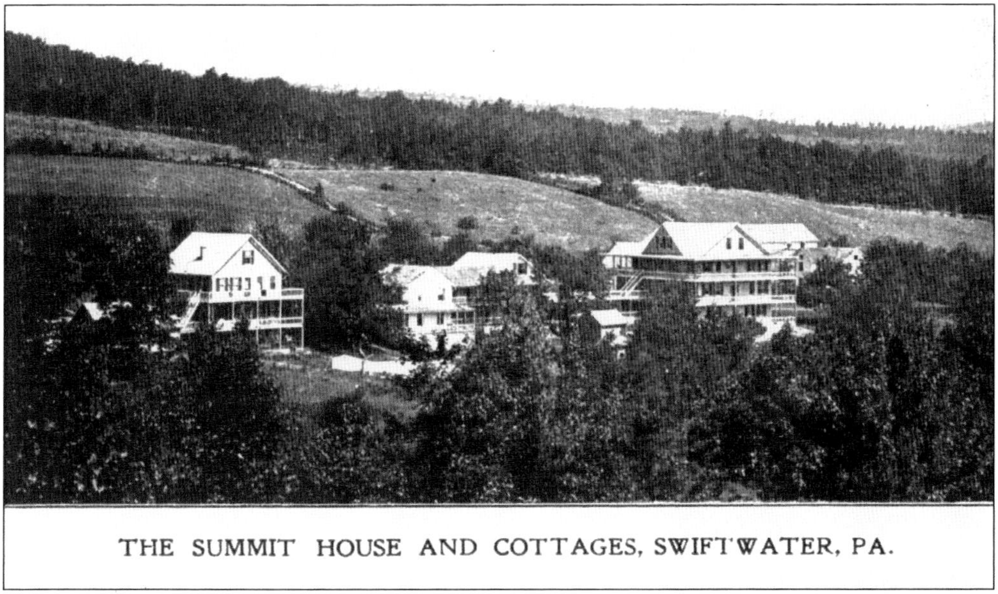

Summit House, located in the most northern corner of Pocono Township, was advertised as having "60 acres which provided ample space for sports on the grounds for tennis and other games; with golf, bowling, riding, and swimming nearby." The same advertisement recommended its good table with the best of meats and the freshest of vegetables. Summit House was torn down and no longer exists. (Courtesy of Diane Davis Abeel.)

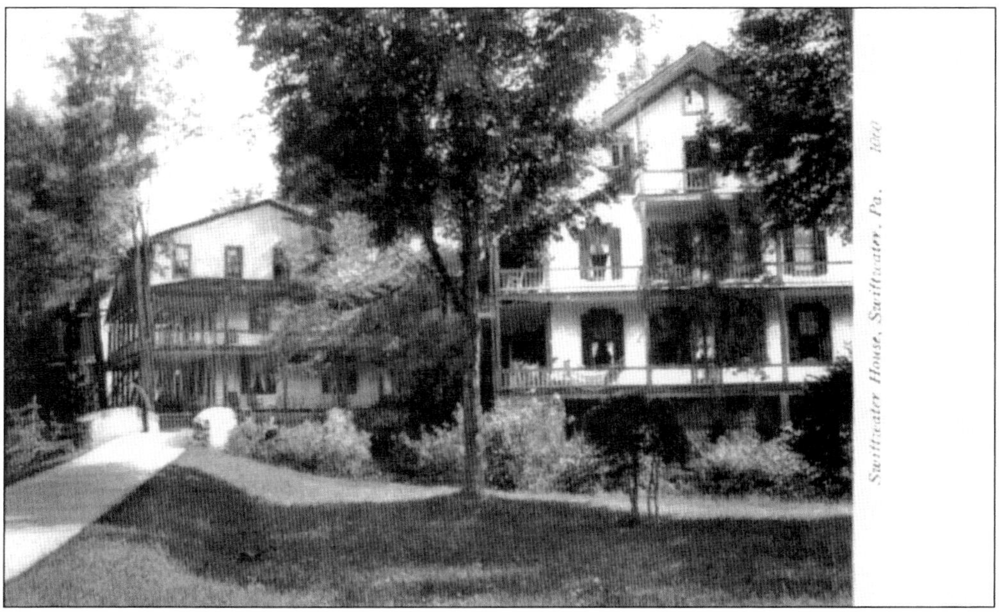

The venerable Swiftwater Inn overlooked its namesake stream at the foot of the hill in Swiftwater from 1778 until 2007, when it was razed to make way for a modern inn. The original deed for the property was purchased at auction by Anthony Maula to be hung in the new establishment. (Courtesy of Jack Hamblin.)

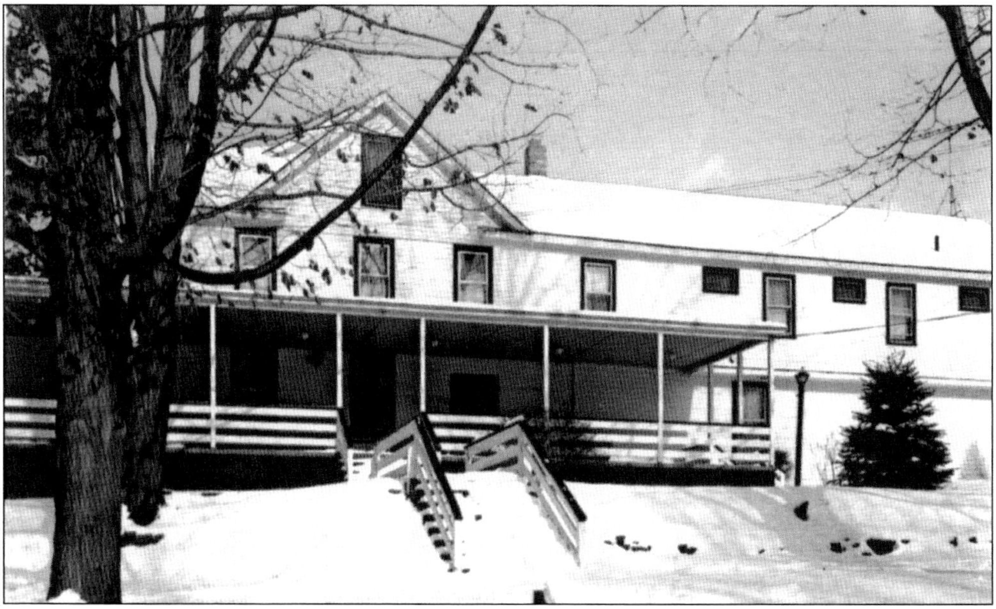

Greenwa Lodge was built as a boardinghouse by Catherine Meiser Vromatr, daughter of John Meiser, in the early 1900s. Each of John Meiser's daughters, of which there were seven, operated an inn catering to tourists. Known as Greenway House, it was renamed Greenwa Lodge by the Sarajian family. The buildings still stand near the Pocono Union Church at the intersection of Route 715N and Route 314. (Courtesy of James Price.)

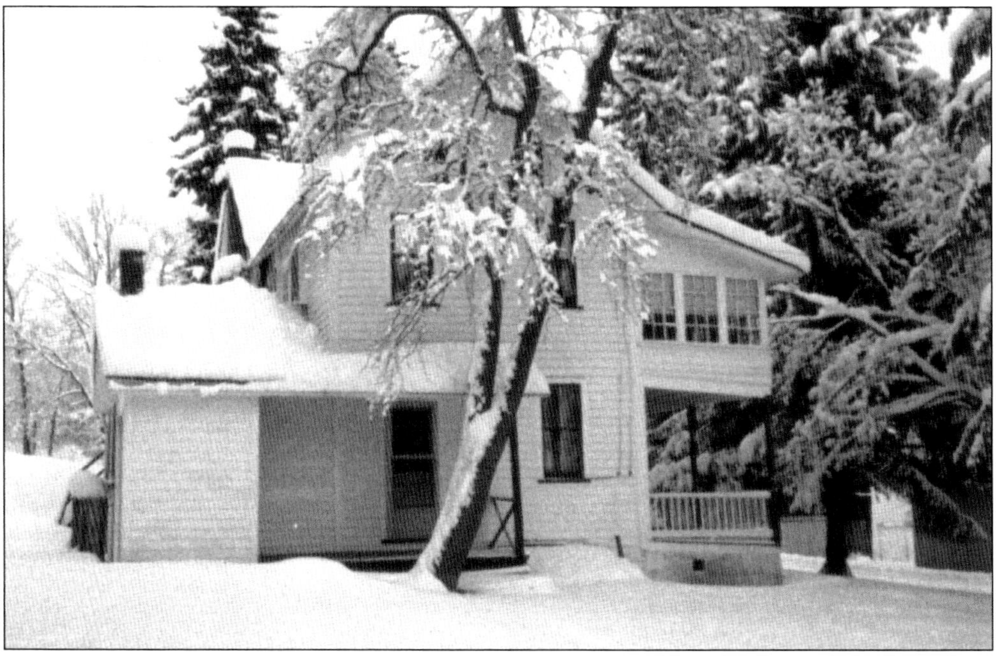

Pedretti Farm consisted of a number of small cottages that dotted the landscape just east of Munch's Boarding House on what is present-day Munch Drive. These cottages provided rest for tourists and families who came to the Pocono Mountains to enjoy the pure country air and peaceful atmosphere. (Courtesy of Mary Pedretti Martinelli.)

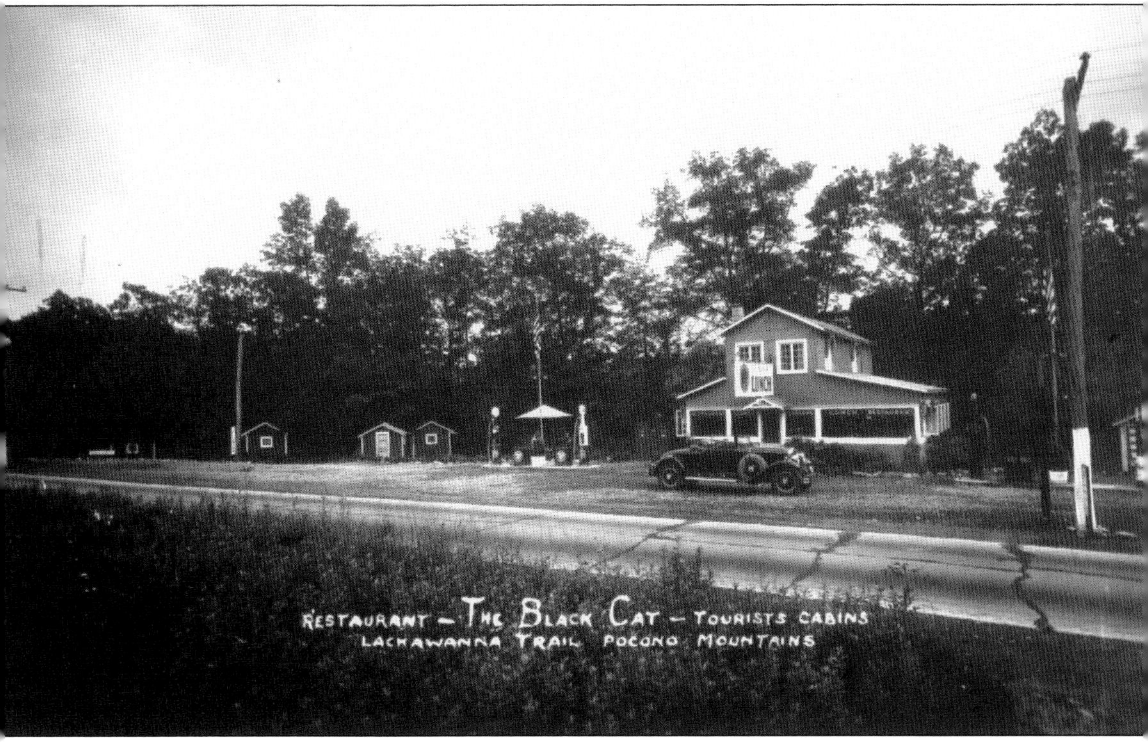

The Black Cat sat along Route 611, or the Lackawanna Trail, serving the motoring public with gasoline sales, tourist cabins, and a restaurant. The site today is located on the northern end of Bartonsville Avenue near its intersection with Route 611. The Black Cat's restaurant and tourist cabins were later renamed the Pocahontas Grill and Cabins, which were operated by Henry and Anna Rohlfs. (Courtesy of John Alleger.)

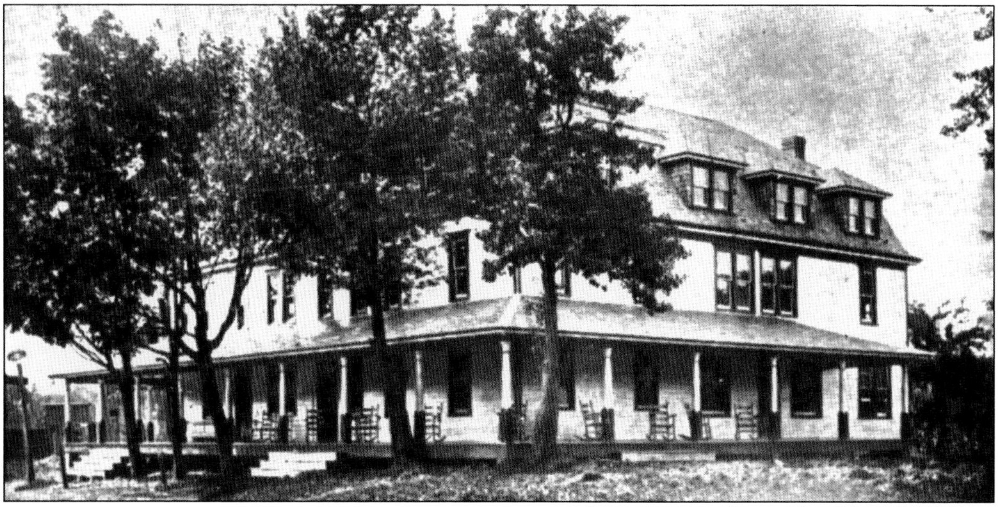

The Forest Inn was located on the northeast corner of the intersection of present-day Route 611 and Bartonsville Avenue. The building is shown above as it appeared around 1905 during the proprietorship of Jervis Hartman. Hartman advertised the hotel extensively, drawing many clients from New York and Philadelphia. Destroyed by fire on March 18, 1906, it was rebuilt at the same location, keeping several features of the old hotel. The photograph below shows the 175 lineal feet of porch that was widely touted as a place to relax and enjoy the "exceptionally pure and invigorating air" of the Pocono Mountains. The new hotel was wired for electricity at the time of the rebuilding and supplied by a power plant on the property. Promotional brochures made special note of the hotel's "modern sanitary plumbing." (Courtesy of John Alleger.)

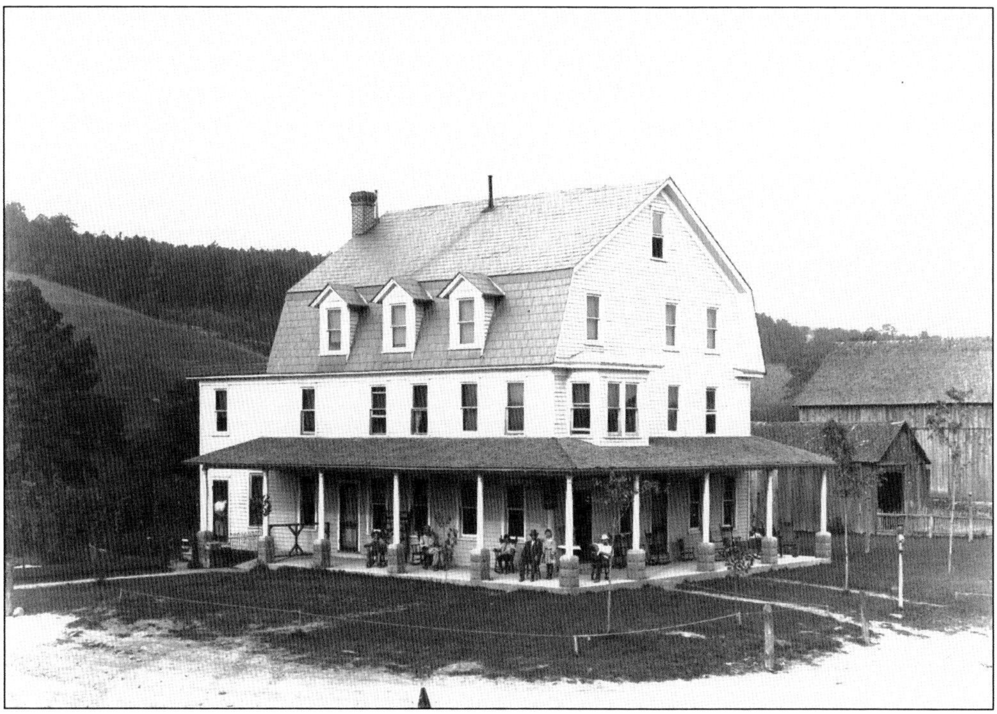

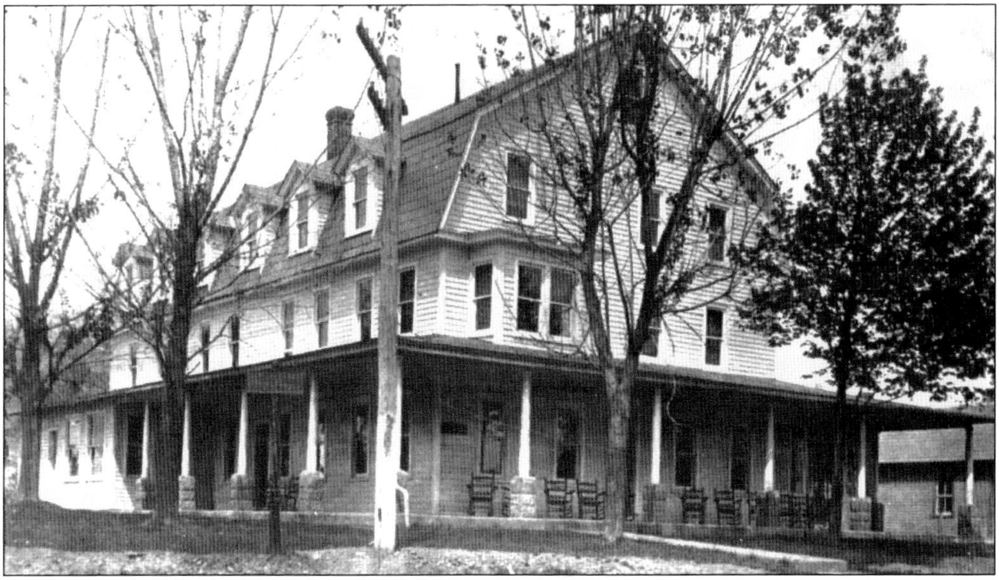

The Forest Inn was destroyed by an early-morning fire on December 31, 1933, as temperatures hovered below zero. At the first sign of the blaze, neighbors called for the fire department from Stroudsburg. By the time firefighters arrived, a hole had been cut in the ice of the nearby millrace, providing a steady source of water. Firefighters were aided in their work to save the structure by a wall that partially separated two sections of the building. Saving a portion of the structure from ruin created the well-known "hanging bathtub," which became visible when several of the hotel's exterior walls were burned away, exposing the interior rooms to view. Following the fire, local teenage boys climbed into the second floor of the partially burned hotel and seated a stuffed, life-size figure on the toilet of the exposed bathroom, causing numerous second glances from those traveling on the nearby Lackawanna Trail. (Courtesy of John Alleger.)

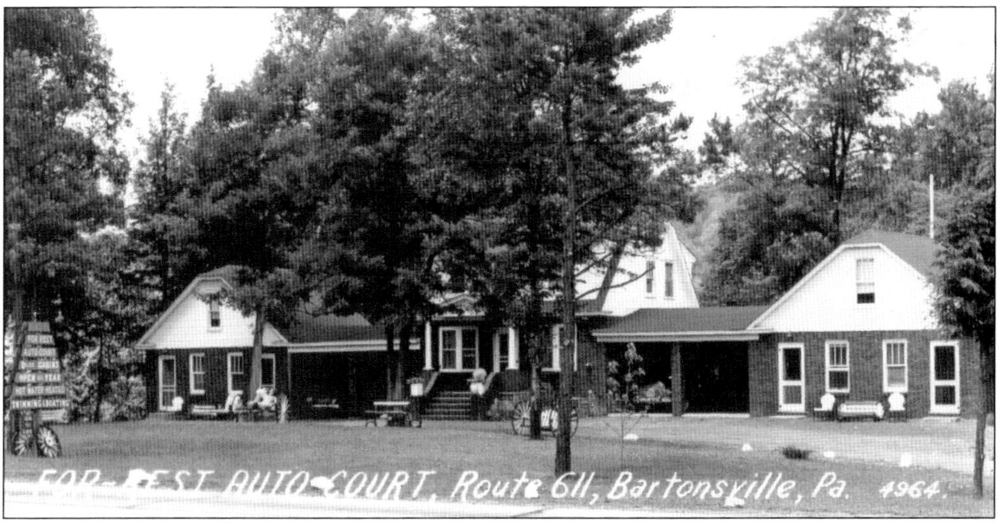

For Rest Auto Court was the predecessor of Knight's Inn along Route 611 in Bartonsville. It was built and operated by Forrest and Ruth Marvin Motts on land purchased from James Canfield Sr., owner of the mill at Bartonsville. The creek at the rear of the building was dammed to provide a water supply for the millrace, which served the mill nearly a quarter mile south. (Courtesy of John Alleger.)

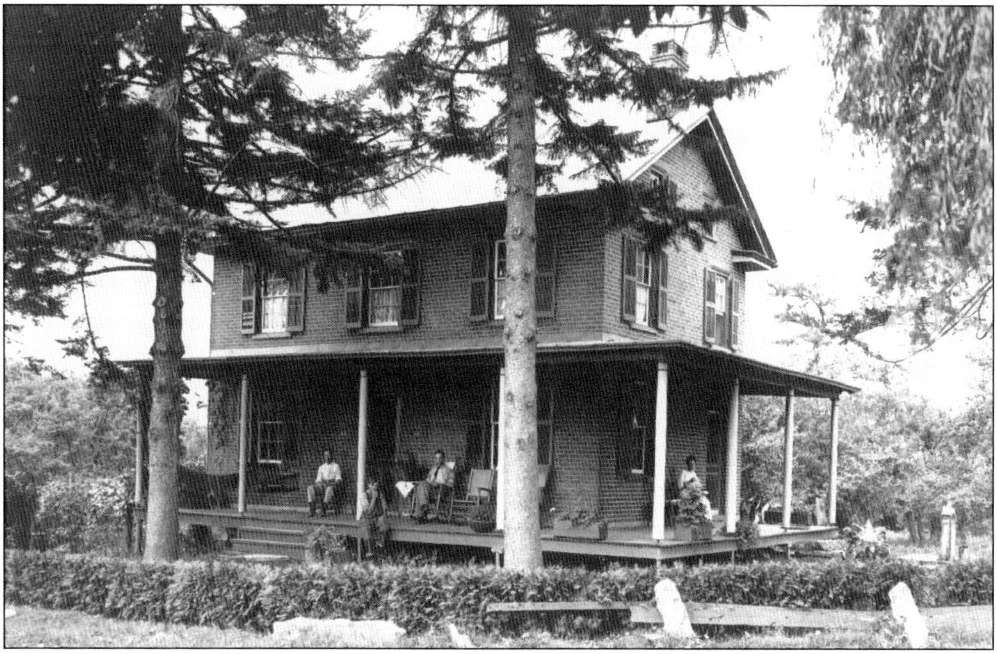

Pokona Farm was the Alleger family homestead. Even after more than 100 years, the well-kept farmhouse and outbuildings still straddle a sharp corner on Beehler Road just north of Bartonsville. During the first half of the 20th century, the farm provided a welcome respite to boarders looking to escape the hustle and bustle of city life. A brochure from about 1940 describes the farm as "a home-like vacation home with old-fashioned country hospitality and home-cooking." Rates of $2.25 per day or $15 per week included a room and three meals per day. The guesthouse era of Pokona Farm ended in 1964 when the farm's owner, Mary Beehler, born in 1886, passed away. Currently a private residence, the property was presented with the Monroe County Historical Association's Preserve, Enhance, and Promote Award in 2009 for residential properties. (Courtesy of John Alleger.)

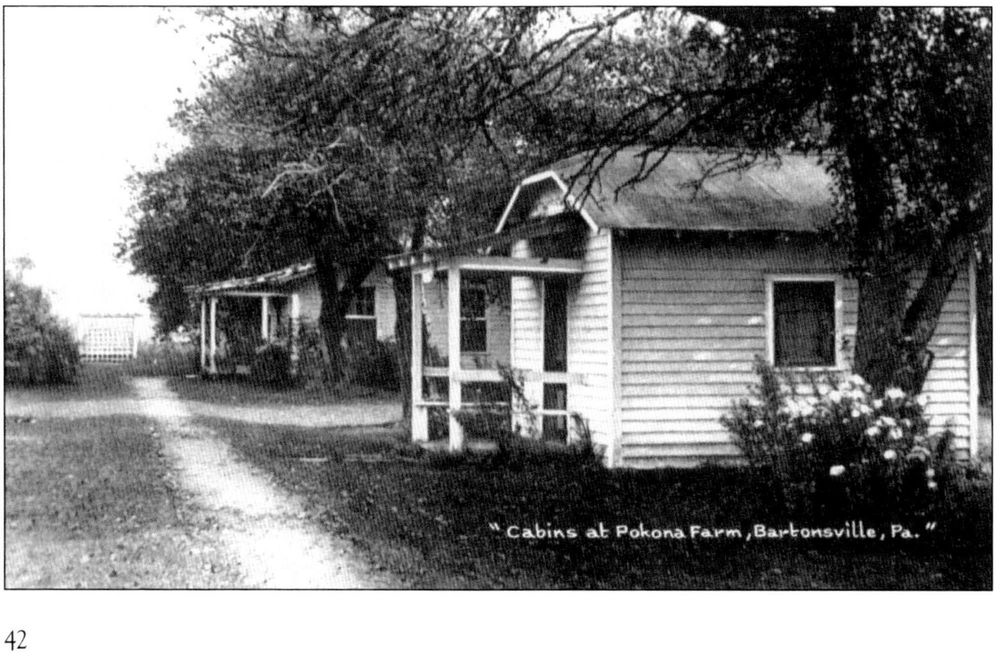

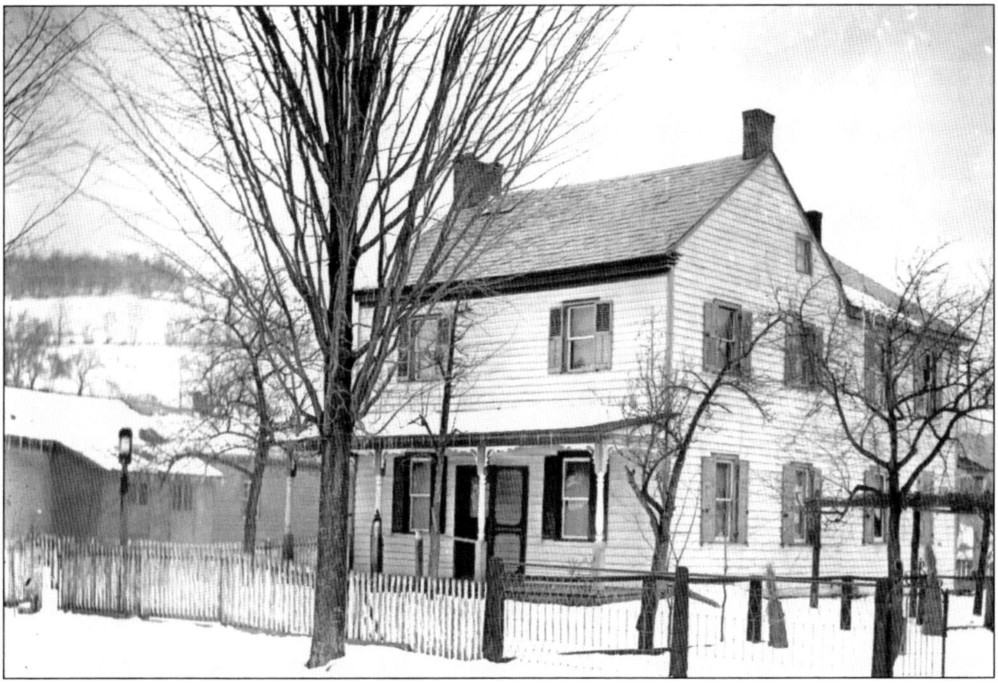

Located just south of Learn's store, this house sat along Tannersville's main road facing the tannery/school property near the intersection of present-day Route 611 and Route 715N. Purchased in 1923 by Rodgers (1889–1983) and Cora Feller Shook (1890–1977), this structure was later razed. The home built in its place during the fall and early winter of 1928 not only became Quando Lodge, a popular boardinghouse, but it also became the home to the Shooks for the rest of their lives. (Courtesy of John Alleger.)

Home for Tourists - Open all year **U. S. Route 611**

QUANDO LODGE

"IN THE POCONOS"

RODGERS C. SHOOK, Prop.

TANNERSVILLE, PA.

Meals by Day or Week **Bath - Hot Water Heat**

Quando Lodge's five bedrooms frequently accommodated as many as a dozen or more guests. While a number of guests visited only once, others came back year after year, becoming family friends. A few continued to spend their vacations in the Poconos with the Shooks several decades after the boardinghouse had been closed to the general public. (Courtesy of John Alleger.)

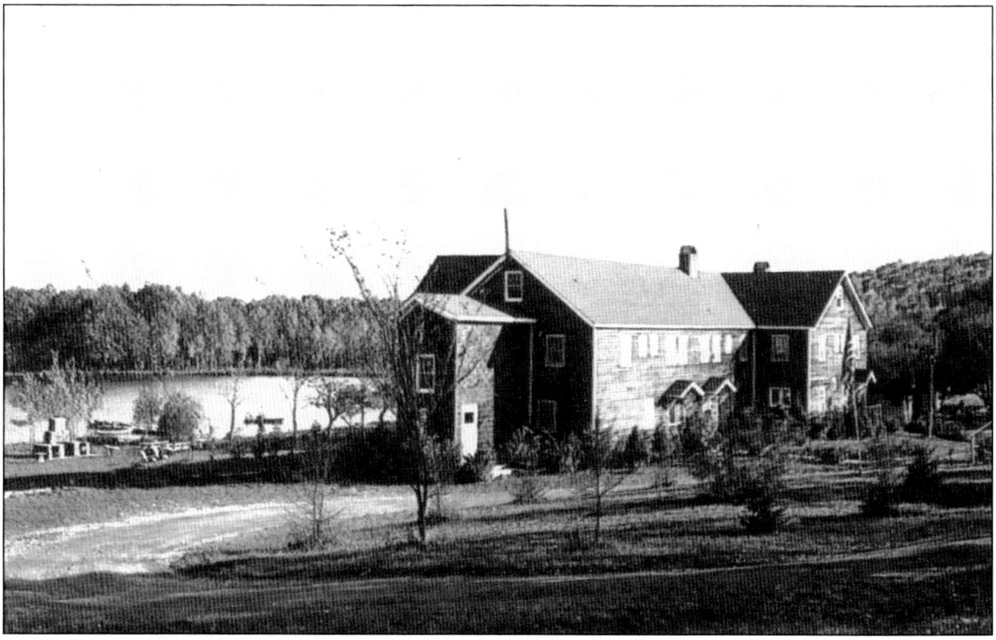

Brookdale-on-the-Lake was a family resort located just off Route 611 in Scotrun. Advertising over the past 80 years described it as "a place to escape from everyday routines; a place to relax together, play together and reconnect." Brookdale-on-the-Lake was recently sold by Caesar's Resorts and is no longer in operation. (Courtesy of John J. Riley.)

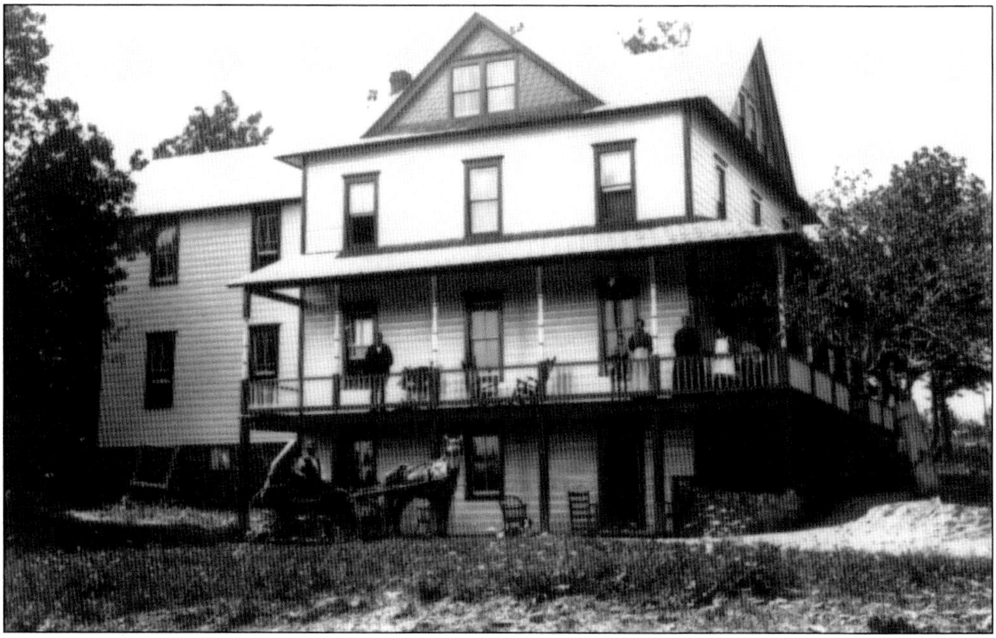

Reeders Hotel was built around 1893 about the same time as construction of the Wilkes-Barre and Eastern Railroad, which ran from Wilkes-Barre to Stroudsburg. Hauling ice from the lakes in Jackson Township, the rail line also brought coal from the mines in the coal region, railroad ties and mine props to the mines, livestock feed, produce, and general freight. (Courtesy of the Pocono-Jackson Historical Society.)

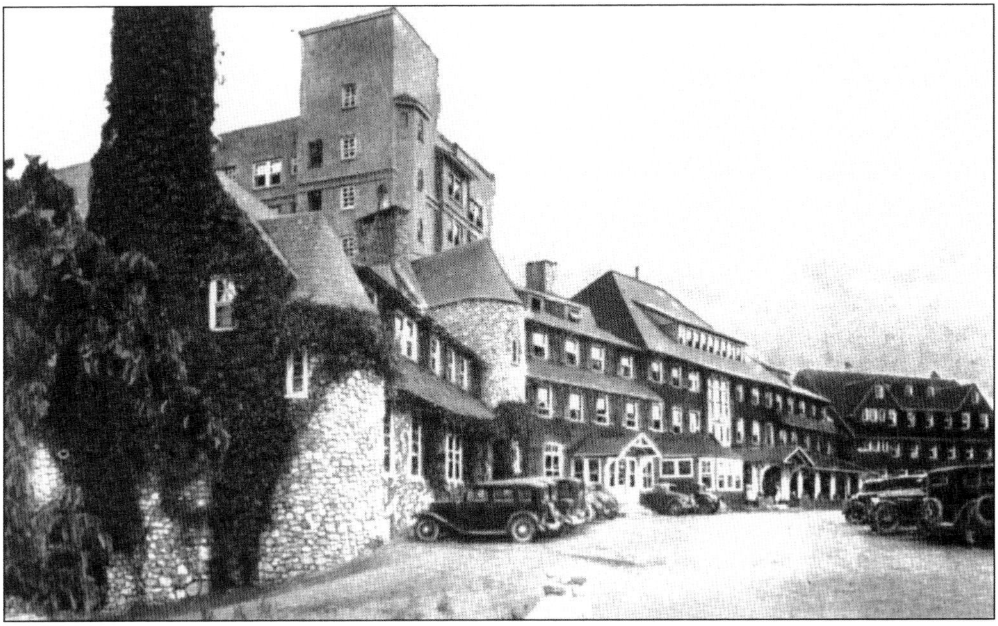

Pocono Manor was built in 1902 by Quaker businessmen from Philadelphia. The original purchase on Little Pocono Mountain was comprised of about 700 to 800 acres. In 1903, it was recorded that the first Friends meeting took place in the auditorium of the west wing. This was to be the only type of church service held at the manor for the next 31 years. The present-day 18-hole golf course was created in 1927. Today the manor is a 3,000-acre resort that has gained a reputation as a top choice for family reunions, getaways, conferences, meetings, weddings, weekend escapes, and so much more. (Courtesy of Linford Werkheiser.)

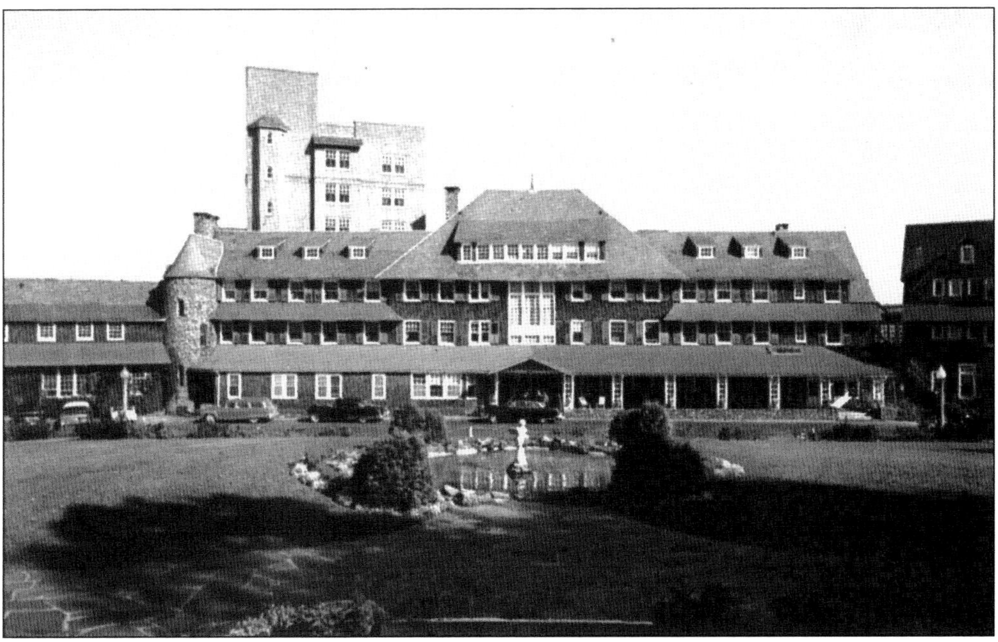

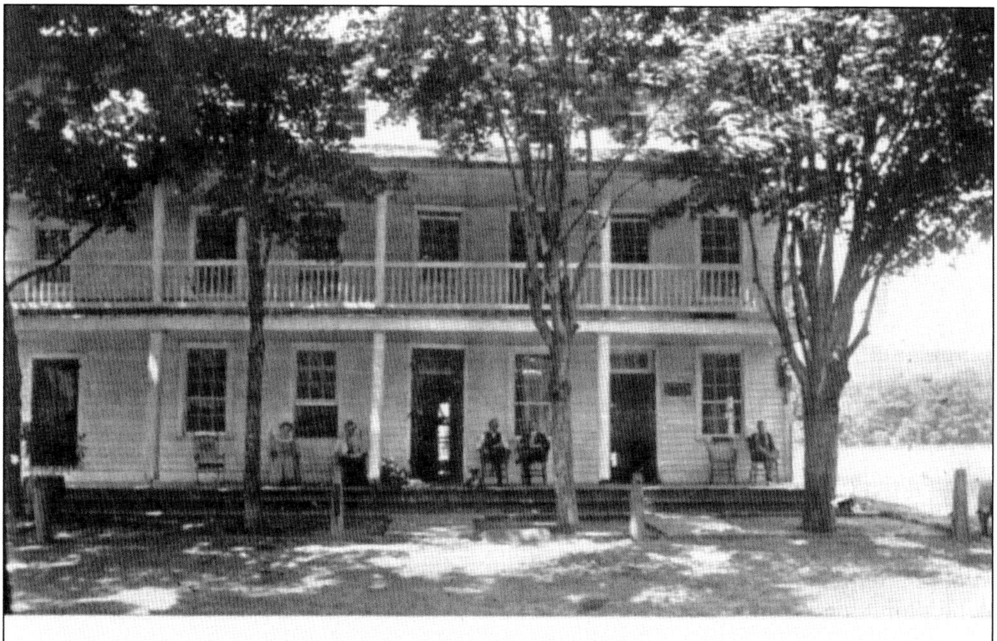

POCONO HOTEL, TANNERSVILLE, PA.

These two photographs show the Pocono Hotel at different eras. It was originally built in 1740 as a small tavern. Its names over the years include Learned's Tavern, Brown's Hotel, Trach's Hotel, Alpen Hof, and Coral Reef. This historic structure burned in the 1990s. At one time, a large red neon *T* was mounted on the roof and was a feature on aerial maps used by pilots. CVS Pharmacy now occupies this site in Tannersville. (Courtesy of Diane Davis Abeel.)

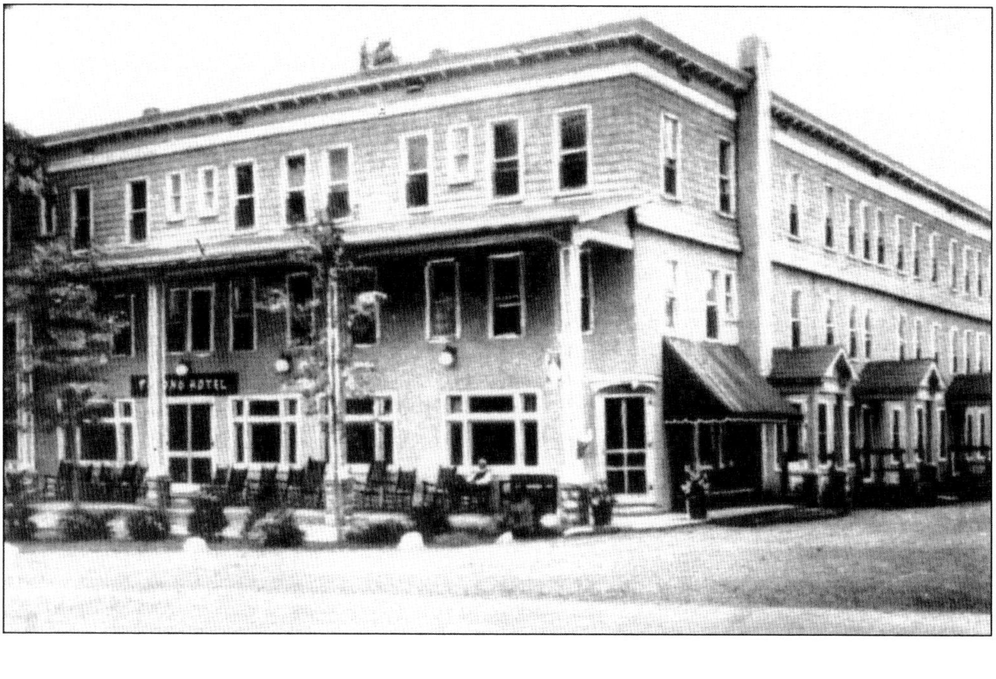

RATES

For the Season

AMERICAN PLAN — ROOM AND MEALS

WEEKLY RATES

One Person —

Single Room - - -	**$19**	**$20**	**$21**	**$22**	**$23**

Per Person —

Double Room - -	**$17**	**$18**	**$19**	**$20**	**$21**

One Person —

Single Room Bath -	**$26.00**	**$27.00**	**$28.00**

Per Person —

Double Room Bath -	**$20.50**	**$21.50**	**$22.50**	**$23.50**

DAILY RATES (*Per Person*)

Week Days —

Single without bath **$3.65**—Single with bath **$4.15**
Double without bath **$3.50** Double with bath **$4.00**

Week-ends and Holidays —

Single without bath **$4.25**—Single with bath **$4.75**
Double without bath **$4.15** Double with bath **$4.65**

MEAL RATES

Week Days —

Breakfast - - **60c** Dinner - - **90c** Supper - - **90c**

Sundays and Holidays —

Breakfast - **60c** Dinner - **$1.50** Supper - **1.25**

Lodging —

Single without bath - - **$1.25**—With bath - - **$1.75**
Double without bath - **$2.25**- With bath - **$3.25**

For Reservations Write to

Trach's Pocono Hotel

On U. S. Route 611 — Tannersville, Penna.

Telephone: Stroudsburg 6083-J-2

During the 1950s, the Pocono Hotel had been sold and was known as Trach's Pocono Hotel. This room rate card has survived to give a glimpse of the reasonable costs for the day, week, and month, including meals. Those rooms with a bath were more expensive. Meal prices are also listed; breakfast cost 60¢. (Courtesy of John Alleger.)

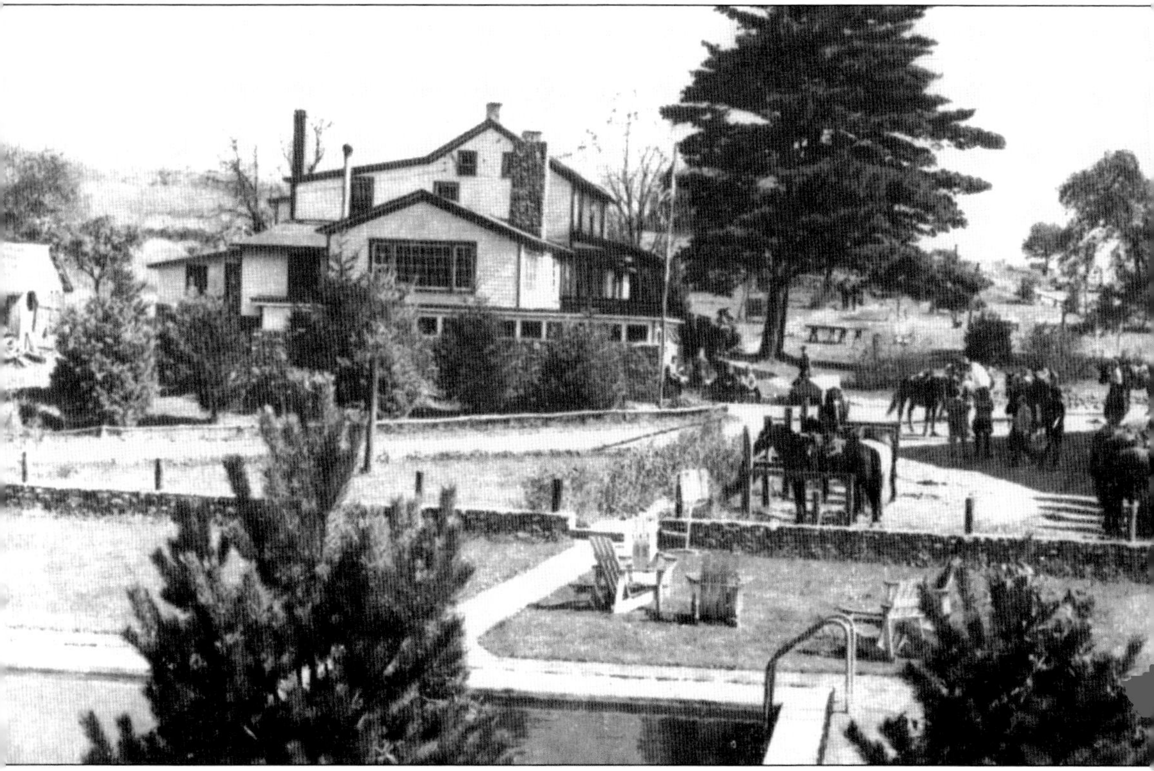

The 1938 sale of a farm in southeastern Jackson Township began a transformation that ended with the creation of a dude ranch known throughout the eastern United States. Owned by Thomas and Elaine Robinson, Twin Pine Lodge and Guest Ranch offered its guests a touch of the Southwest in eastern Pennsylvania. The weeklong vacations of aspiring cowboys and cowgirls were filled with riding lessons, cookouts, square dances, and western entertainment. Advertisements encouraged would-be guests to join in the fun and make Twin Pine Lodge and Guest Ranch their "Home on the Range." Today Twin Pines Camp, Conference and Retreat Center, a ministry of the Evangelical Congregational Church, occupies this 205-acre hilltop location. (Courtesy of John Alleger.)

Three

Reading, Writing, and Arithmetic

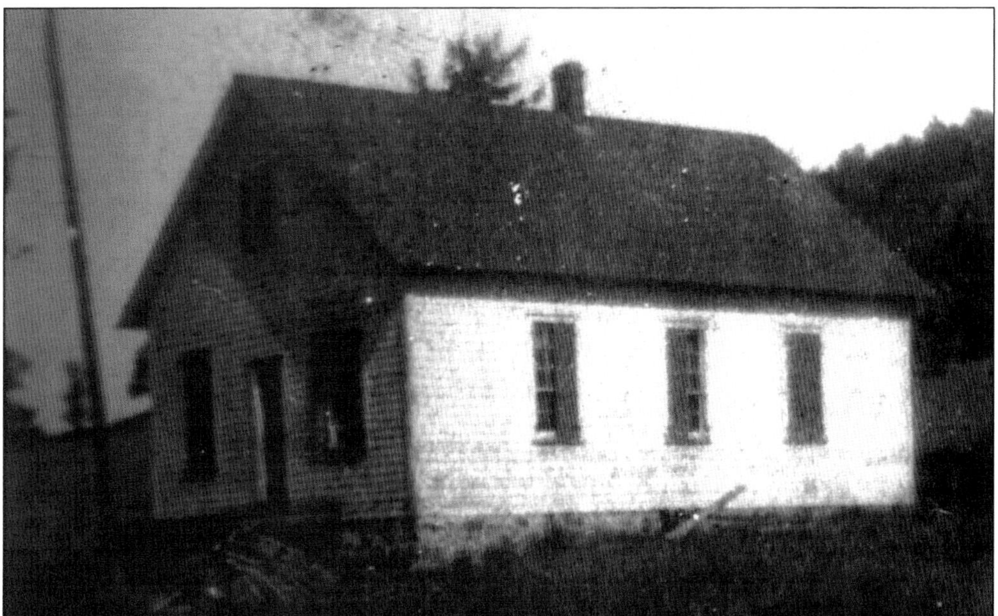

The original Neola (Rinkerville) one-room schoolhouse was torn down in the late 19th century and replaced with a larger school to accommodate the many students from the area. (Courtesy of Diane Davis Abeel.)

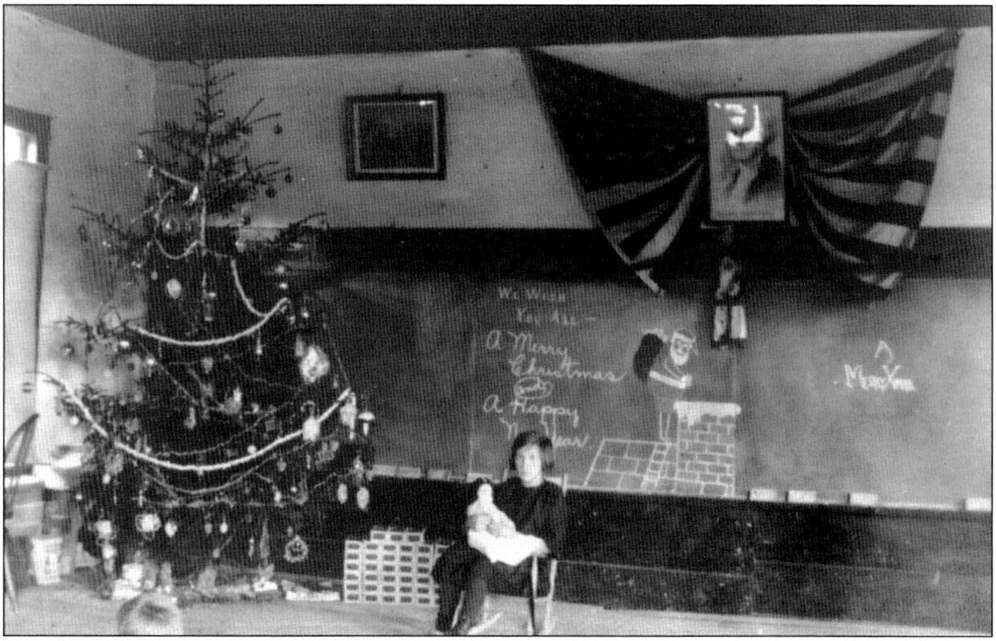

Hazel Butz is shown holding a doll at Christmastime in the Appenzell one-room school about 1920. Notice how the American flag is draped using a portrait of George Washington to hold the center, and the chalk drawing on the blackboard is depicting Santa Claus ready to go down the chimney. (Courtesy of Robert Wallingford.)

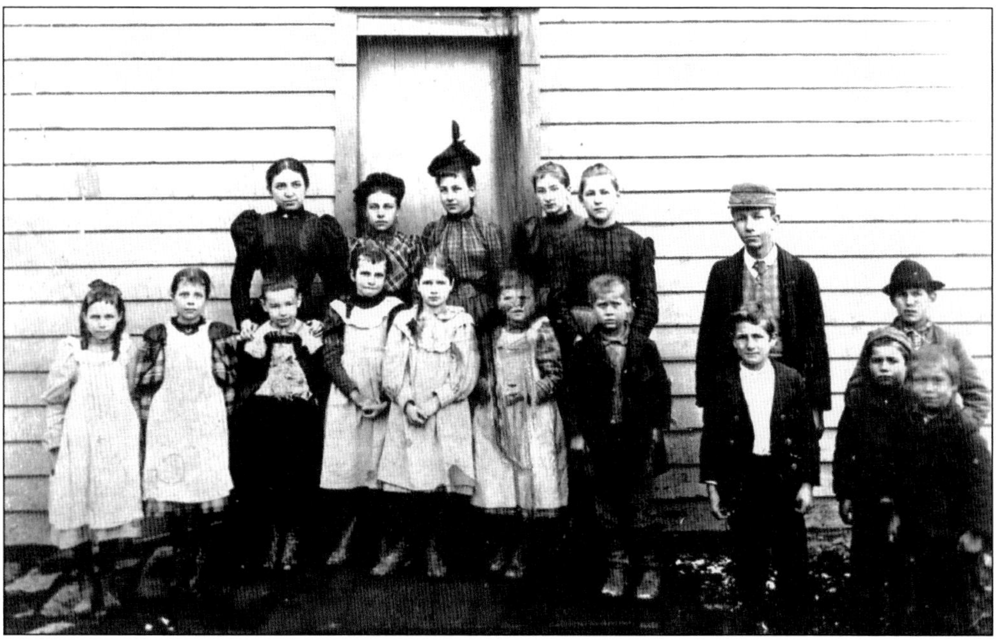

Pupils line up in front of the Pocono Township one-room schoolhouse at Swiftwater around 1900. The school operated until 1920 in a small white building two doors east of the former Swiftwater United Methodist Church on Upper Swiftwater Road. Following closure in 1920, the building was utilized for storing apples harvested from the adjacent William J. Hamblin farm. The schoolhouse now houses a day care center. (Courtesy of Jack Hamblin.)

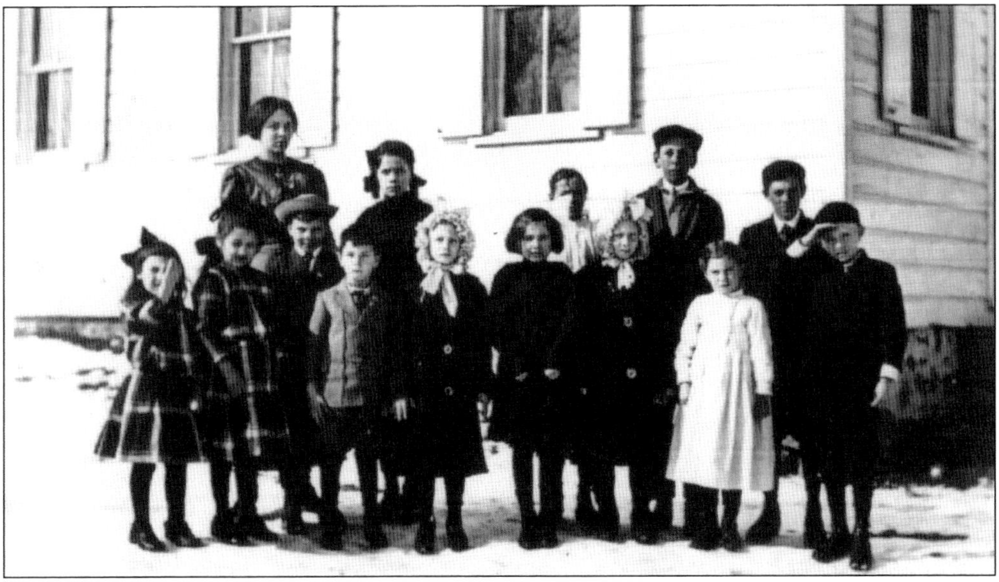

White Oak Run School was located along Sullivan Trail near the border with Coolbaugh Township. A known teacher was Lulu Schiffer. The Grace Reformed Chapel was located in the area. The two girls in plaid outfits pictured in the first row may be sisters Rose and Nora Hawk, whose family lived nearby. The school has since been converted to a private home. (Courtesy of Mike Iby.)

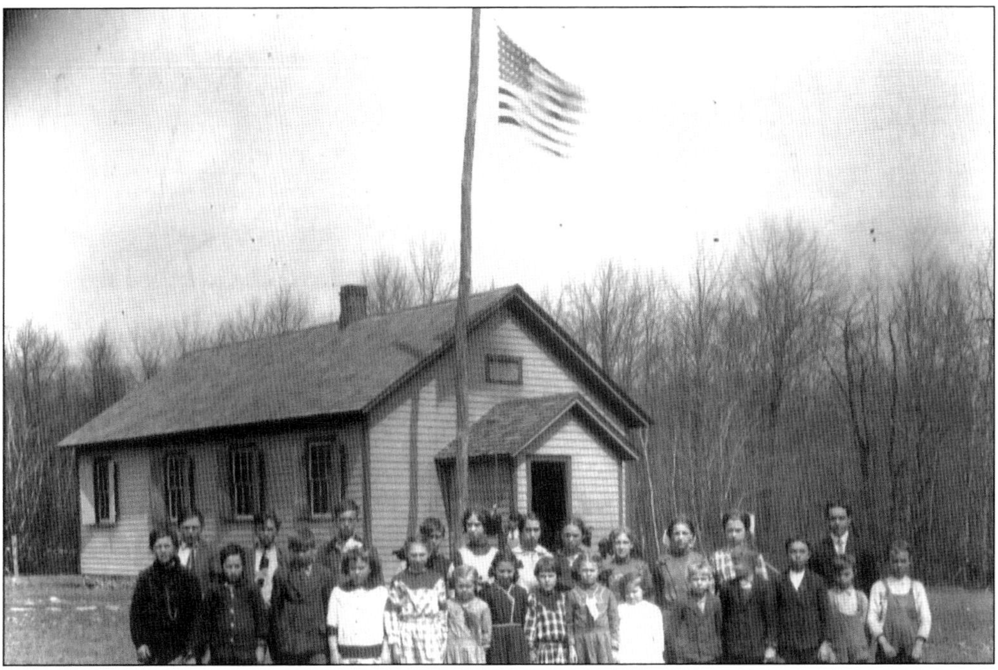

The Mountain School was built about 1900 for 18 to 30 students. Notable teachers were James Butz, Thomas Possinger, Claude T. Shupp, Adam Meckes, Floyd E. Shupp, Earl Doll, Samuel Reimel, Verna C. Hillard, Bessie D. Grover, Gladys George, Alice Wilson, Burton A. Shupp, and Romaine Reimel. It has since been converted into a private home. (Courtesy of Olive Metzger Learn.)

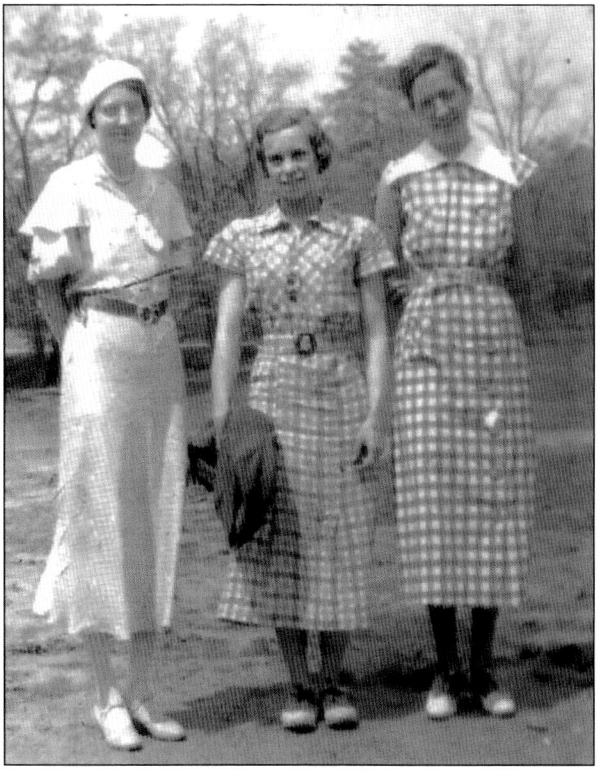

Many students have memories of the teachers at the Pocono Township Consolidated and High School. Pictured here are, from left to right, Mabel Singer, Margaret Bryson, and Helen Shick. (Courtesy of Leeanne Dyson.)

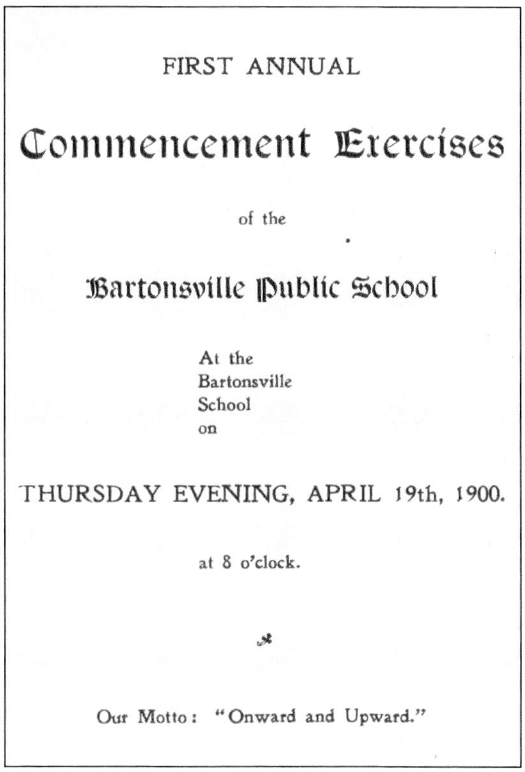

FIRST ANNUAL

Commencement Exercises

of the

Bartonsville Public School

At the
Bartonsville
School
on

THURSDAY EVENING, APRIL 19th, 1900.

at 8 o'clock.

Our Motto: "Onward and Upward."

The Bartonsville Public School was located in the most southern part of Pocono Township. This program from April 19, 1900, marks the first commencement exercises. The graduating class consisted of two pupils, valedictorian Daisy Shook and salutatorian Ira Hay. Several other persons listed as having taken part in the exercises are teacher C. B. Musselman and students Mary Metzgar, Hattie Bisbing, Frank Marvin, Mary Alleger, and Mabel Shook. (Courtesy of John Alleger.)

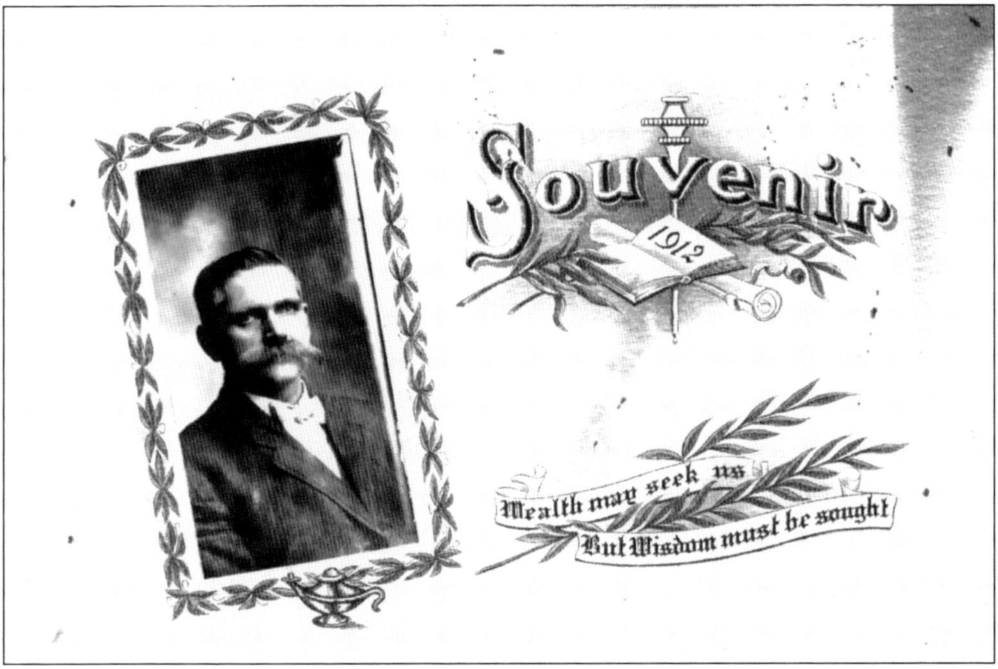

These pages are from the 1912 Cherry Lane School souvenir booklet with a photograph of teacher Thomas Possinger pasted on the front cover. The school was located along Cherry Lane and was later owned by Judge Davis, who converted it to a private dwelling. (Courtesy of Diane Davis Abeel.)

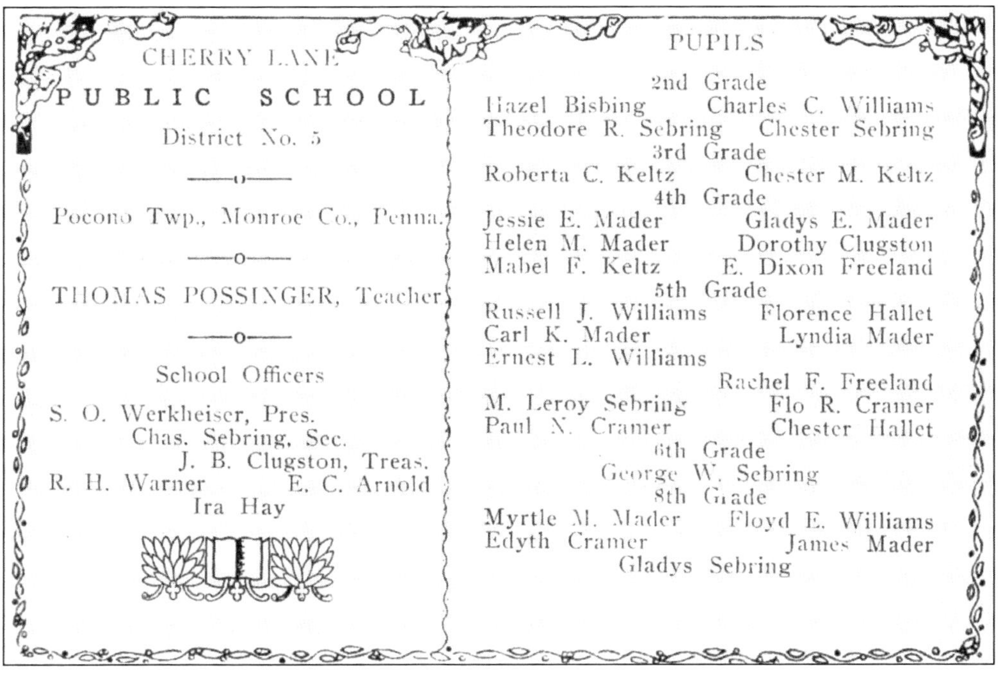

CHERRY LANE
PUBLIC SCHOOL
District No. 5

—o—

Pocono Twp., Monroe Co., Penna.

—o—

THOMAS POSSINGER, Teacher

—o—

School Officers

S. O. Werkheiser, Pres.
Chas. Sebring, Sec.
J. B. Clugston, Treas.
R. H. Warner E. C. Arnold
Ira Hay

PUPILS

2nd Grade
Hazel Bisbing Charles C. Williams
Theodore R. Sebring Chester Sebring
3rd Grade
Roberta C. Keltz Chester M. Keltz
4th Grade
Jessie E. Mader Gladys E. Mader
Helen M. Mader Dorothy Clugston
Mabel F. Keltz E. Dixon Freeland
5th Grade
Russell J. Williams Florence Hallet
Carl K. Mader Lyndia Mader
Ernest L. Williams
Rachel F. Freeland
M. Leroy Sebring Flo R. Cramer
Paul N. Cramer Chester Hallet
6th Grade
George W. Sebring
8th Grade
Myrtle M. Mader Floyd E. Williams
Edyth Cramer James Mader
Gladys Sebring

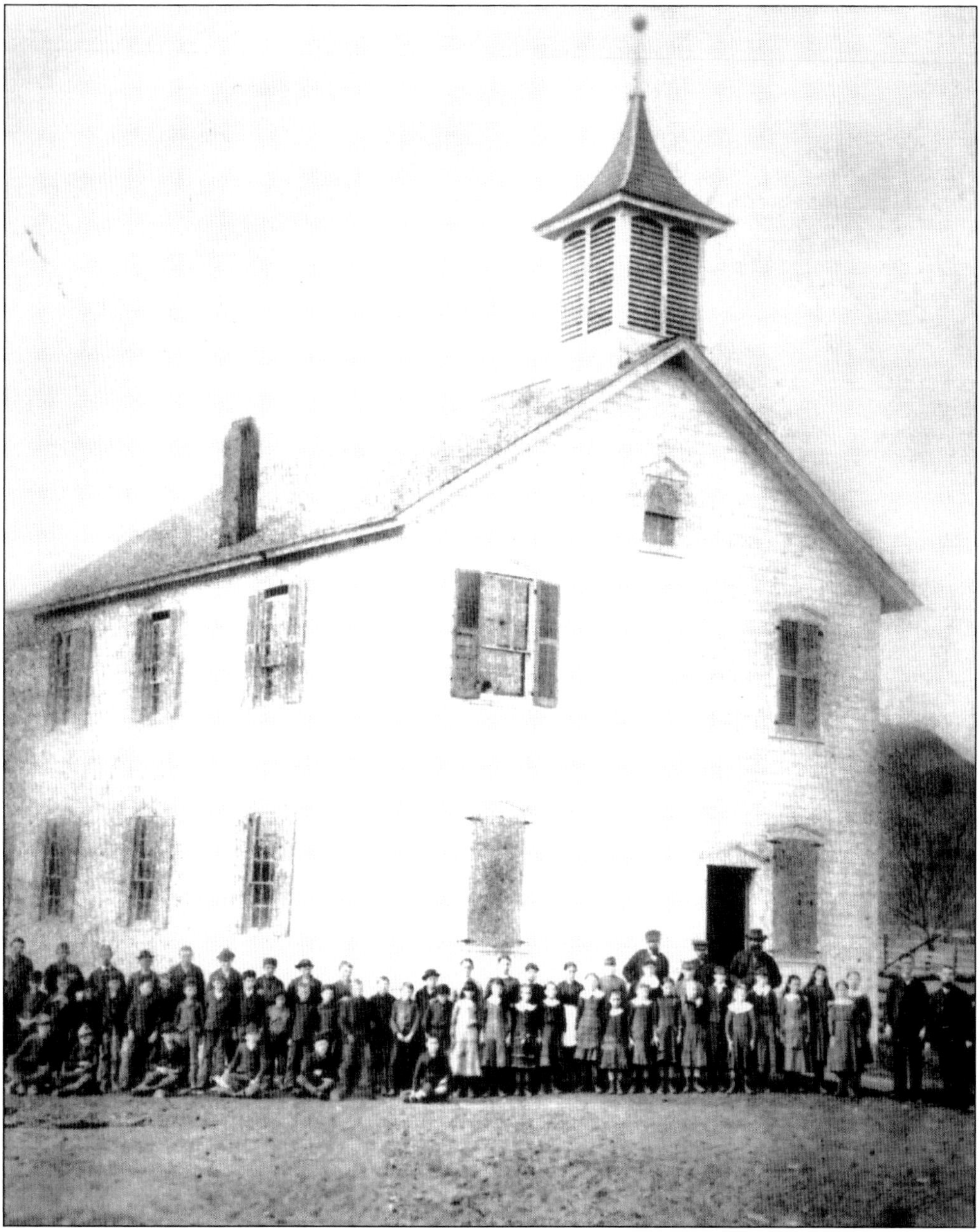

Tannersville Graded School, a two-story building, was located next to the Methodist church and cemetery on old Route 611. They were behind what are now Carquest Auto Parts and a delicatessen, which are located where Metzger's Nu-Way Market was previously. The first floor housed the school, and the second floor was used by the Pokono Grange. Eventually the first floor housed grades one through four, and the second floor held grades five through eight. The first graduate, Emma Singer, went on to be a teacher at the Scotrun Graded School. The original rectangular heating stove is now located in the restored Appenzell one-room school. Among the many teachers were Mary S. Royer, F. F. Marvin, Dr. Elsie Longacre, Florence Gantzhorn, Mary Bryson, Floyd Hay, Lillian Learn, and a Mrs. Shaw. (Courtesy of the Monroe County Historical Society.)

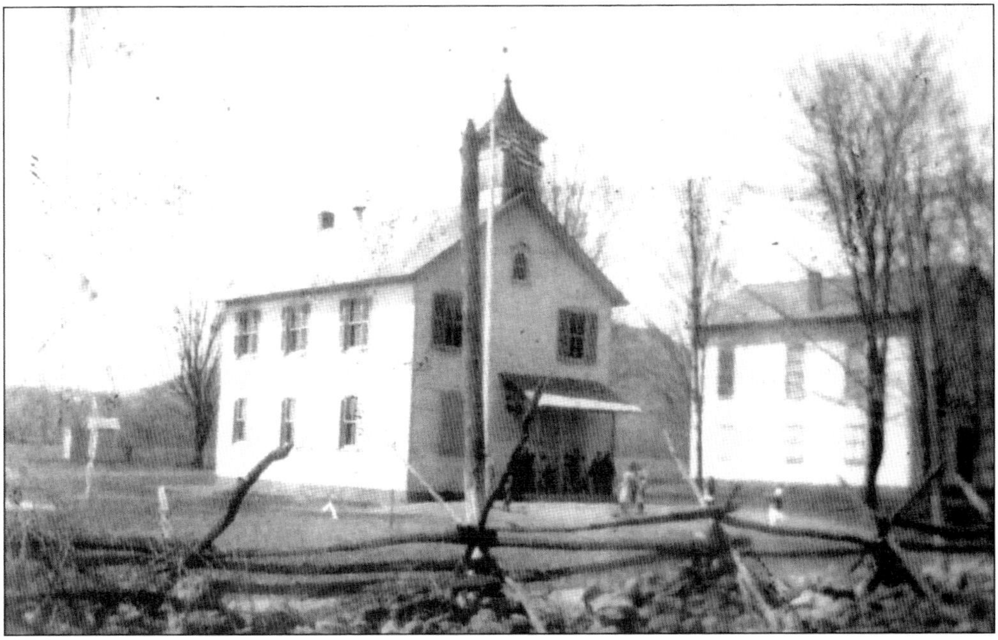

Tannersville Graded School, built in 1879, housed a bell in the cupola. This photograph has William H. Miller listed as teacher. The school closed in 1925 when the new Pocono Township School opened, and the building was sold to the Pocono Grange. The first teacher at the school was Rev. L. M. Hobbs. Both the old school and the neighboring Methodist church were torn down in the 1970s. (Courtesy of the Monroe County Historical Society.)

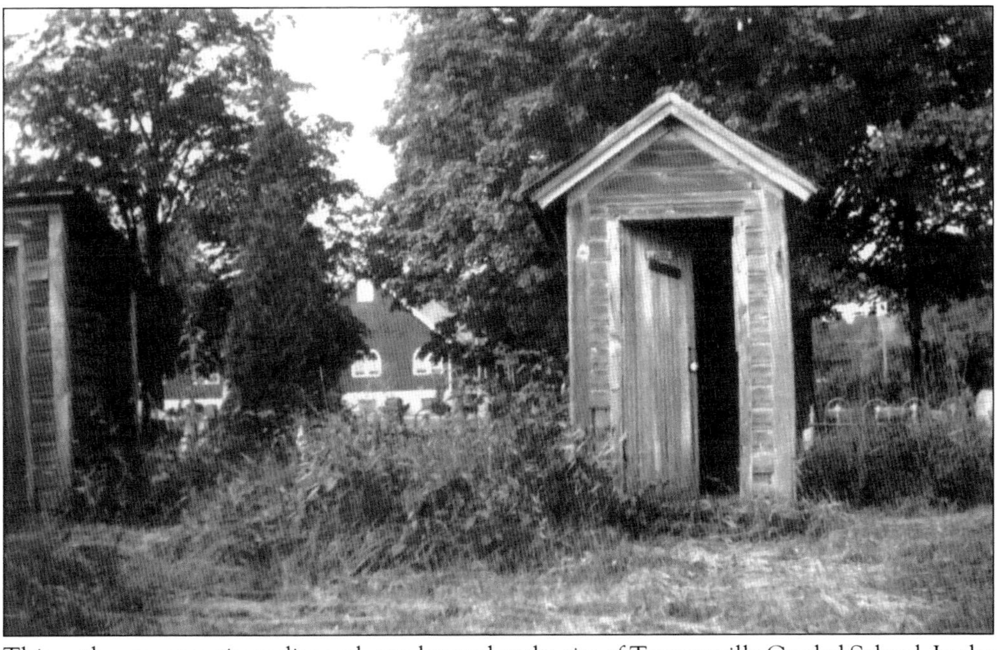

This outhouse, or sanitary disposal, was located at the site of Tannersville Graded School. In the background are the Our Lady of Victory Catholic Church and the Methodist church cemetery. The graded school was abandoned in 1925 when the Pocono Township Consolidated and High School was constructed. (Courtesy of the Pocono-Jackson Historical Society.)

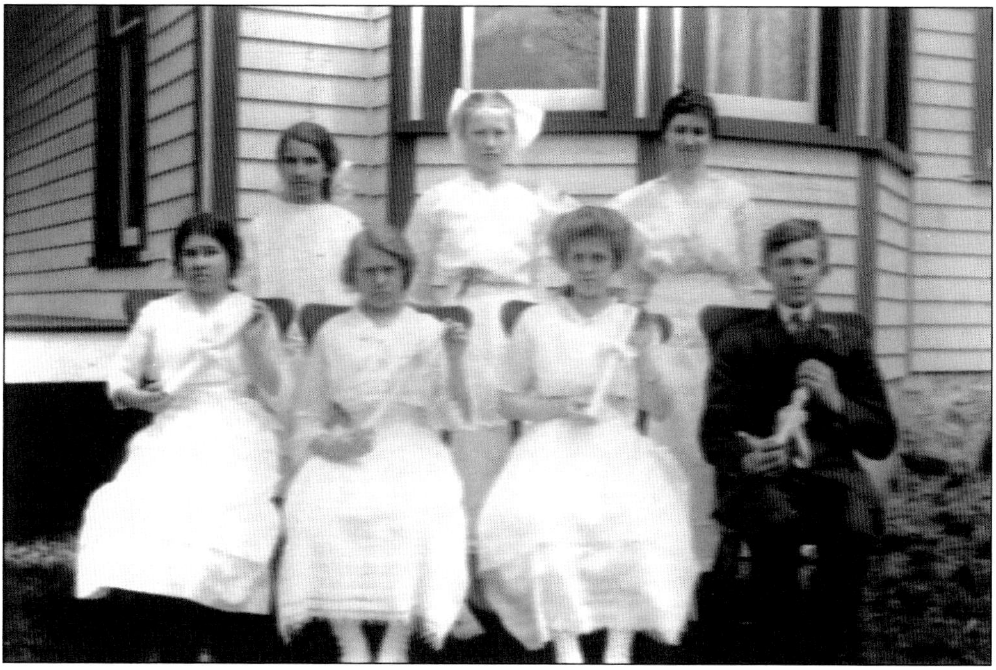

Taken at the Clyde Paul homestead, this photograph shows the eighth-grade graduation at the Appenzell one-room school. Pictured are, from left to right, (first row) Alice Motz, Verna Hillard, Alberta Baltz, and Paul Whelan; (second row) Catherine Motz, Mabel J. Miller, and teacher Etta Paul. (Courtesy of Olive Metzger Learn.)

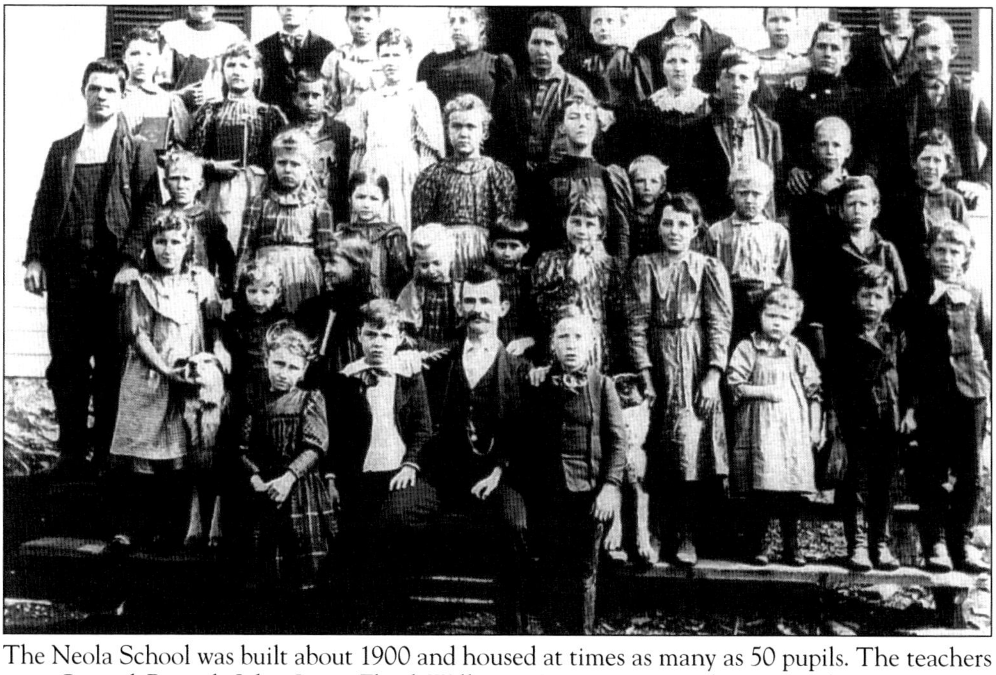

The Neola School was built about 1900 and housed at times as many as 50 pupils. The teachers were Samuel Reimel, John Litts, Floyd Williams, Mary A. Reimel, Etta Paul, and Franklin Everett. It has since been converted to a private home. Seen on the left in the second row are Essie Olive Smith and her dog Shep. (Courtesy of Diane Davis Abeel.)

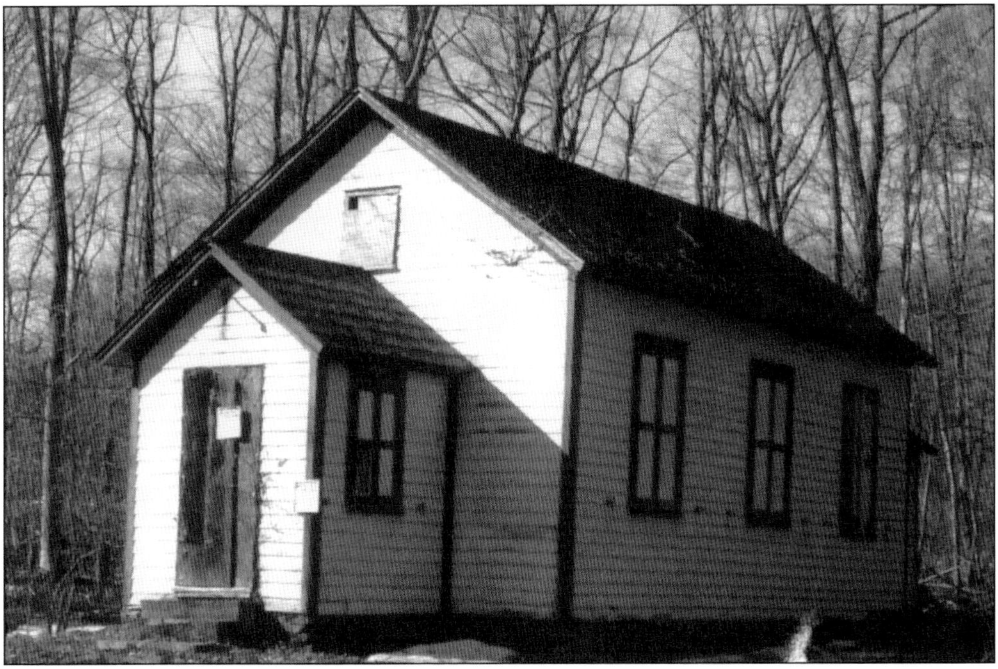

The Butz Run one-room schoolhouse is still standing on what is now Route 715 on the road from Tannersville to Meisertown. It was closed in 1925, when schools in Pocono Township consolidated. The building is boarded up and has been unused since it closed. (Courtesy of Marie Starner Guidry.)

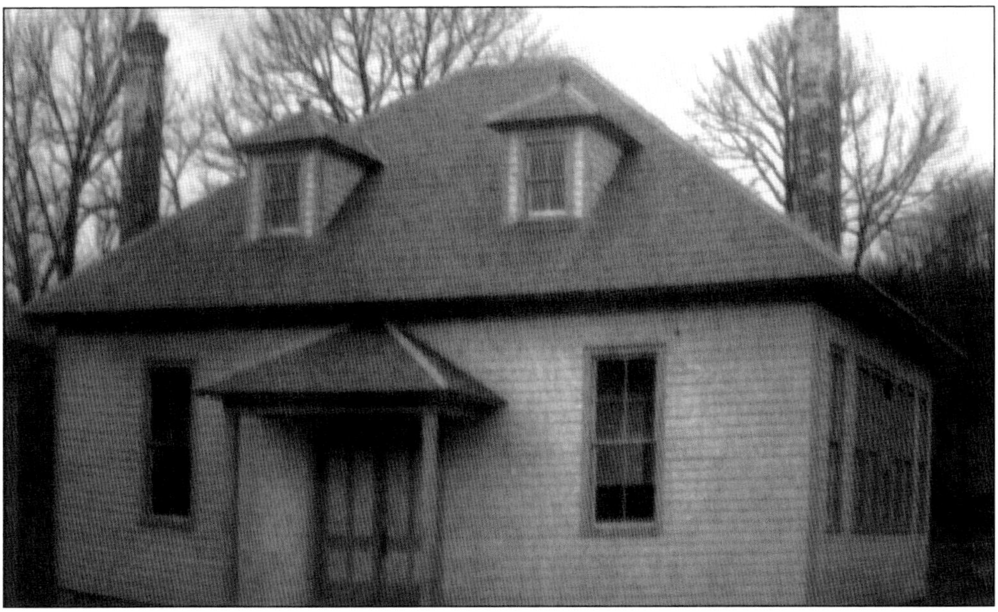

The Scotrun School was originally a one-room building constructed in 1840. It was replaced with this two-room schoolhouse built in 1915. The old one-room school was then torn down. Teachers were Ethel Bisbing, Harry Bisbing, Floyd Hay, Mabel Learn, Cora Raish, Charles Werkheiser, Keturah Mader, Florence Gantzhorn, Pearl Warner, Emma Singer, and Ruth Learn. (Courtesy of Linford Werkheiser.)

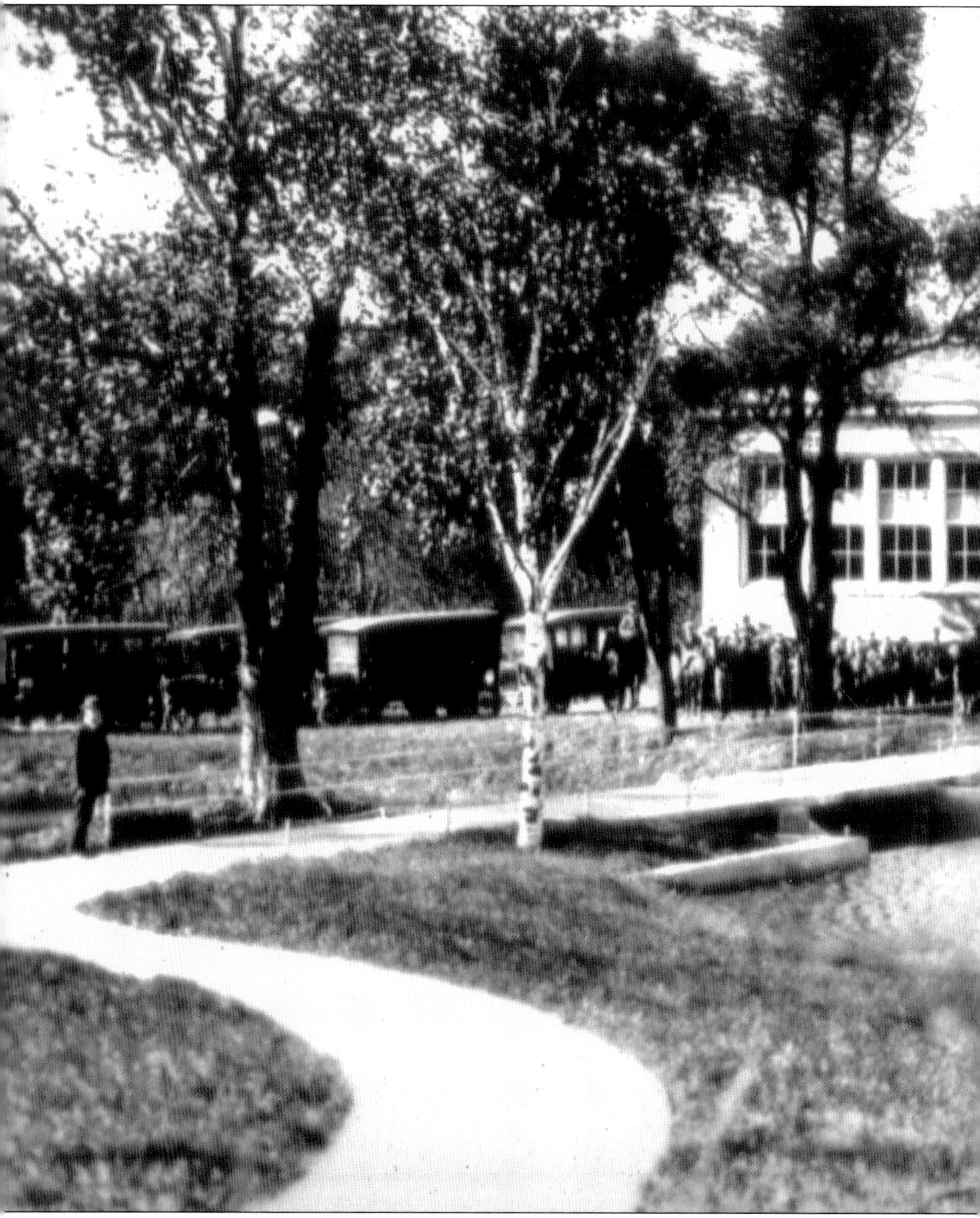

The opening day of the brand-new Pocono Township Consolidated and High School was in 1925. To the left rear are the school buses shining and lined up waiting for students. The students are in their first day finery. Dr. A. A. Wertman is standing on the sidewalk by the old millpond. Kistler's Mill was torn down to make way for the school. The tannery that burned in 1888 was

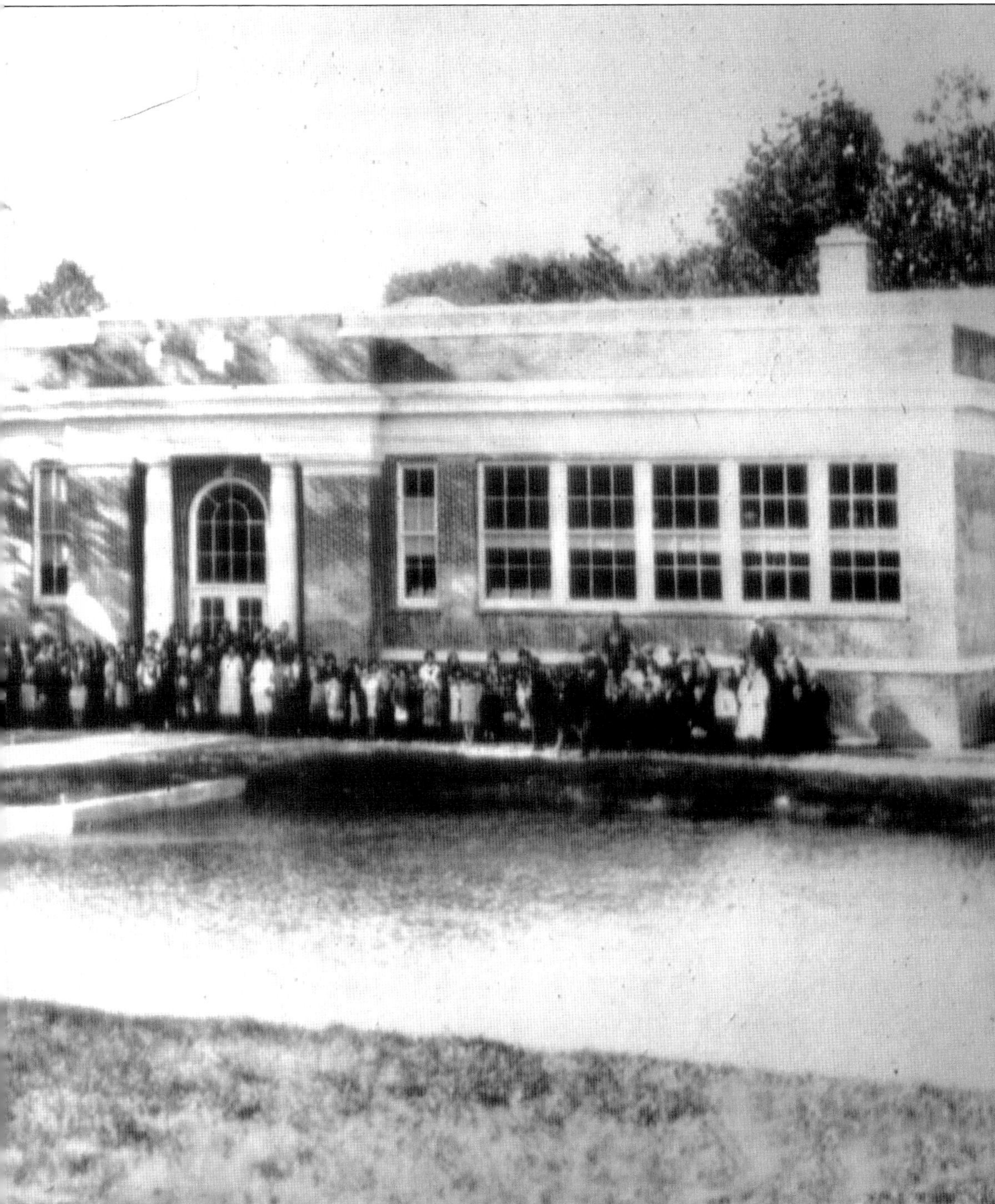

located directly behind the school. The leading citizens of the village conducted a fund drive and constructed the building with voluntary donations. No taxes were levied. (Courtesy of the Pocono-Jackson Historical Society.)

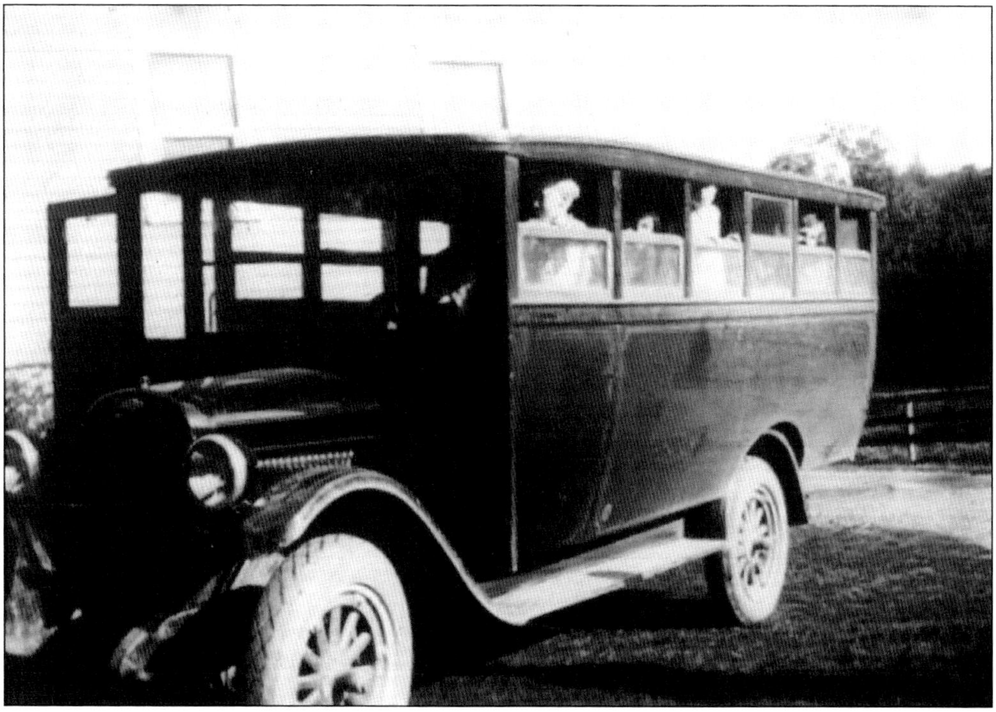

This 1930 Chevrolet school bus was owned and operated by Floyd DeHaven of Scotrun, and it transported students to the Tannersville School. His son John followed in his footsteps and drove a school bus for many years. (Courtesy of the Pocono-Jackson Historical Society.)

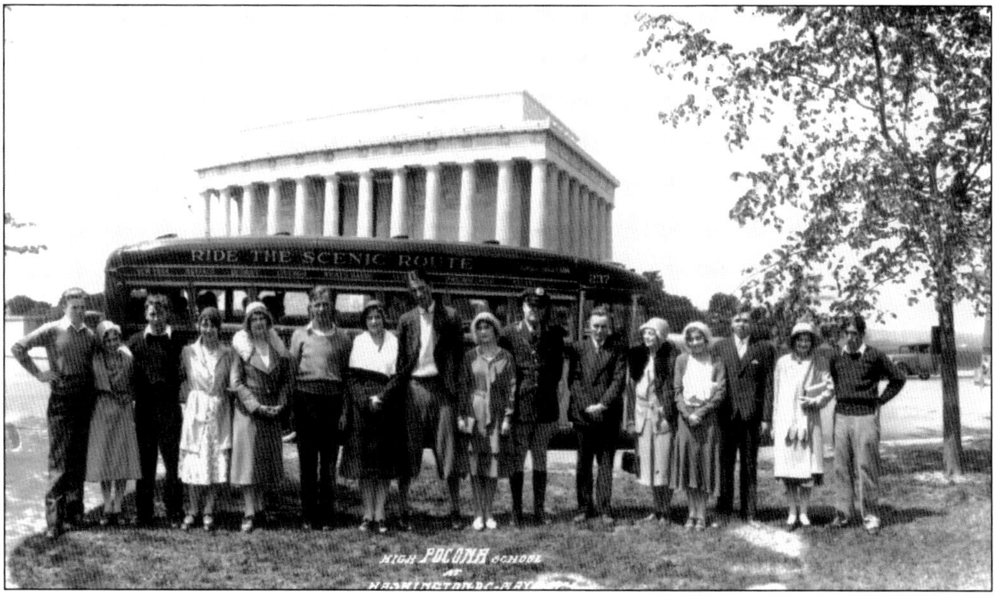

Members of the Pocono Township senior class of 1931 made the trip to Washington, D.C., where they are pictured in front of the Lincoln Memorial. Shown are, from left to right, Harry Litts, Thelma Metzgar, Max Warner, Jesse Dailey, Mabel Halstead, Bob Frailey, Alice Halstead, Gerald Tyreman, Beulah Butz, the bus driver, Wilbur Hay, teacher Alice Cook, Miranda Peechatka, Wilson Christman, Anna Bryson, and Harry Trach. (Courtesy of Ann Lichtenwalner.)

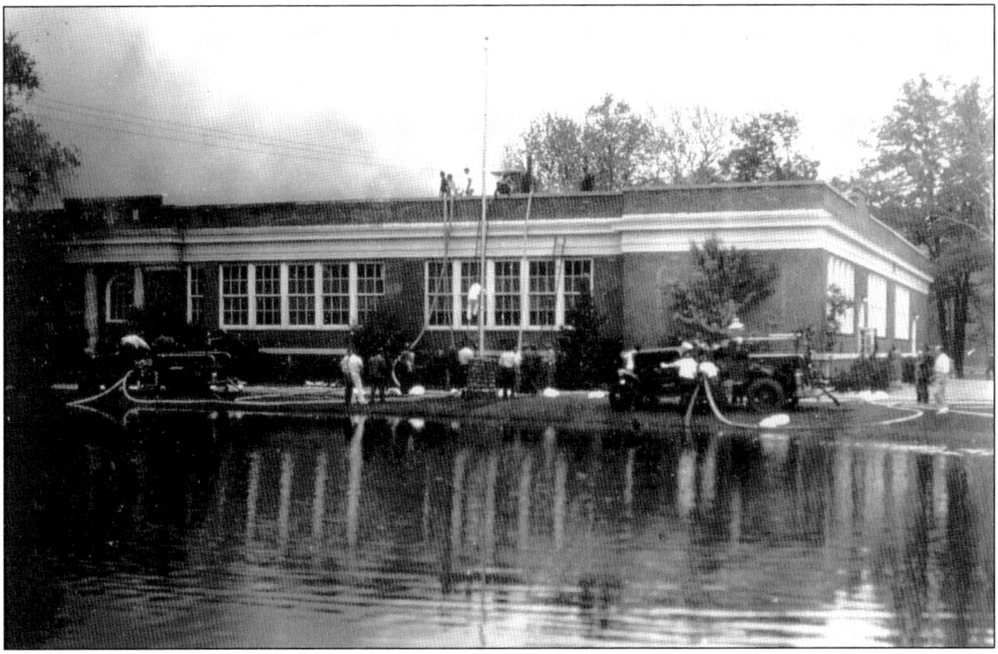

These photographs of the Pocono Township Consolidated and High School were taken on Saturday, May 20, 1939. They show firefighters battling a blaze at the school. Newspaper accounts published shortly after the fire credited the nearness of water from the ponds at the front of the school and the quick response of companies from Mount Pocono, Pocono Manor, Stroudsburg, and East Stroudsburg as factors in the limited damage. The rear view of the building shows two sets of open doors located in the gymnasium/auditorium of the school. A large window that opened onto the stage can be seen just to the left of the chimneys. Shortly after the blaze was extinguished, school officials were of the opinion that the fire had begun in the wiring near the roof of the stage. (Courtesy of John Alleger.)

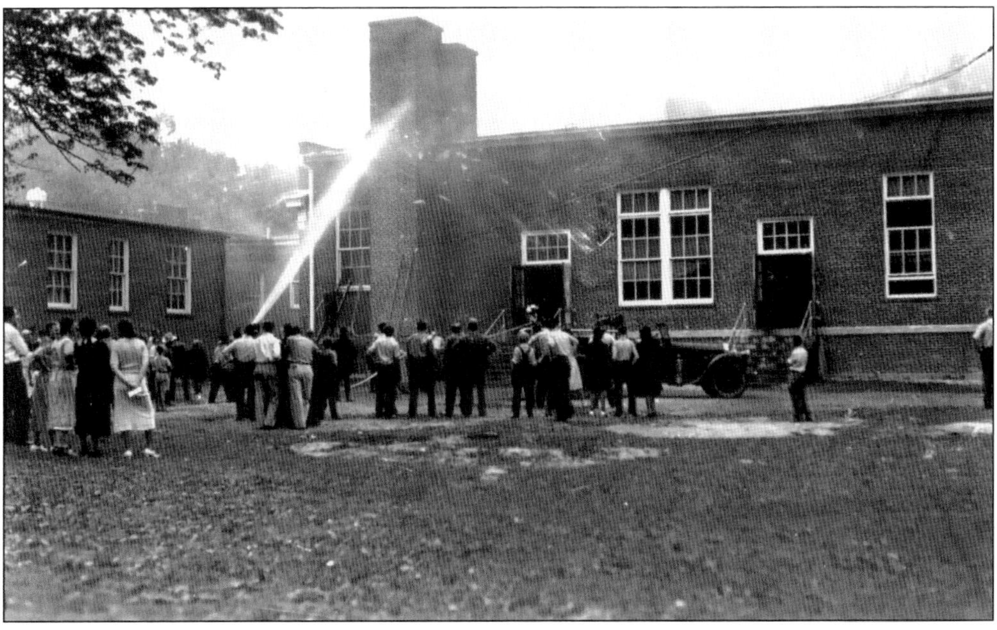

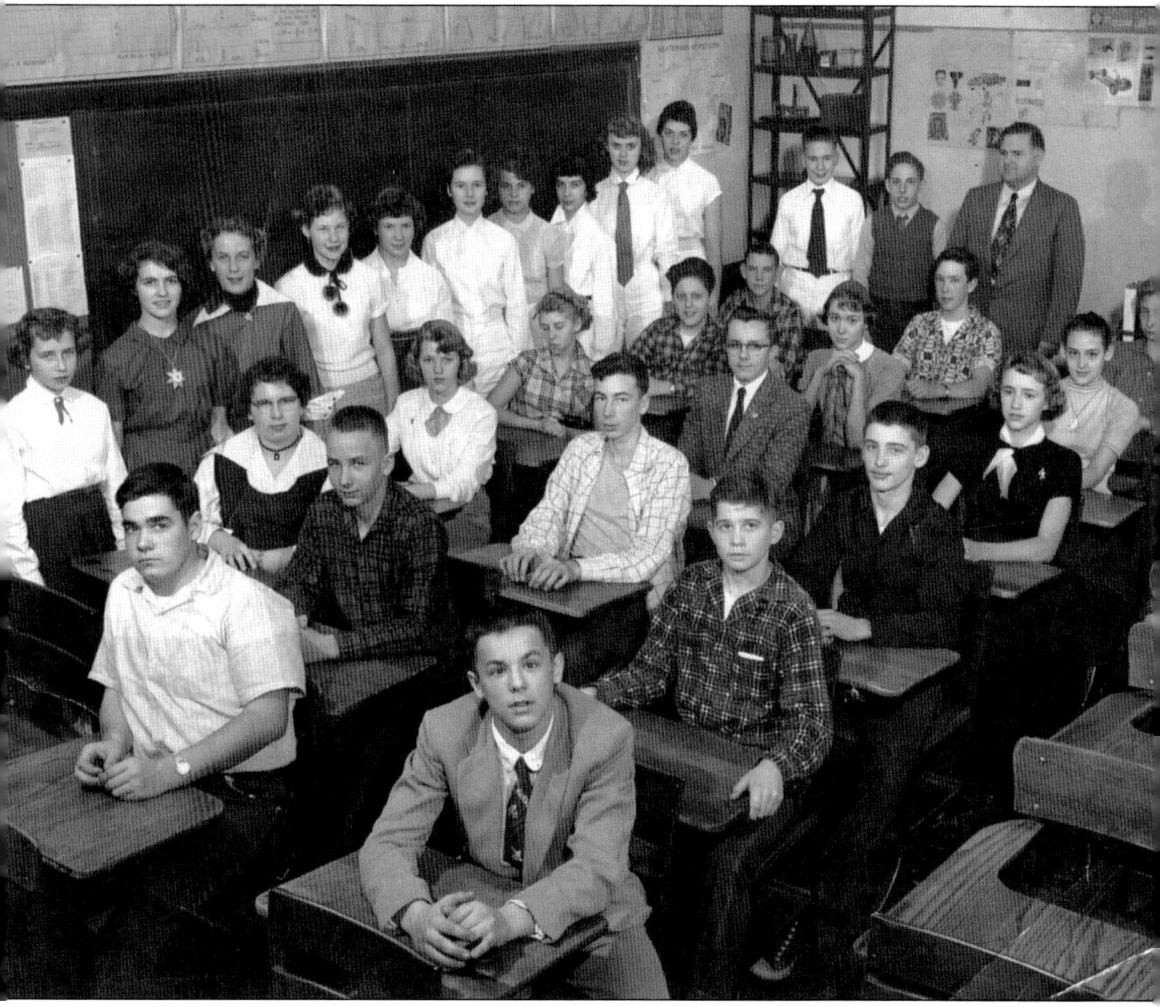

This photograph from 1955 of Pocono Township School's ninth-grade class, taught by John Montgomery, has signatures of students on the back, including Edward Pooley, Nancy Canfield, Lois Strand, Nellie Ruehlman, Marie Besecker, Carol Peechatka, Jane Law, Harrison "Shotgun" Stewart, Judy Singer, Jerry Adkins, Larry Starner, Walt Rohrbach, Doug Bauman, Allen Raish, Ronald Martinell, JoAnn Terry Lloyd, Fred Nidland Jr., Linda Strand, Ronnie Shick, Ruthann Rustine, and Barbara Metzger. (Courtesy of James Price.)

Four

Getting There by Wagon, Train, and Automobile

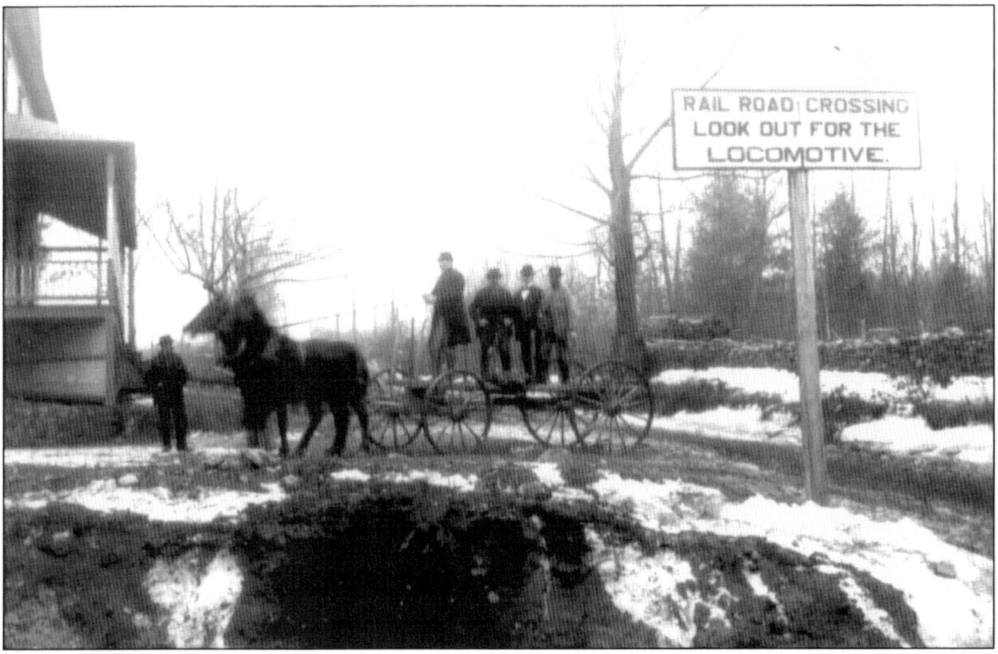

These daring men were photographed standing on the bed of a buckboard at the Reeders Railroad crossing prior to 1927 when present-day Route 715 was improved and paved for the first time. The Reeders Hotel is shown in the background. (Courtesy of the Pocono-Jackson Historical Society.)

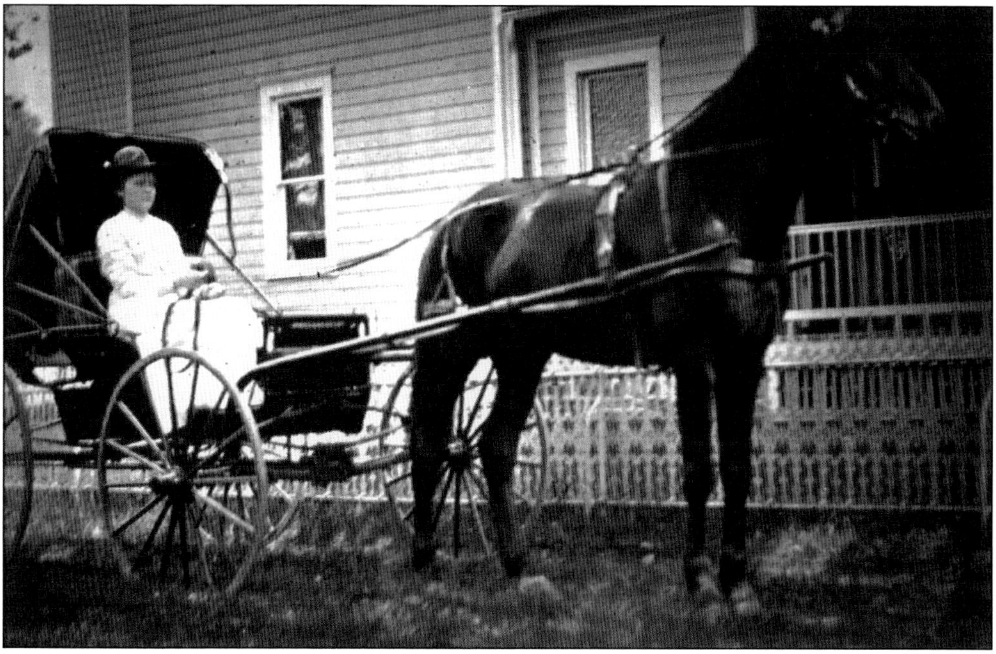

Dr. Elsie Longacre is shown in this undated photograph. She was the first woman physician who served the Tannersville area, graduating from Tannersville High School and the Pennsylvania Woman's Medical College in 1909. She was the stepdaughter of Dr. A. A. Wertman and died during the 1918 Spanish influenza epidemic after contracting the disease while serving her patients. (Courtesy of the Pocono-Jackson Historical Society.)

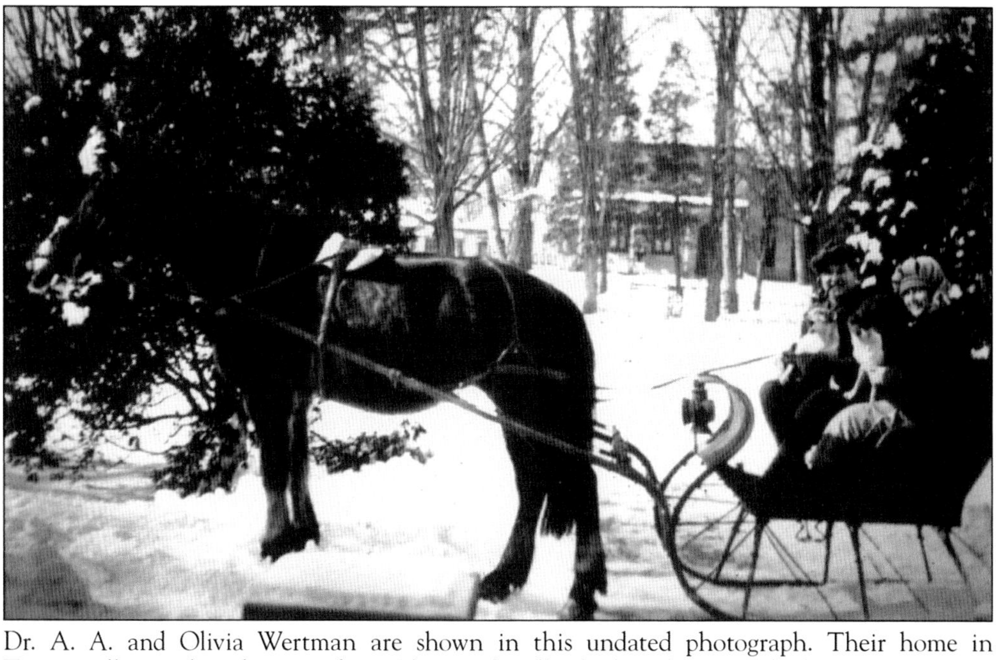

Dr. A. A. and Olivia Wertman are shown in this undated photograph. Their home in Tannersville was directly across from Glenwood Hall, which is shown in the background of the photograph. The Wertmans' home is now occupied by the retail store Imaginations. (Courtesy of the Pocono-Jackson Historical Society.)

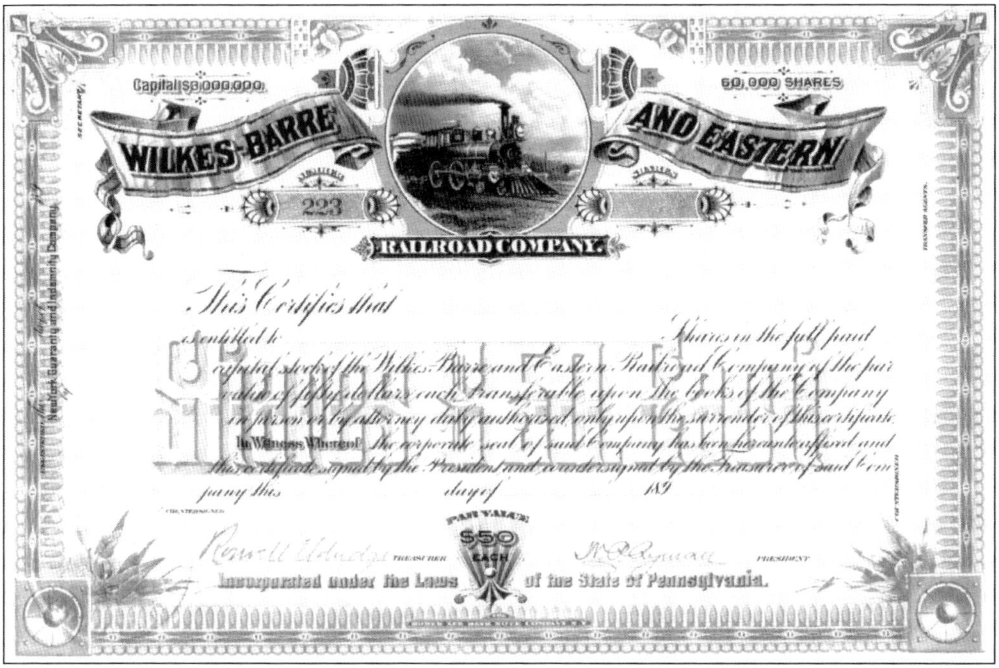

The Wilkes-Barre and Eastern Railroad received its charter on March 8, 1892. Built to connect the coal fields of the Wyoming Valley with the large cities of the East, the railroad carried not only coal but also ice, huckleberries, and passengers. Stations, stops, and sidings found along the right-of-way from south to north were Bartonsville, Trout Lake, Reeders, Mountain Spring Lake, Rinkers, Tannersville, Coolmoor, Half Moon, and Crescent Lake. The last train ran over the line in 1939. The tracks were removed in 1940. (Courtesy of John Alleger.)

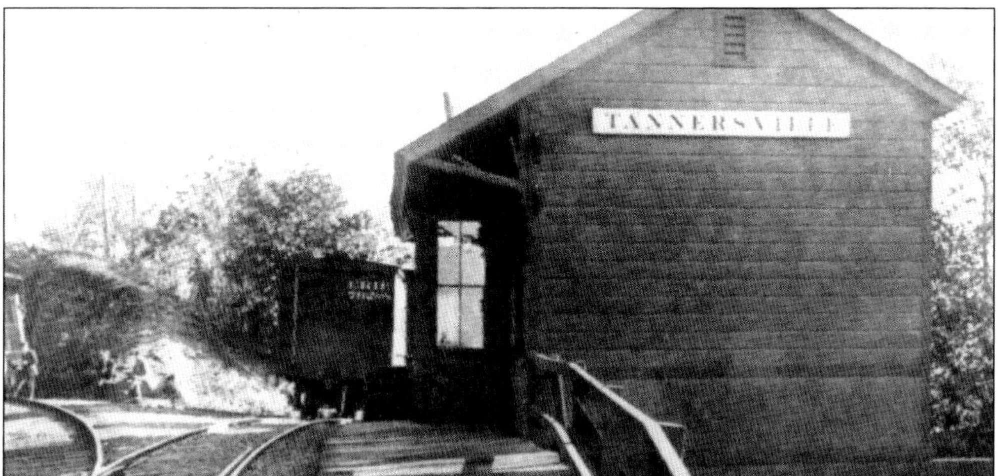

The Tannersville station was built in the 1890s along a rock cut into the side of Camelback Mountain, or as local residents call it, "Big Pocono." Stories tell of the stationmaster hearing the whistle blow at Reeders and walking to the Tannersville station to meet the train. (Courtesy of the Pocono-Jackson Historical Society.)

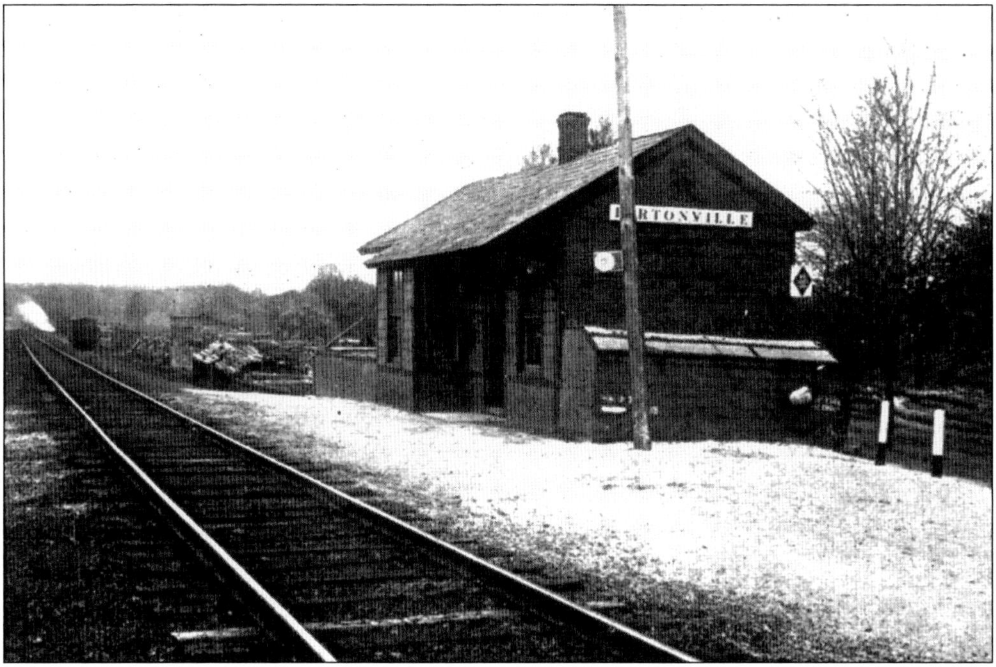

In the photograph above, the Bartonsville (note the spelling on the sign as Bartonville) station is on the Wilkes-Barre and Eastern Railroad line. The railway ran from New York through Stroudsburg and on to Wilkes-Barre, with many stations, sidings, and stops along the way. The close-up view of the Bartonsville railroad station in the photograph below shows large bags, which may be filled with flour or animal feed. The gristmill was only 100 feet away. Note the telegraph wires going into the station on the left side and back to the pole on the right. (Courtesy of the Pocono-Jackson Historical Society.)

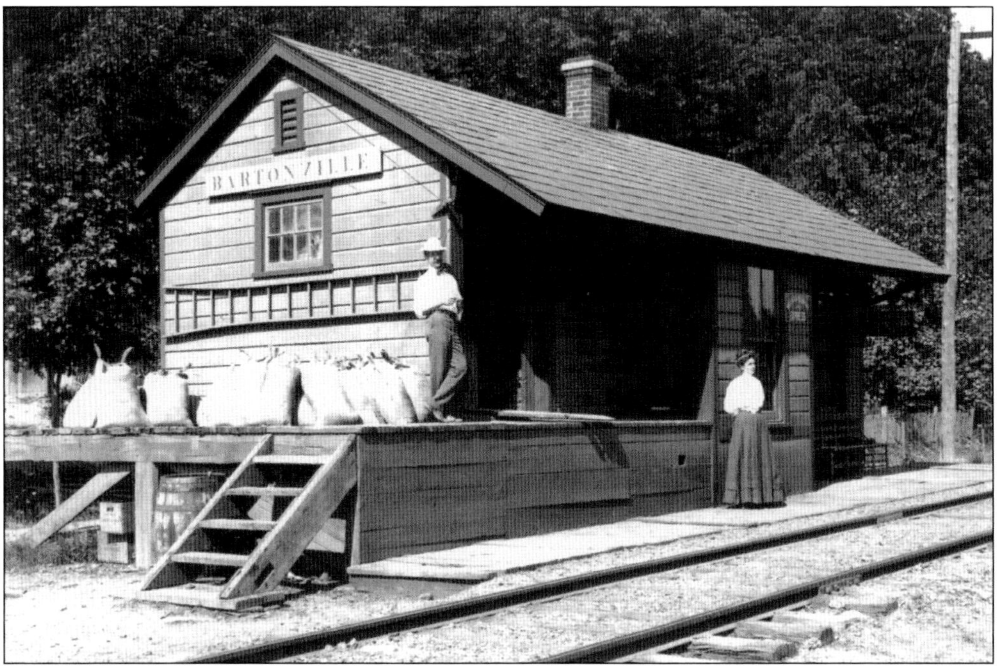

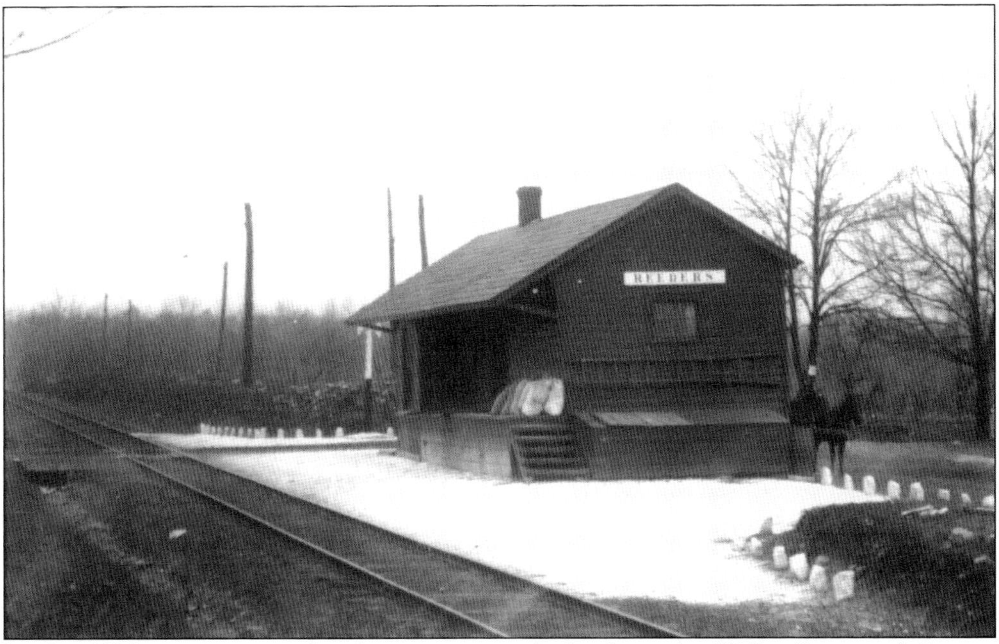

In the 1890s, numerous railroad stations were built along the Wilkes-Barre and Eastern Railroad line. The Reeders station provided freight service for ice, grain, and blueberries, among other supplies. Note the team of horses just visible to the right rear of the station. This photograph was taken looking toward Camelback Mountain. (Courtesy of the Pocono-Jackson Historical Society.)

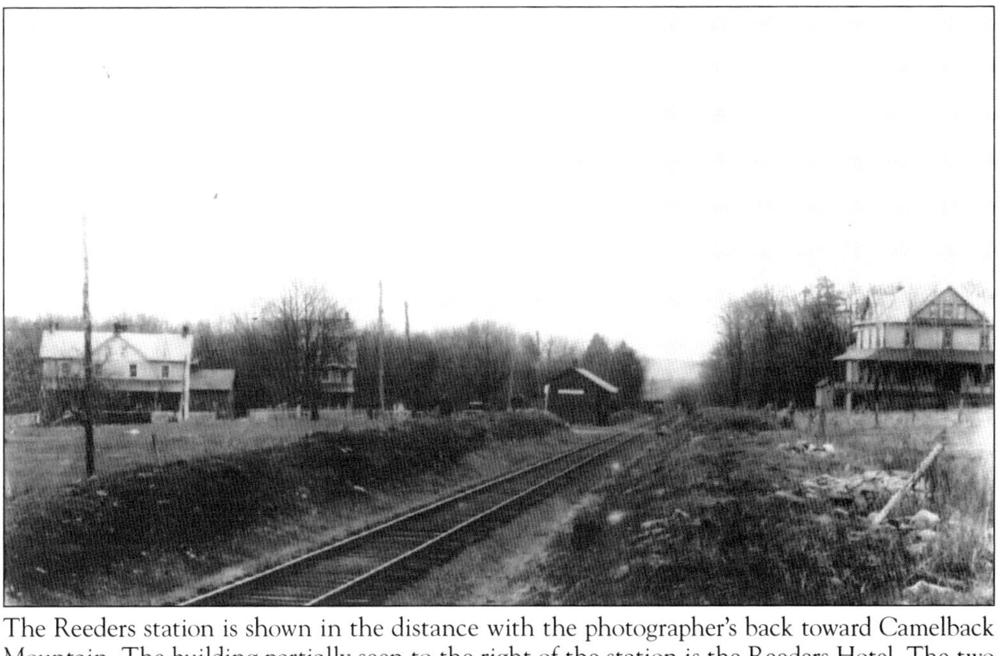

The Reeders station is shown in the distance with the photographer's back toward Camelback Mountain. The building partially seen to the right of the station is the Reeders Hotel. The two buildings to the left of the station are the Reeders store (left) and the home of stationmaster Ben Smiley. The station no longer exists, but the other buildings still stand. (Courtesy of the Pocono-Jackson Historical Society.)

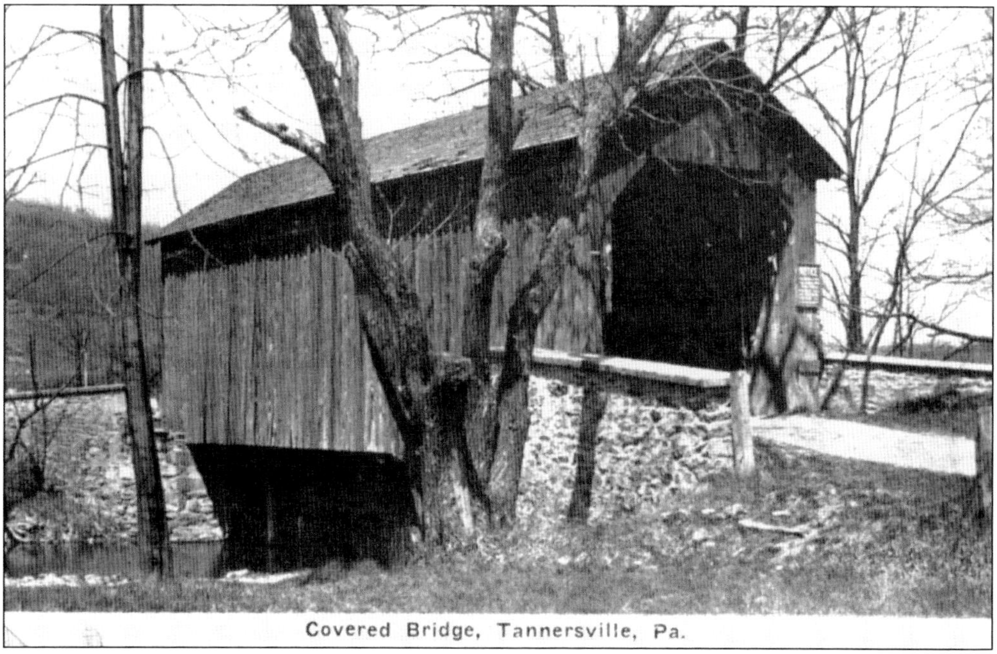

Just north of the current-day Route 715S bridge crossing the Pocono Creek at Tannersville are the abutments for the covered bridge shown in the photograph. (Courtesy of the Pocono-Jackson Historical Society.)

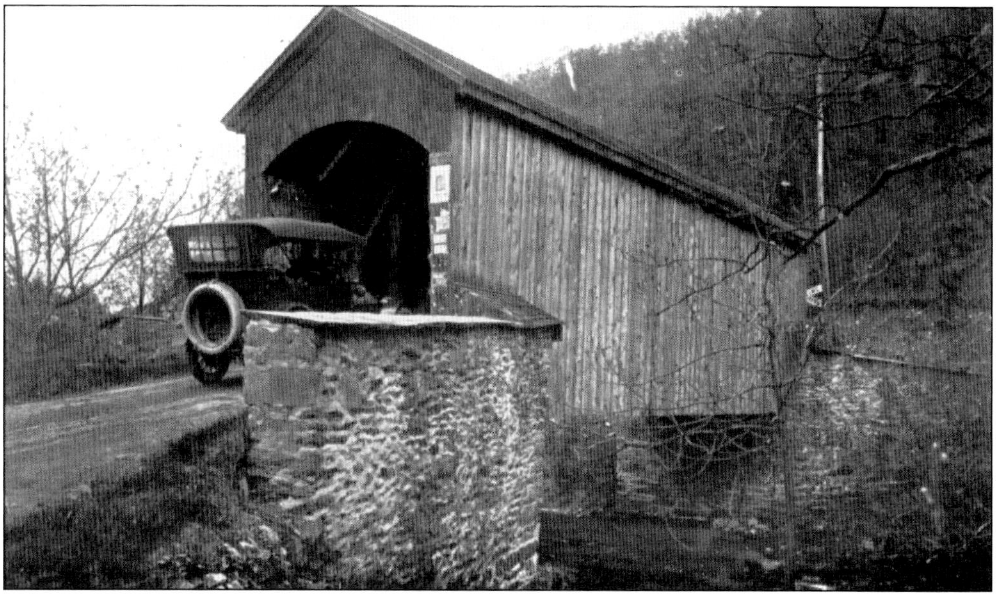

The Bartonsville covered bridge crossed the Pocono Creek just west of the present bridge on Rimrock Road. An abutment for this bridge is mentioned in the deed to the Bartonsville Mill as a corner in the property boundary. The railroad crossing sign is partially visible in the right center of the photograph. Hanging precariously over the Pocono Creek, the bridge's southern abutment can still be seen today. (Courtesy of John Alleger.)

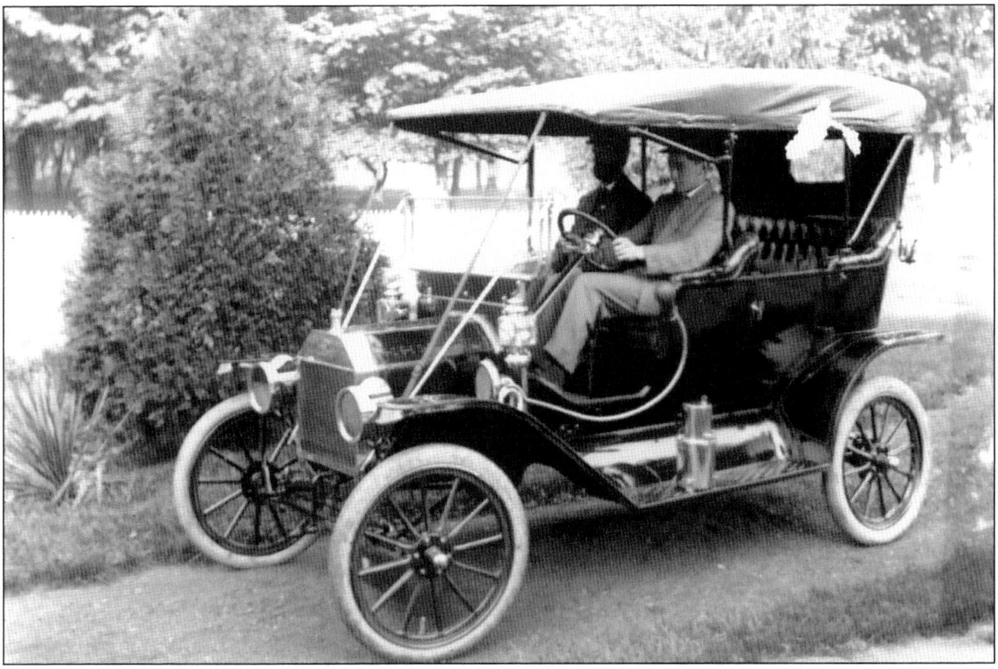

Dr. A. A. Wertman (left) and Dr. George Zehner are shown in a 1910 or 1911 Ford. They were family practitioners in Pocono and Jackson Townships. (Courtesy of Olive Metzger Learn.)

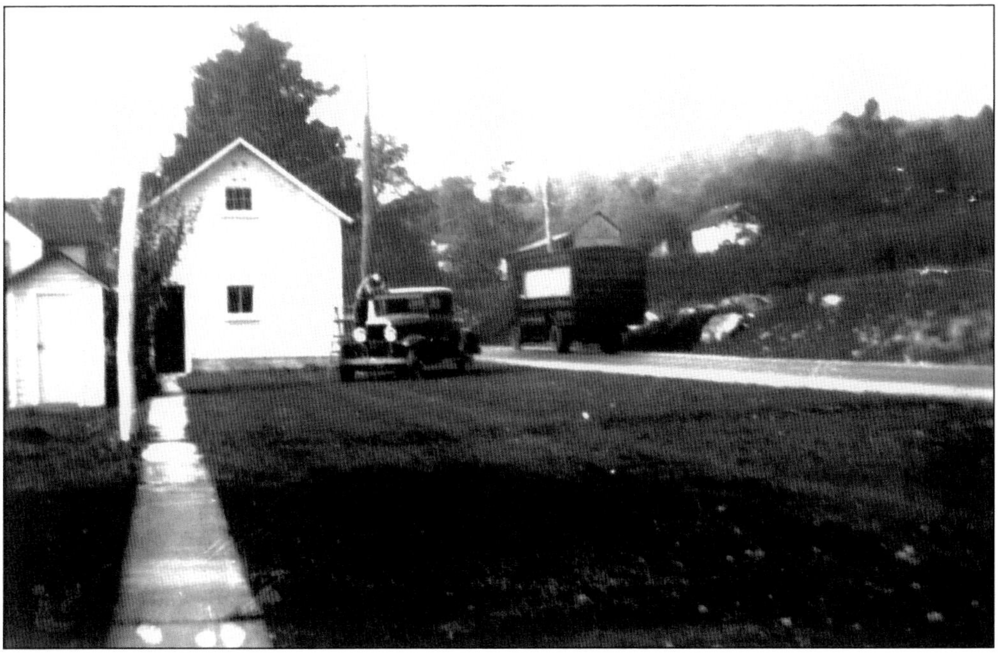

This view looks north on present-day Bartonsville Avenue just north of the village center. Lifelong resident William Joseph (Joe) Dunbar (1911–1989) works on his automobile next to the family garage. An early school bus headed north to Tannersville's Pocono Township Consolidated and High School is seen passing by on the Lackawanna Trail. The garage shown at left still stands. (Courtesy of Joanne Pirzer.)

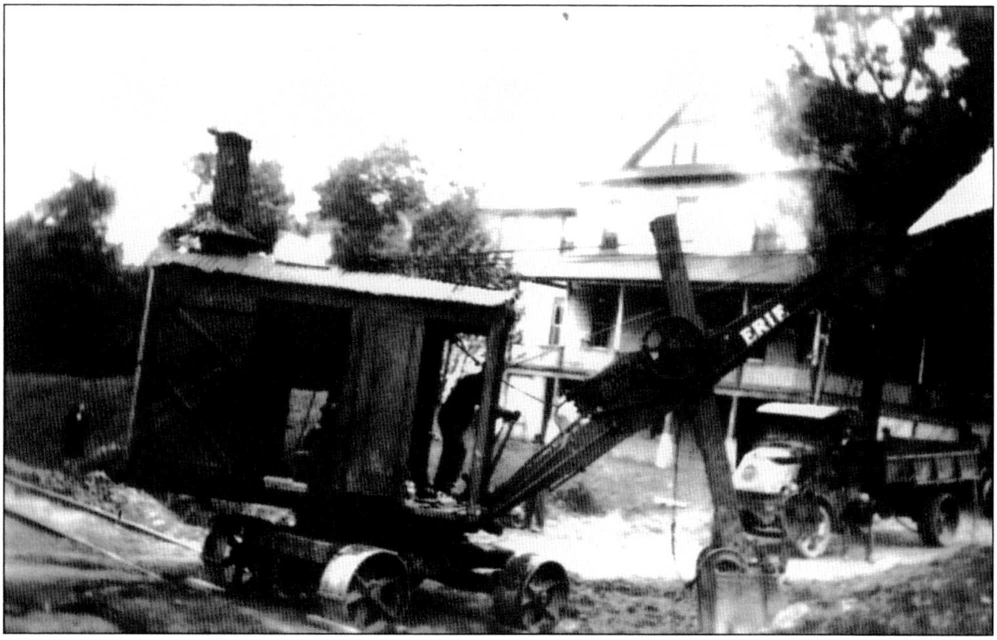

Prior to the 1920s, Route 715S was a dirt road. These two photographs record the paving operation in Reeders, with the workers using a large Erie power shovel (above), which is straddling the railroad tracks. A Mack dump truck is nearby. In the background is the Reeders Hotel. In the photograph below, the Mack dump trucks are parked for the night alongside the Reeders railroad station. (Courtesy of Verdon Rustine.)

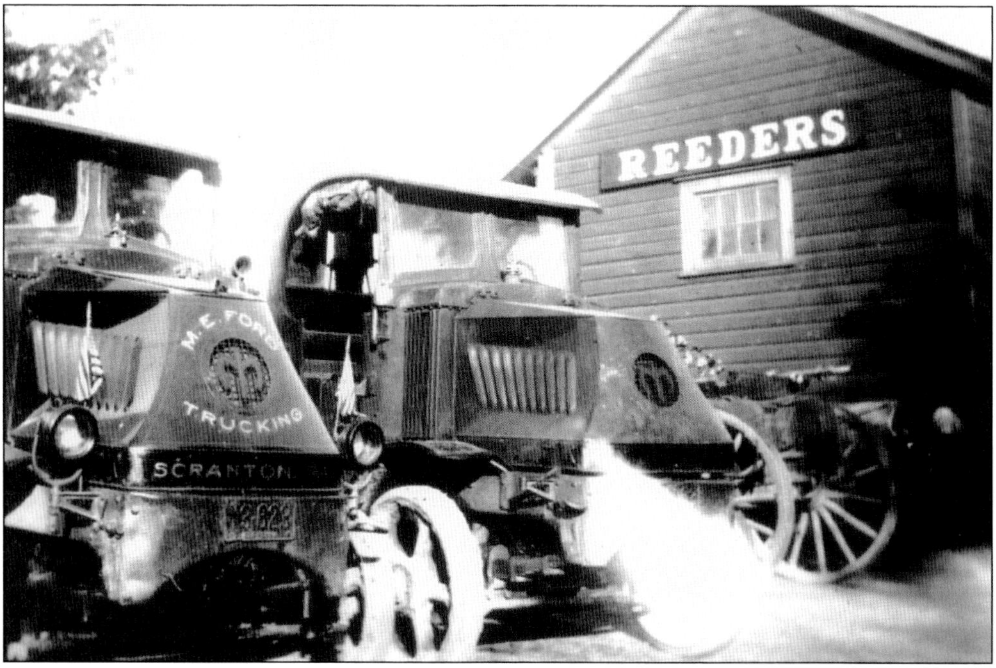

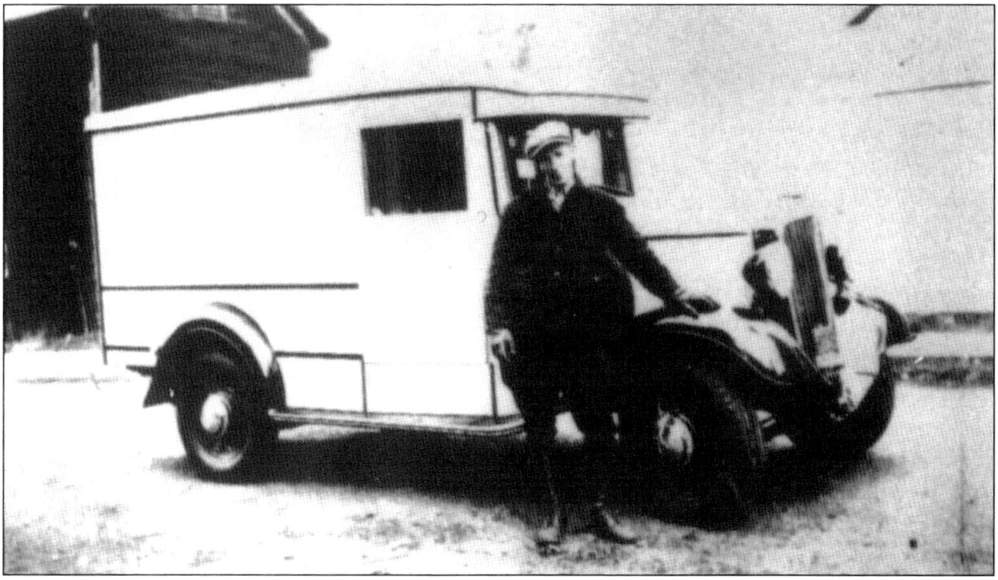

In this photograph, Mack Roeber stands beside William Niering's 1939 Chevrolet meat wagon that was used to deliver meats from their store located in Scotrun. (Courtesy of the Pocono-Jackson Historical Society.)

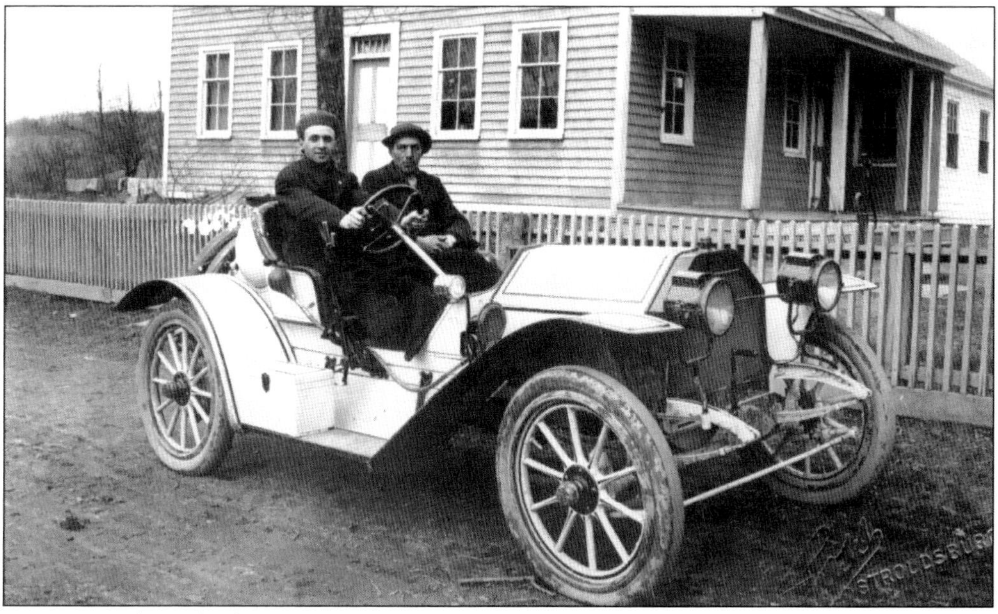

Herman Paul, on the left, and a friend pose for this photograph taken by Ross Photography of Stroudsburg. (Courtesy of Robert Wallingford.)

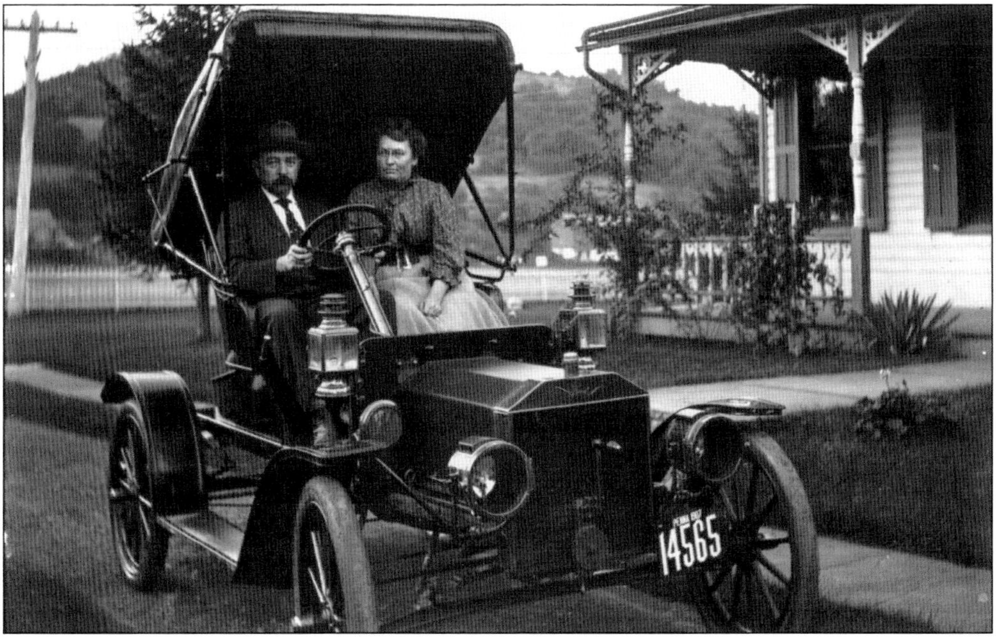

Dr. A. A. and Olivia Wertman are shown in this photograph taken in front of their house in Tannersville. The Pennsylvania license plate is from 1907. (Courtesy of George Learn.)

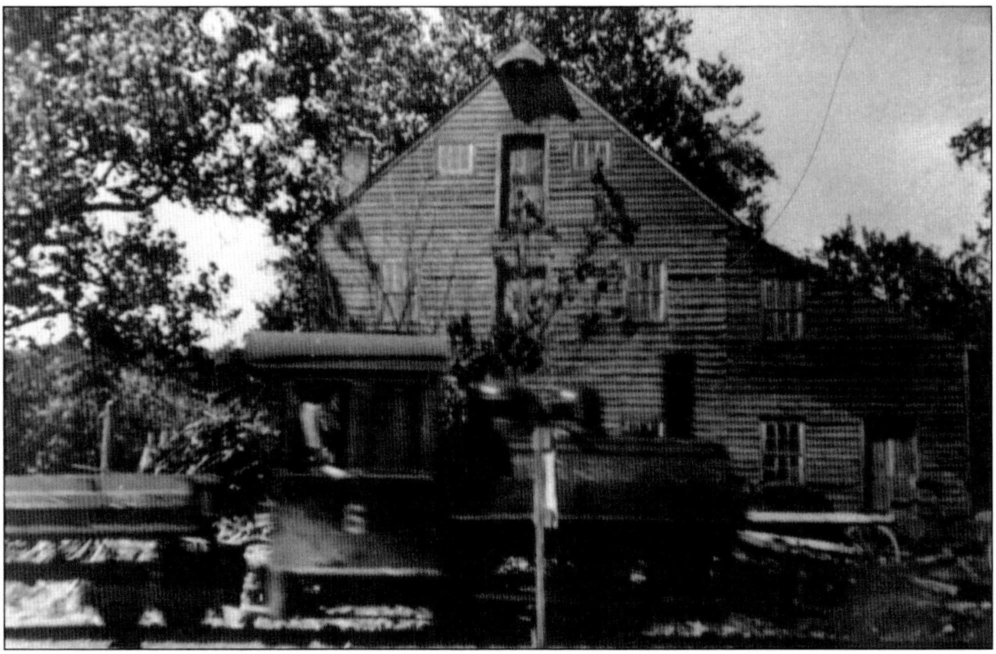

During the initial paving of Route 611, a small railroad spur was built to haul materials used in the construction. This photograph captures the train passing Kistler's Mill in Tannersville. (Courtesy of the Pocono-Jackson Historical Society.)

Five

Along the Scenic Byways

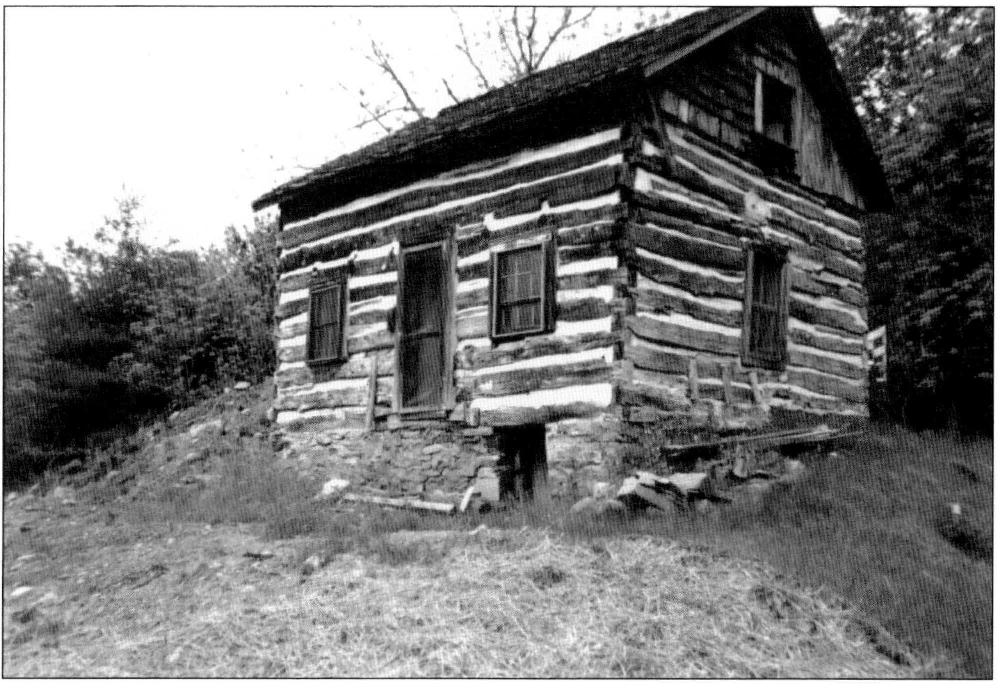

The Robert Buskirk log house stood along present-day Route 715 traveling out of Reeders on the way to Appenzell. (Courtesy of James Price.)

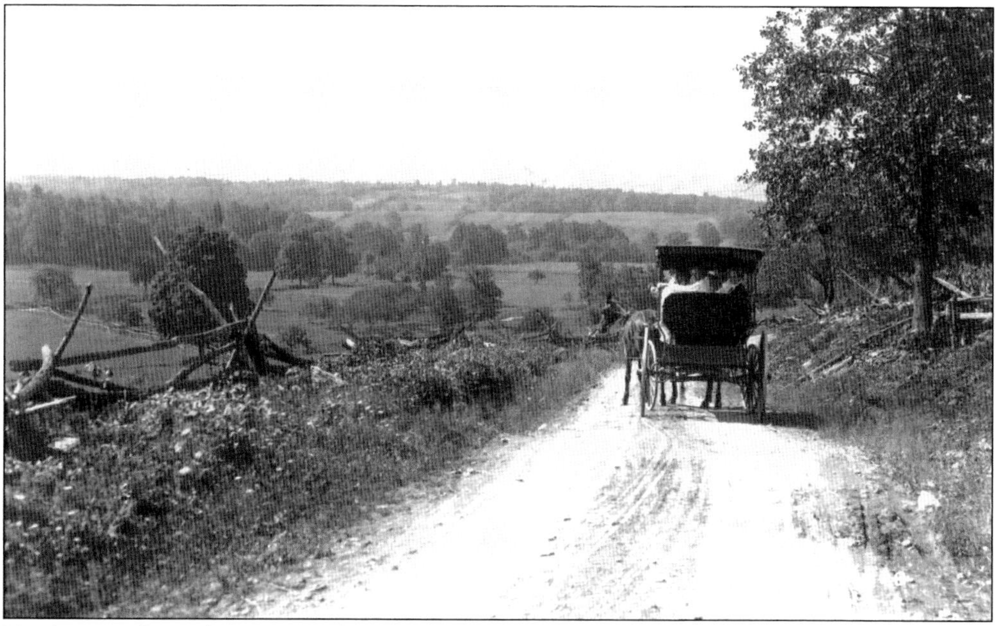

Heading north on the Easton-Belmont Pike (present-day Beehler Road), just after the last sharp corner, Big Pocono fills the distant view today as it did nearly a century ago. Forrest and Claribel Frailey Sebring live along this section of Beehler Road today. (Courtesy of John Alleger.)

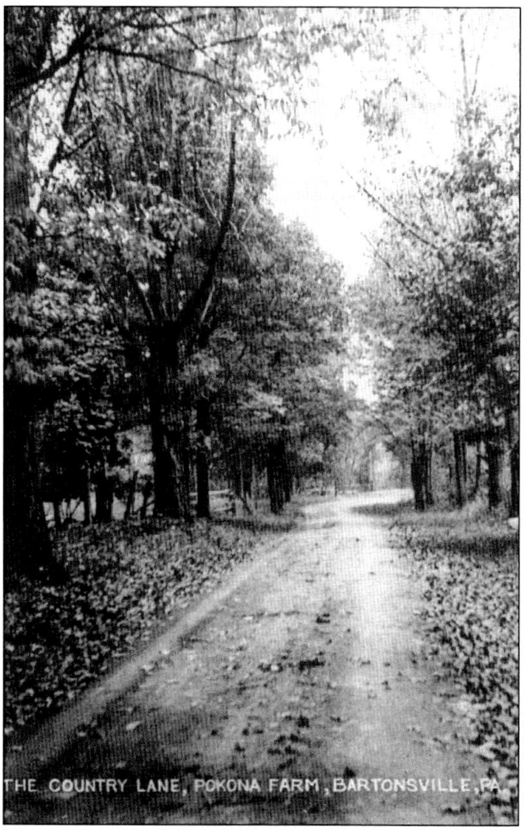

Present-day Beehler Road just north of Pokona Farm looks much today like it did early in the 20th century. In this view, the brick farmhouse and cabins are to the photographer's left. The barn, carriage shed, chicken coops, and other farm buildings are just to the right. (Courtesy of John Alleger.)

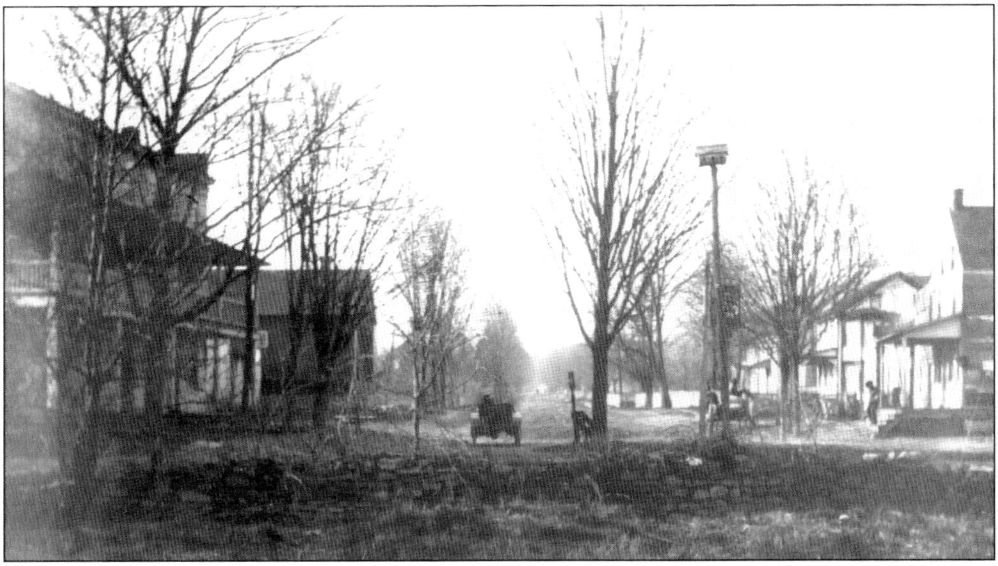

This photograph was taken looking north along what is present-day Route 611. The building to the left is the Pocono Hotel, while across the street to the right is William Kresge's store and the post office. The building behind the Pocono Hotel is Arthur Christman's barn. The unpaved road dates the photograph prior to 1921. (Courtesy of George Learn.)

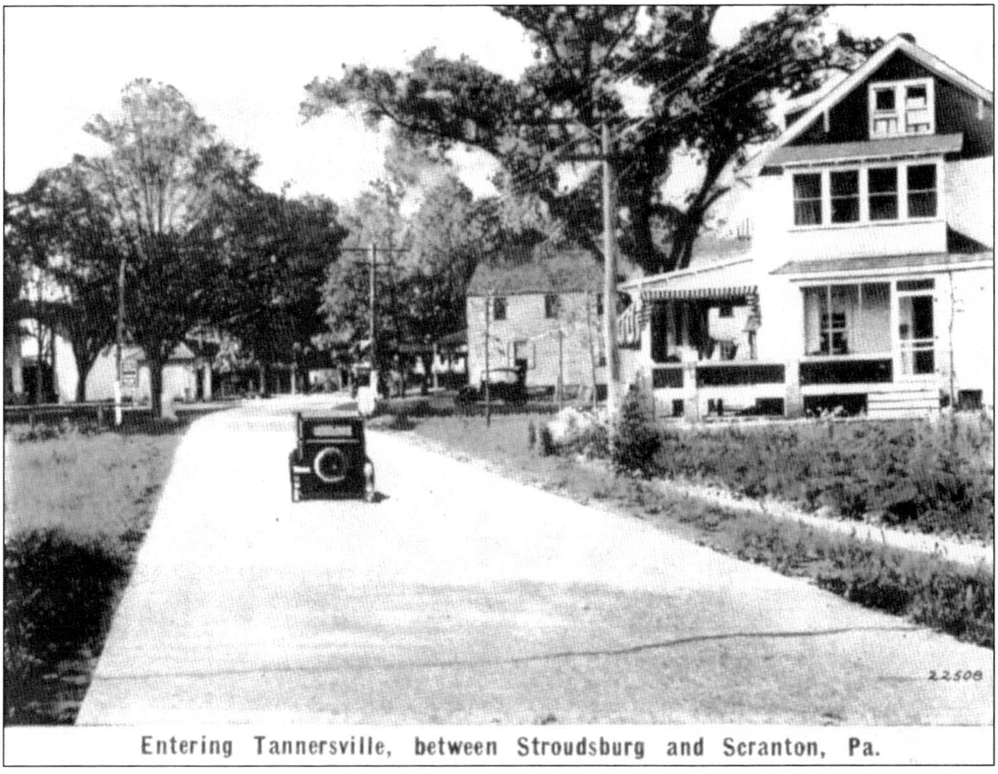

Approaching the Pocono Hotel on the left, two-lane Route 611 makes a slight right-hand turn to head north toward Scotrun. Kresge's store is on the left just north of the John Lesoine home in the right foreground. (Courtesy of George Learn.)

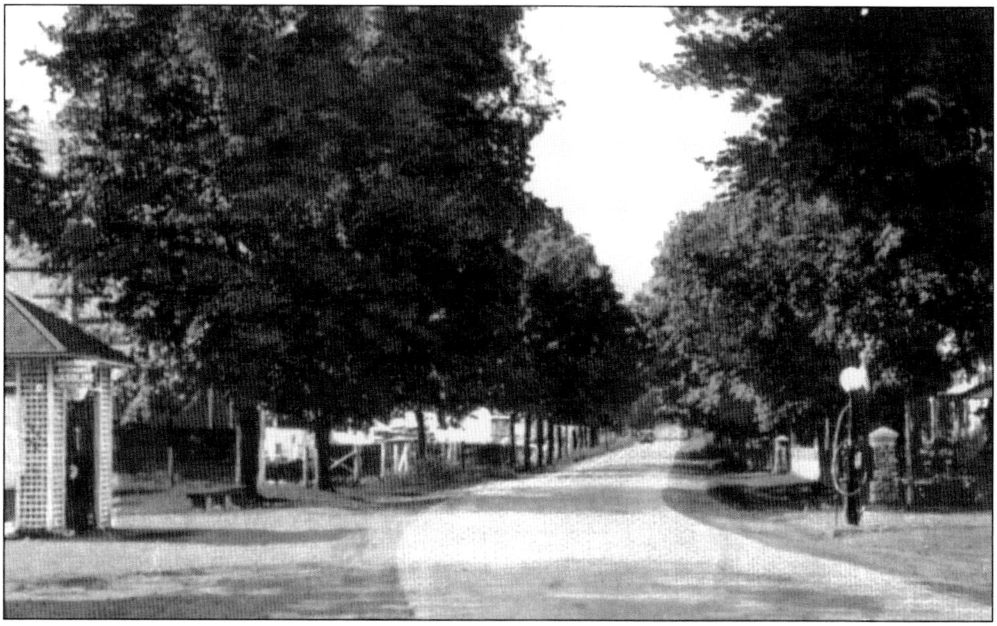

Route 611 is now paved and tree lined, unlike the photograph on page 75. Notice the gasoline pump in front of William Kresge's store. When the post office closed at the store after Kresge passed away, Grace Ludwig lived in the apartment created in the space. (Courtesy of George Learn.)

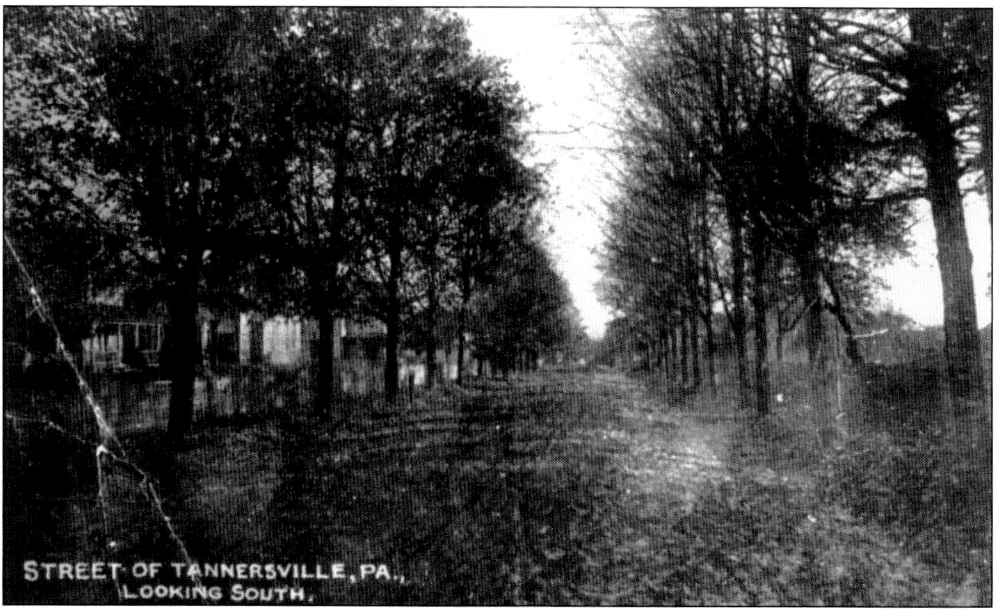

An old postcard shows the main road through Tannersville as it heads south. The road appears to be unpaved. Lined by trees with a fence surrounding the property on the left, it is a very picturesque scene. (Courtesy of the Pocono-Jackson Historical Society.)

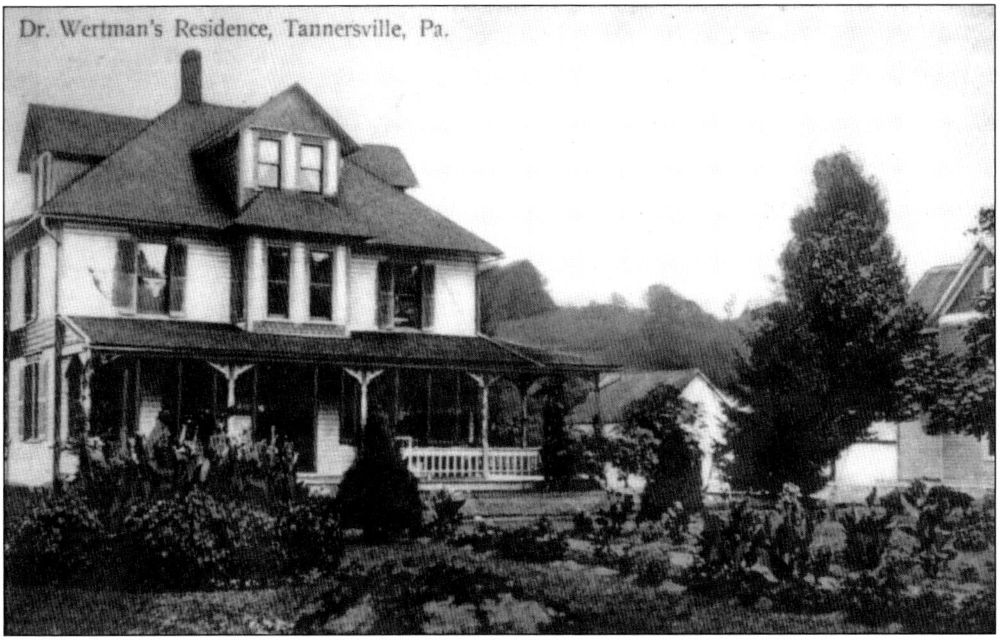

Dr. A. A Wertman built this house in Tannersville around 1900. He and his stepdaughter, Dr. Elsie Longacre, treated patients in the attached doctor's office. After her death in 1918, Dr. George Zehner joined the practice. The home now houses the retail store Imaginations. (Courtesy of the Pocono-Jackson Historical Society.)

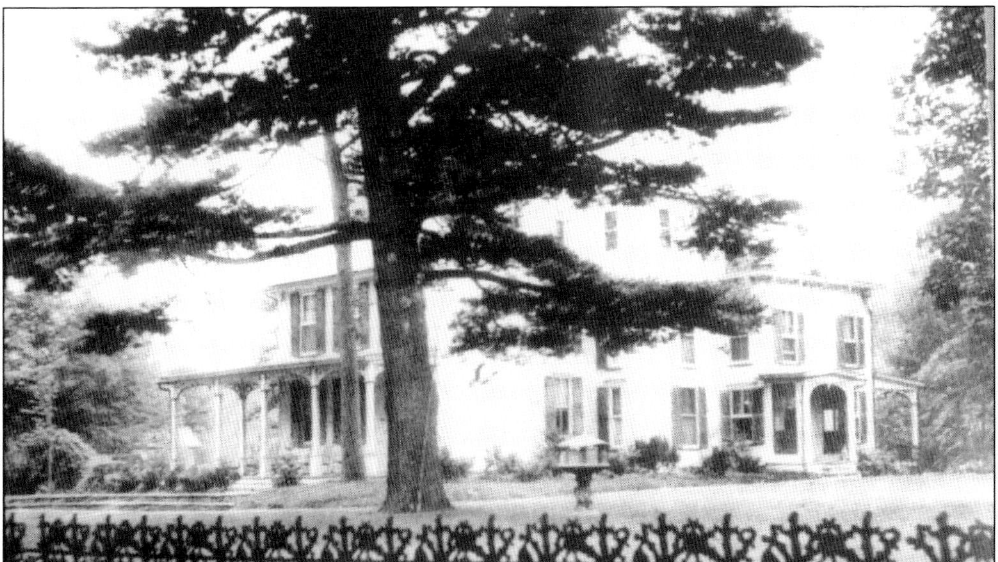

Glenwood Hall started its existence in 1836 as the home of Jacob Singmaster, builder and owner of the tannery in Tannersville. The tannery last burned in 1884 and was not rebuilt. Glenwood Hall still stands across Route 611 from the old homesteads of Dr. A. A. Wertman and John Montgomery. (Courtesy of the Pocono-Jackson Historical Society.)

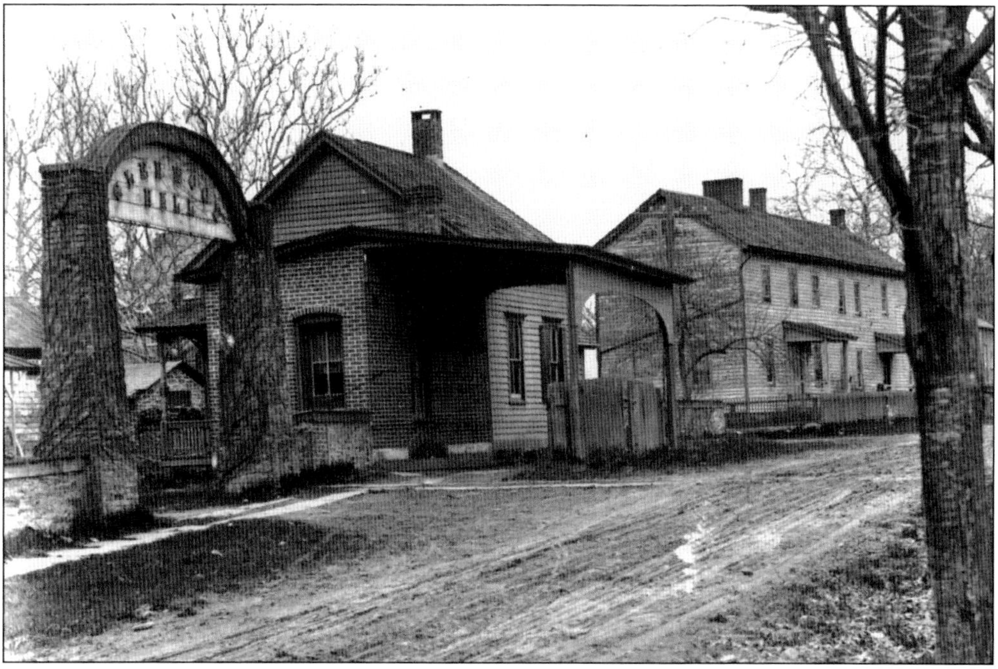

The entrance to Glenwood Hall, home of Stephen Kistler, builder and owner of the gristmill in Tannersville, is topped by an arched, ornate iron sign. The building to the right is the weigh scale for the mill. (Courtesy of George Learn.)

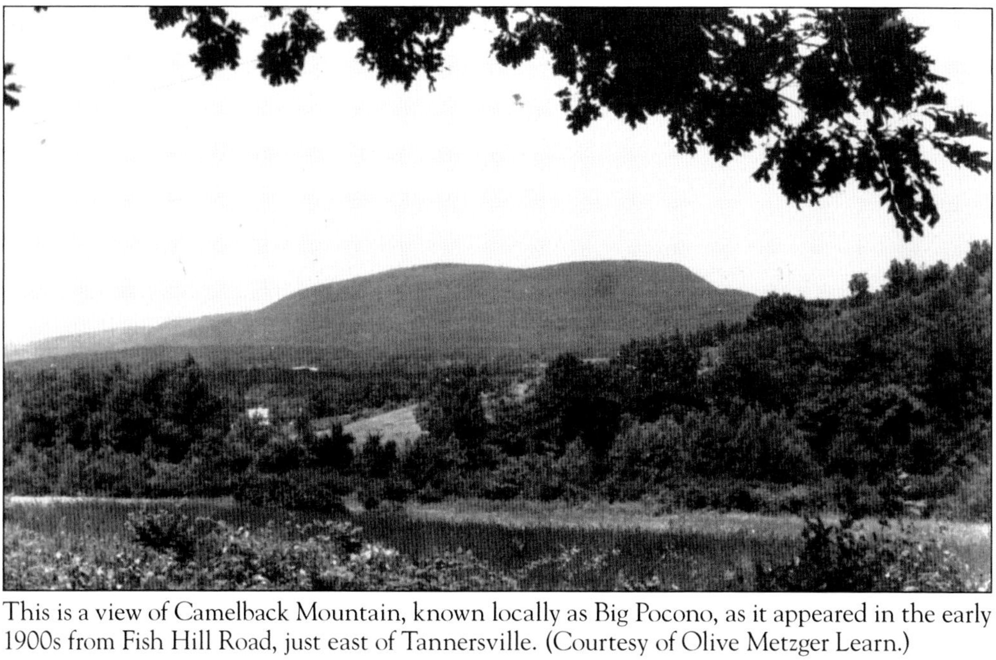

This is a view of Camelback Mountain, known locally as Big Pocono, as it appeared in the early 1900s from Fish Hill Road, just east of Tannersville. (Courtesy of Olive Metzger Learn.)

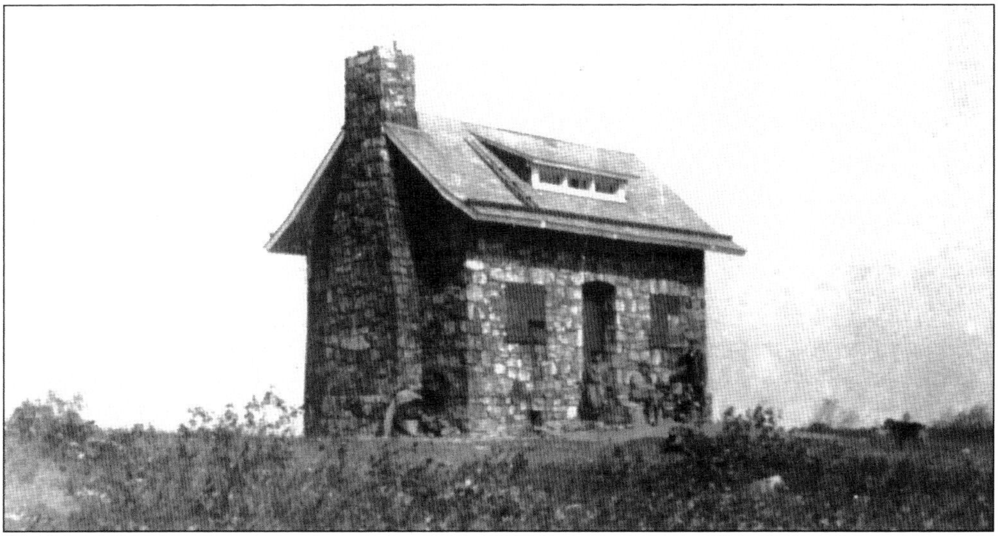

Henry Cattell called Pocono Manor his "home away from home" during the early part of the 20th century. Cattell spent many days riding horseback over the Old City Road, a trail from the manor to the top of Camelback Mountain. He purchased the property and in 1908 hired local stonemason Oscar Peechatka, his son Earl as the water boy, and Harry E. Werkheiser as the carpenter. This little stone house was the result and became a haven for anyone who needed shelter. Twelve years after Cattell's death, the property was purchased by the Pennsylvania Game Commission and is now known as Big Pocono State Park. The fire tower in the photograph below was manned by Esther "Pocono Pete" Motts, Sam DeHaven, and Russell DeHaven for many years to watch for forest fires. (Courtesy of James Price.)

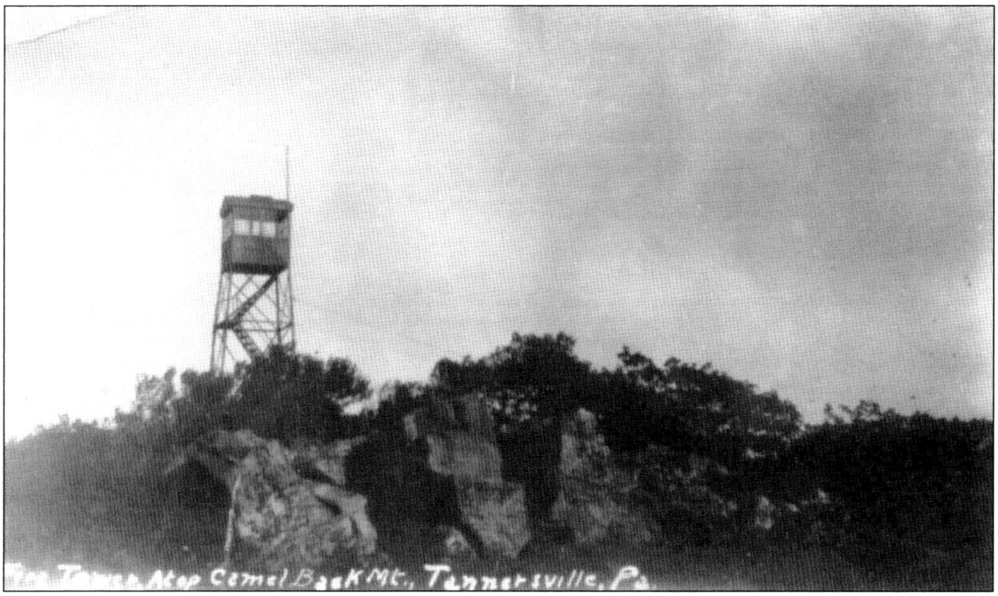

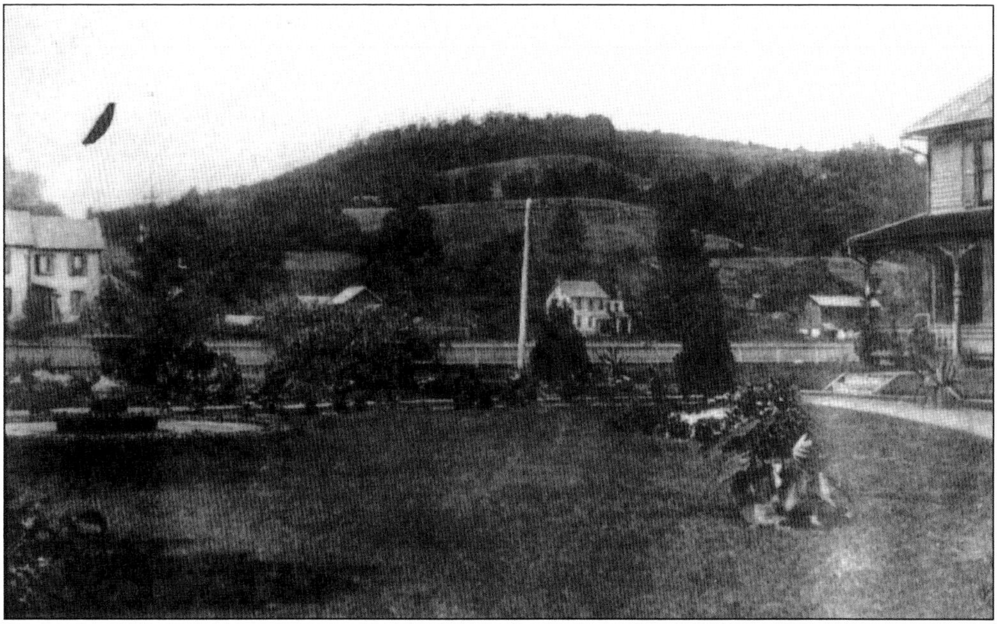

In this view of Tannersville taken from the area of St. Paul's Lutheran Church, Dr. A. A. Wertman's house is on the right. (Courtesy of George Learn.)

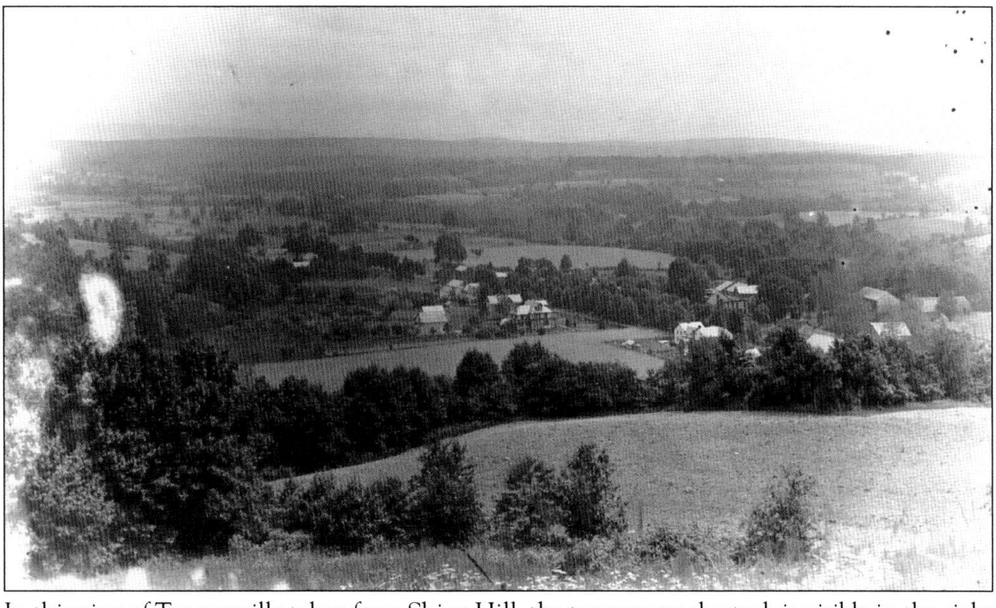

In this view of Tannersville taken from Shine Hill, the tannery smokestack is visible in the right center. To the left, the house with the circular driveway is the home of Dr. A. A. Wertman. St. Paul's Lutheran Church is absent from the photograph, thus the photograph was taken prior to 1910, before the church was built. (Courtesy of George Learn.)

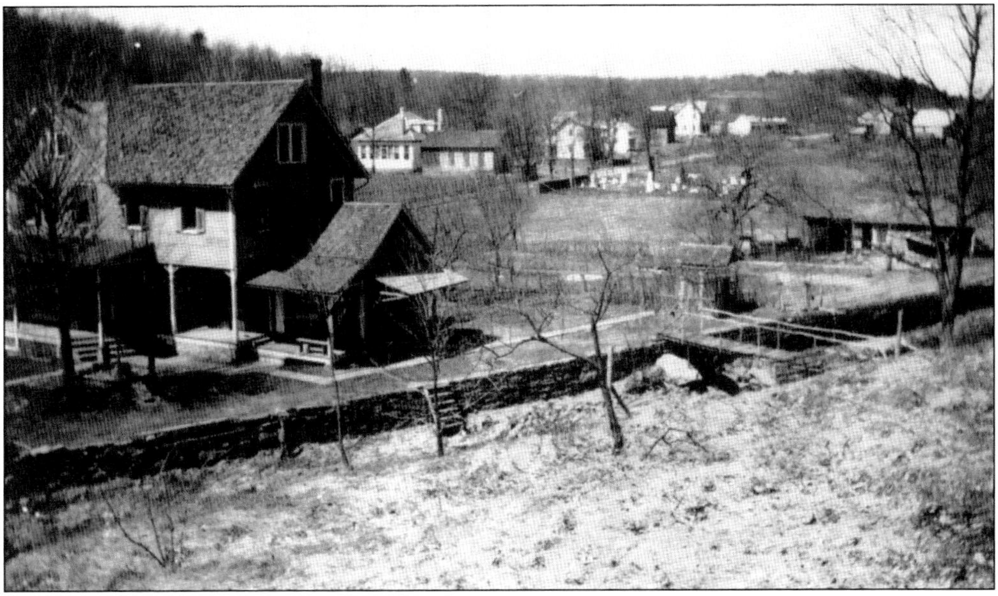

This view of Scotrun was taken from behind the home of Arthur F. Heckman, known as Brookhaven or Pohokomo. Heckman's former home now houses the Scotrun Post Office and a number of apartments. The Scotrun two-room school (built in 1870) and an earlier one-room school (1840) are visible, as is St. John's Lutheran Church. The Brookhaven woodshed and small ice shed are seen at right. (Courtesy of Linford Werkheiser.)

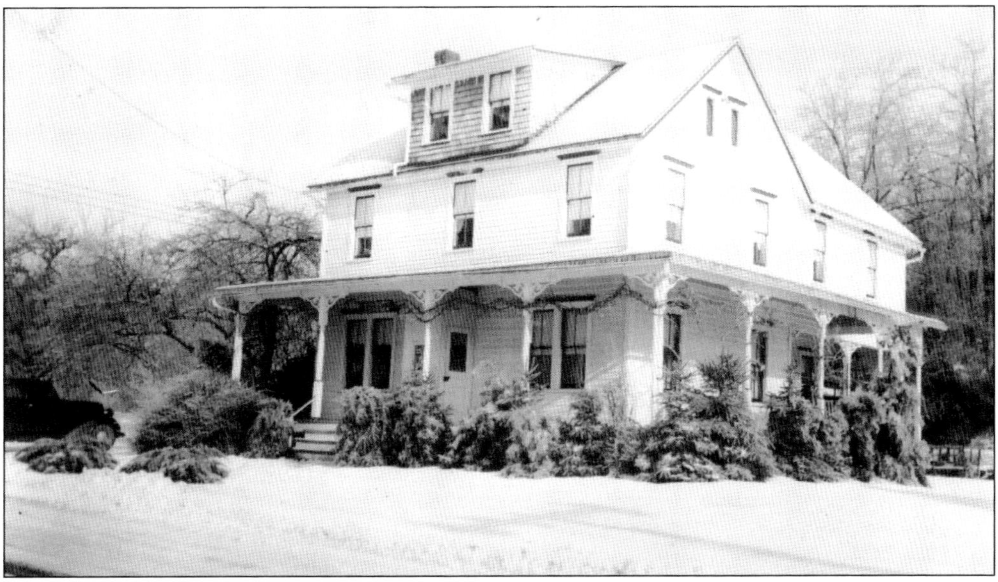

Brookhaven was built by George Kerst in Scotrun. Later it was owned and operated as a boardinghouse by Arthur F. Heckman and his wife, Eleanor (Kerst) Heckman. It was on the two-lane Route 611, which is now Scotrun Avenue. The building now houses the Scotrun Post Office and a number of apartments. (Courtesy of Linford Werkheiser.)

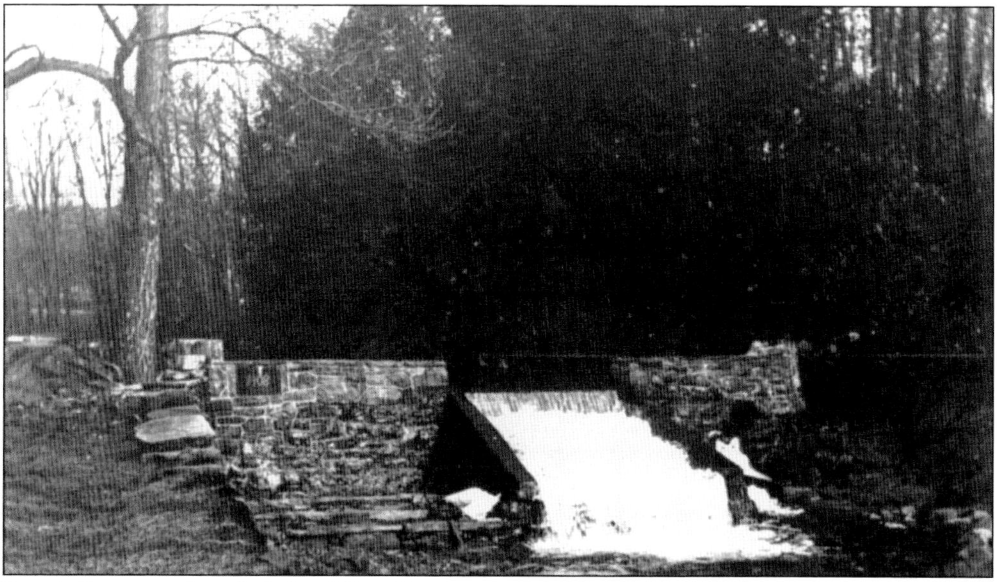

Kerst's Dam was directly behind Brookhaven in Scotrun. The swimming and fishing spot was created by damming Scotrun Creek. Brookhaven is now the Scotrun Post Office. (Courtesy of Linford Werkheiser.)

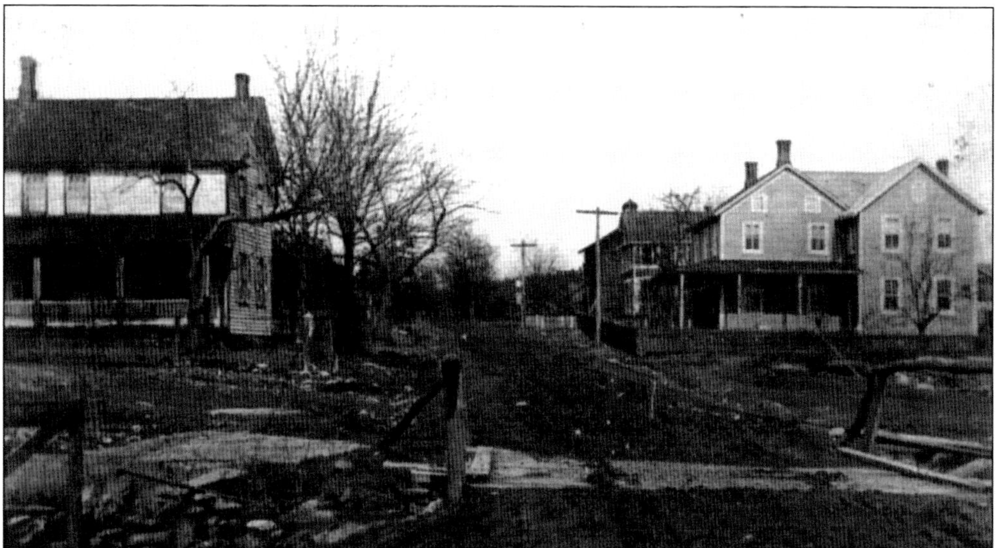

The main road from Scotrun to Mount Pocono passed through the village of Scotrun. It appears the road is not paved in this photograph taken prior to 1921, the year the two-lane Route 611 was first paved. The house on the left was the home of the Niering family and still stands today. (Courtesy of Linford Werkheiser.)

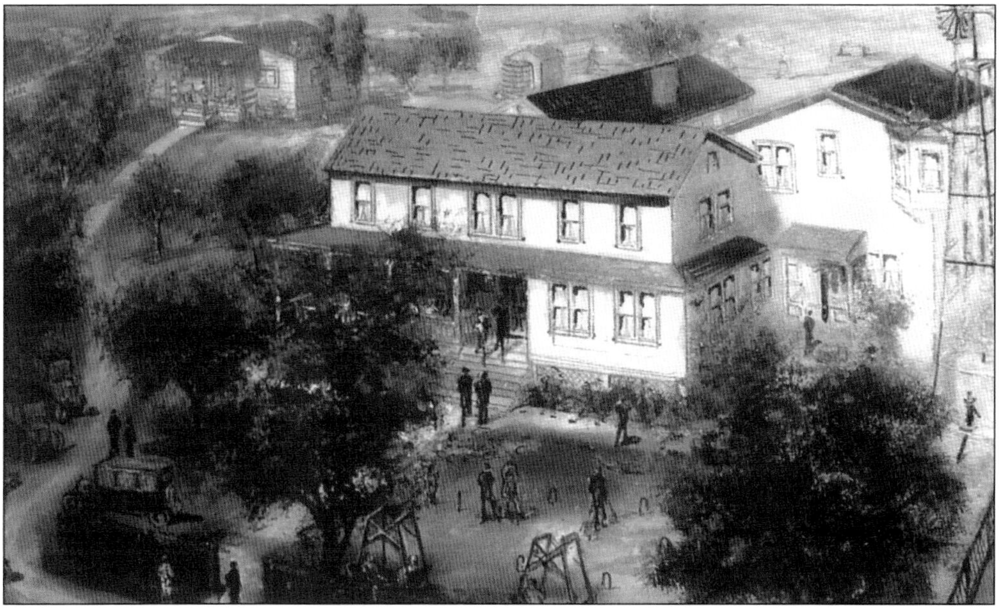

Rose Tree Inn was located along Lower Swiftwater Road on the hill above the Swiftwater store owned by Thomas McGuire. It was a resort for African Americans. (Courtesy of Jack Hamblin.)

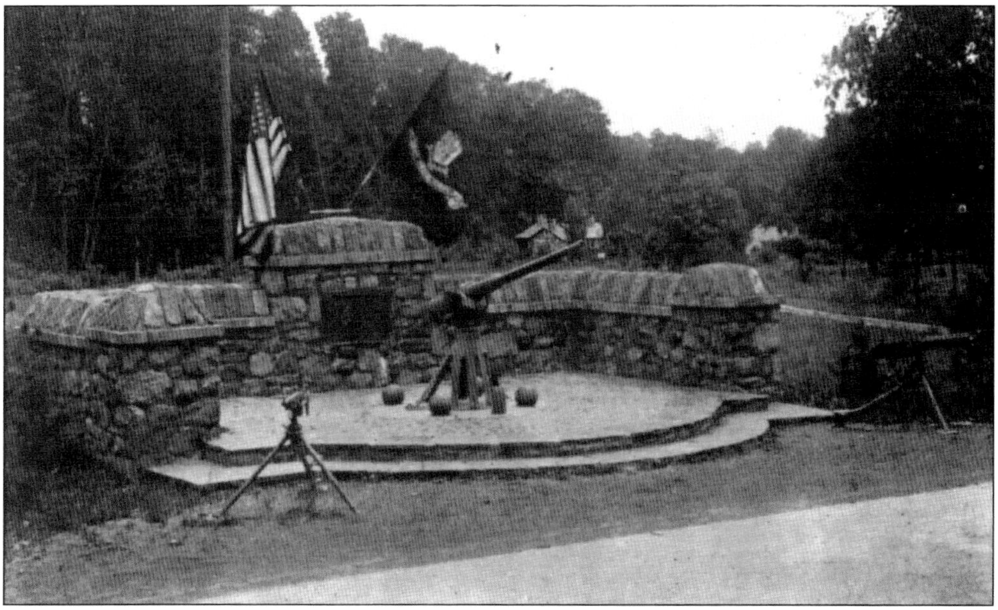

This soldiers' memorial was dedicated on September 6, 1912, as a memorial to the "men of the Swiftwater Valley who served during World War I." The project was spearheaded and completed by Col. Richard Slee. The memorial was moved in the 1990s to its present location in Tannersville. (Courtesy of James Werkheiser.)

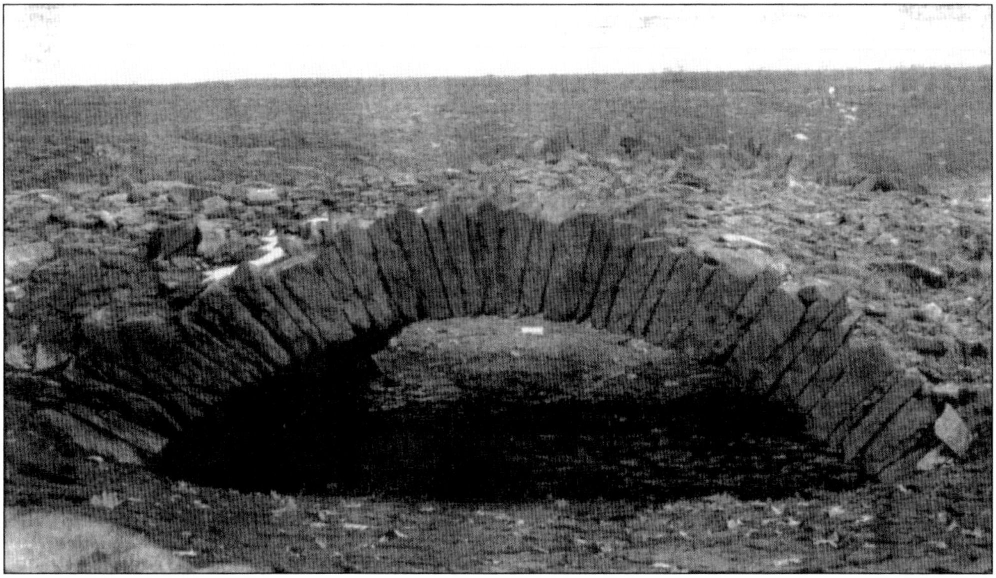

This old bridge became visible on the bottom of Trout Lake off Route 715 in Reeders, when the lake was drained to build a new dam. The bridge once spanned Twin Lake Road. The bridge was built before World War I, when ice was harvested from the lake. (Courtesy of the Pocono Record.)

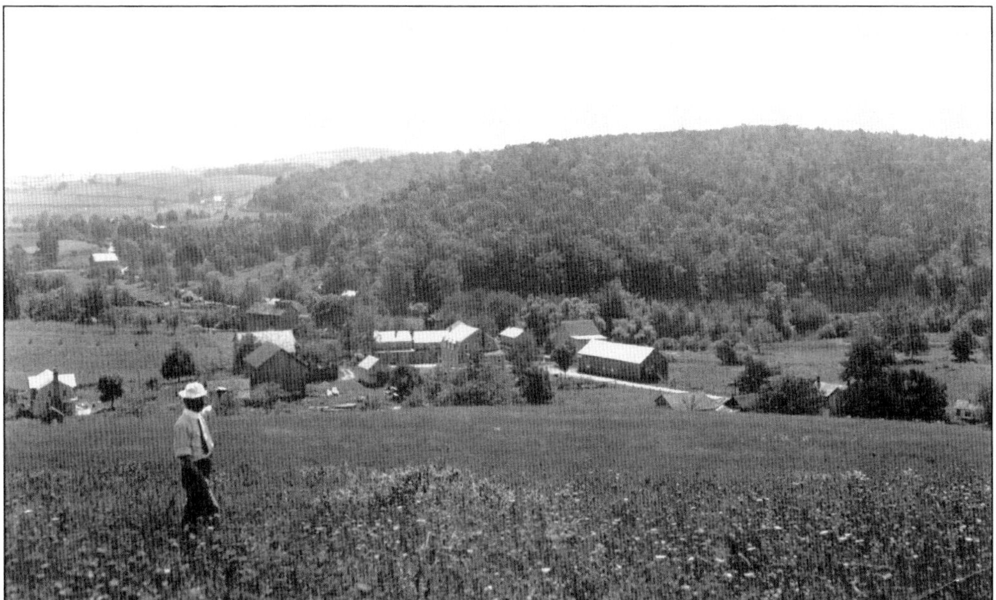

Looking southwest from a hill, this view from about 1910 shows much of the Bartonsville village center. Larger structures near the center of the photograph include the Forest Inn, a gristmill, a covered bridge, and several dwellings. Nearly a mile to the south, the roof of St. John's Church can be seen amid the fields in the upper left of the photograph. (Courtesy of John Alleger.)

Six

Community Churches

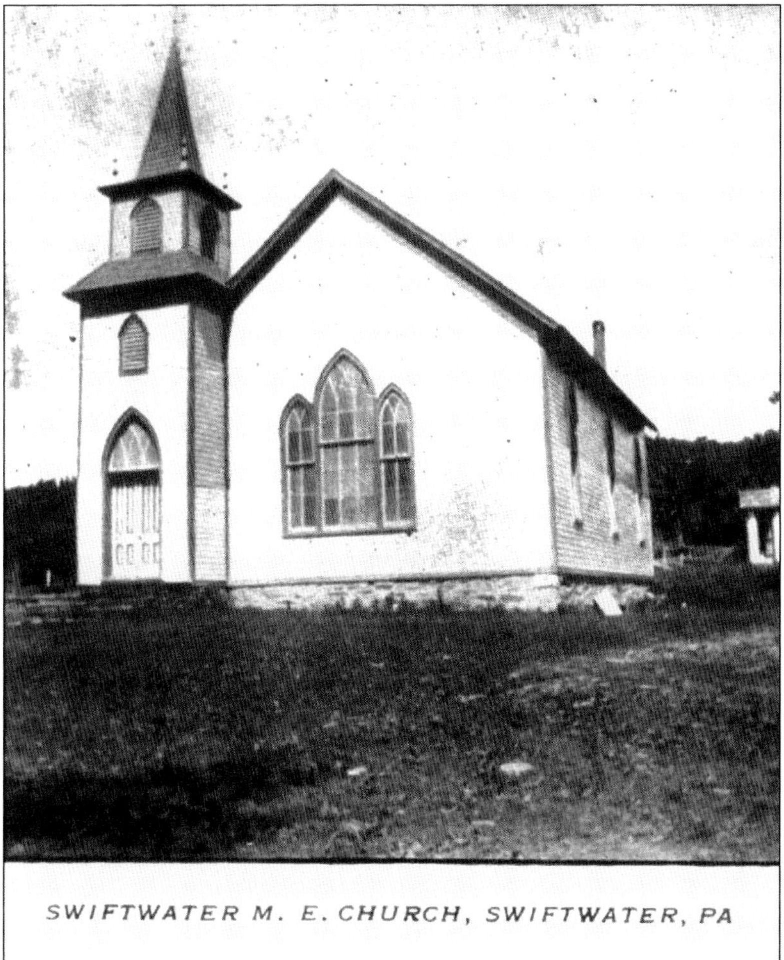

The Swiftwater Methodist Episcopal Church was erected in 1891. The congregation disbanded in 2006. (Courtesy of Jack Hamblin.)

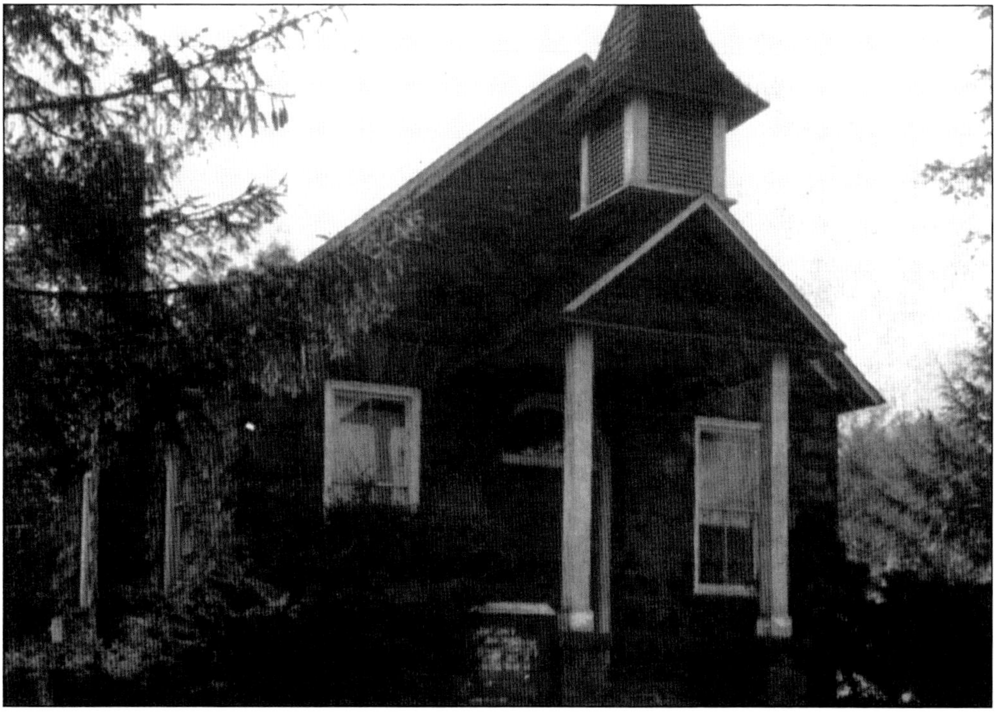

During the 50th anniversary celebration of St. John's Sunday school and church held in Scotrun on October 25, 1953, the efforts of the Ladies' Aid Society told an amazing story. Pledges were taken following a declaration in 1901 to build a chapel. The church was built with a total cost of $1,208.86 and dedicated in 1904. The last payment on the church debt was made in 1909. (Courtesy of Linford Werkheiser.)

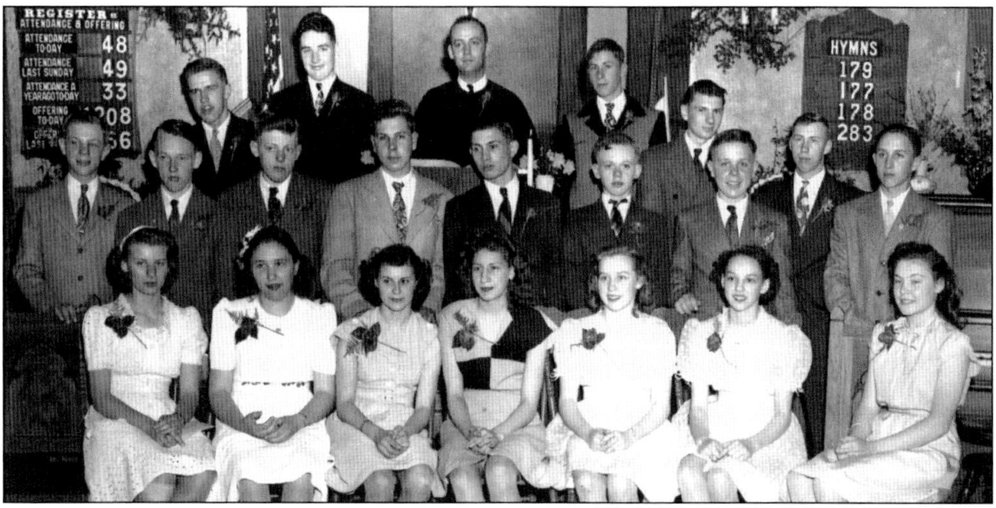

The confirmation class at St. John's Church in Scotrun was photographed in 1944. From left to right are (first row) Mae DeHaven, Geraldine Warner, Phyllis Bloss, Arlene Johnson, Helen Detrick, Emily Detrick, and Dawn Peechatka; (second row) Harold Warner, James Price, Dayton Frantz, Allan Rinker, Arthur Shick, Bruce Frantz, John Rinker, Melvin Johnson, and Arthur Youngken; (third row) Sharon Peechatka, William Storch, Rev. William Wunder, Horace Johnson, and Floyd DeHaven Jr. (Courtesy of James Price.)

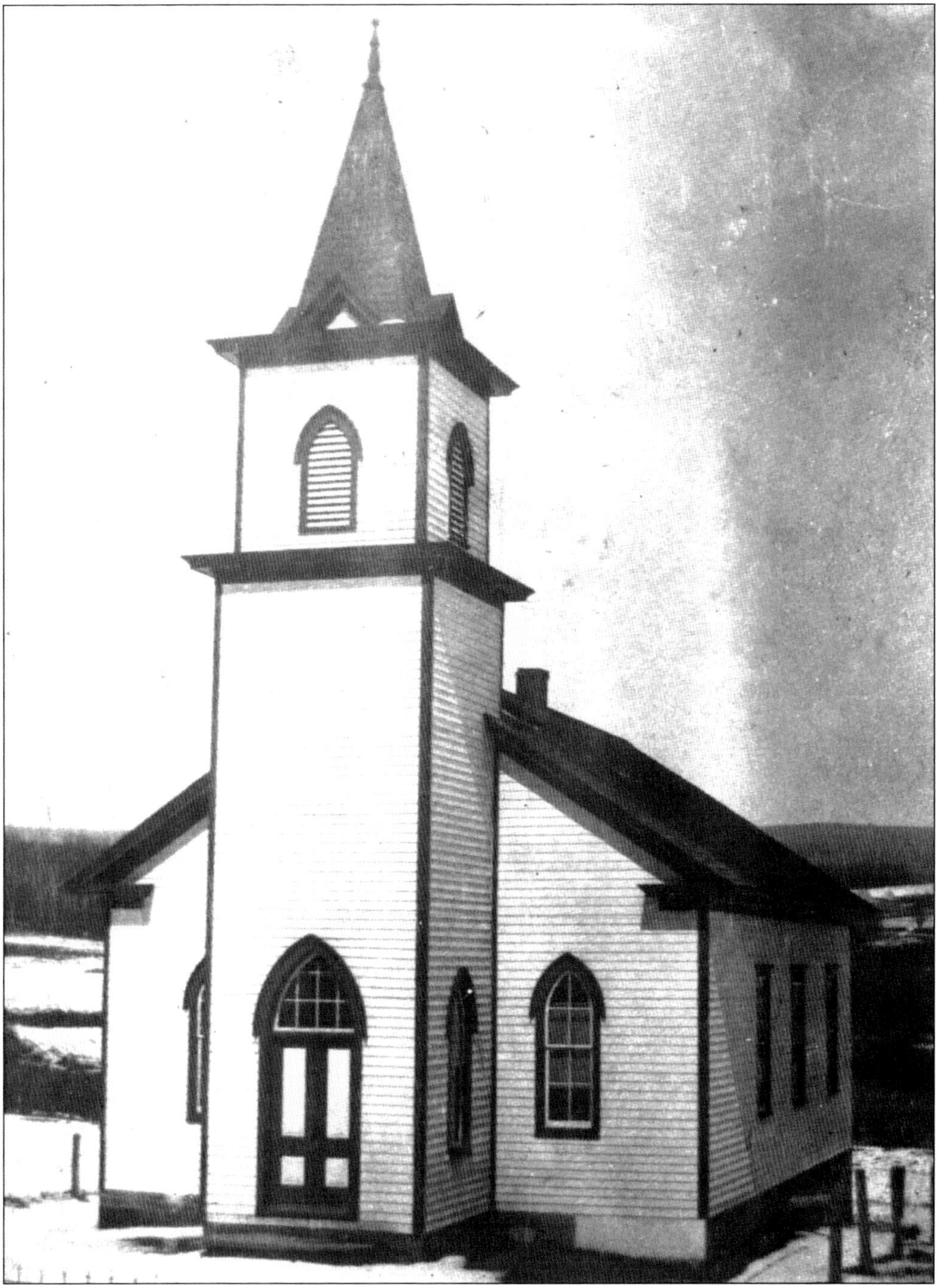

This picture is of St. Mark's Lutheran and Reformed Church in Appenzell, built in 1850. Prior to the construction of this church, the congregation members shared the one-room schoolhouse, which was built in 1820 just below the site of the new church. (Courtesy of Robert Wallingford.)

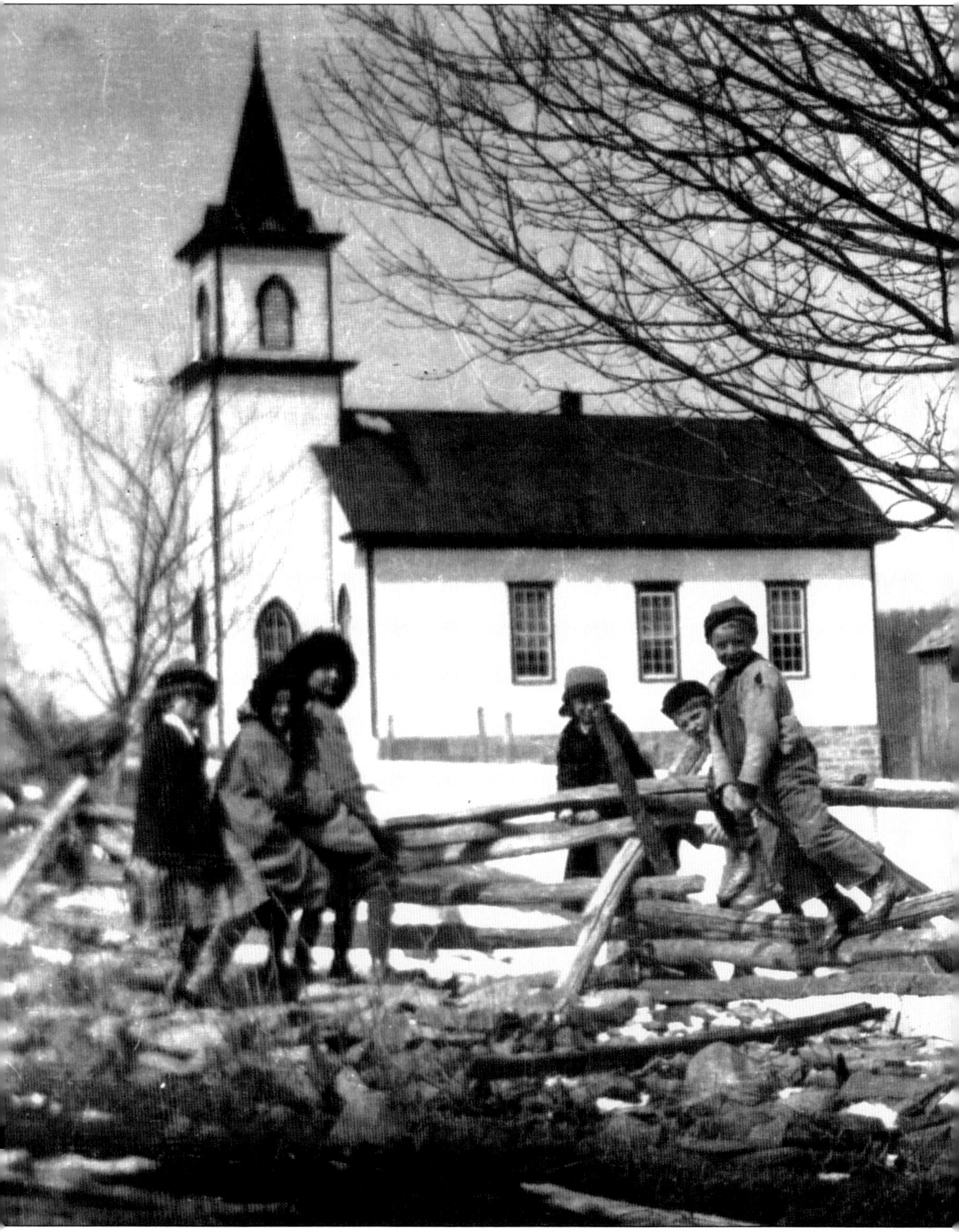

Schoolchildren pose on the split-rail fence between the Appenzell one-room schoolhouse and St. Mark's Lutheran and Reformed Church. The snow is on the ground and the trees are bare,

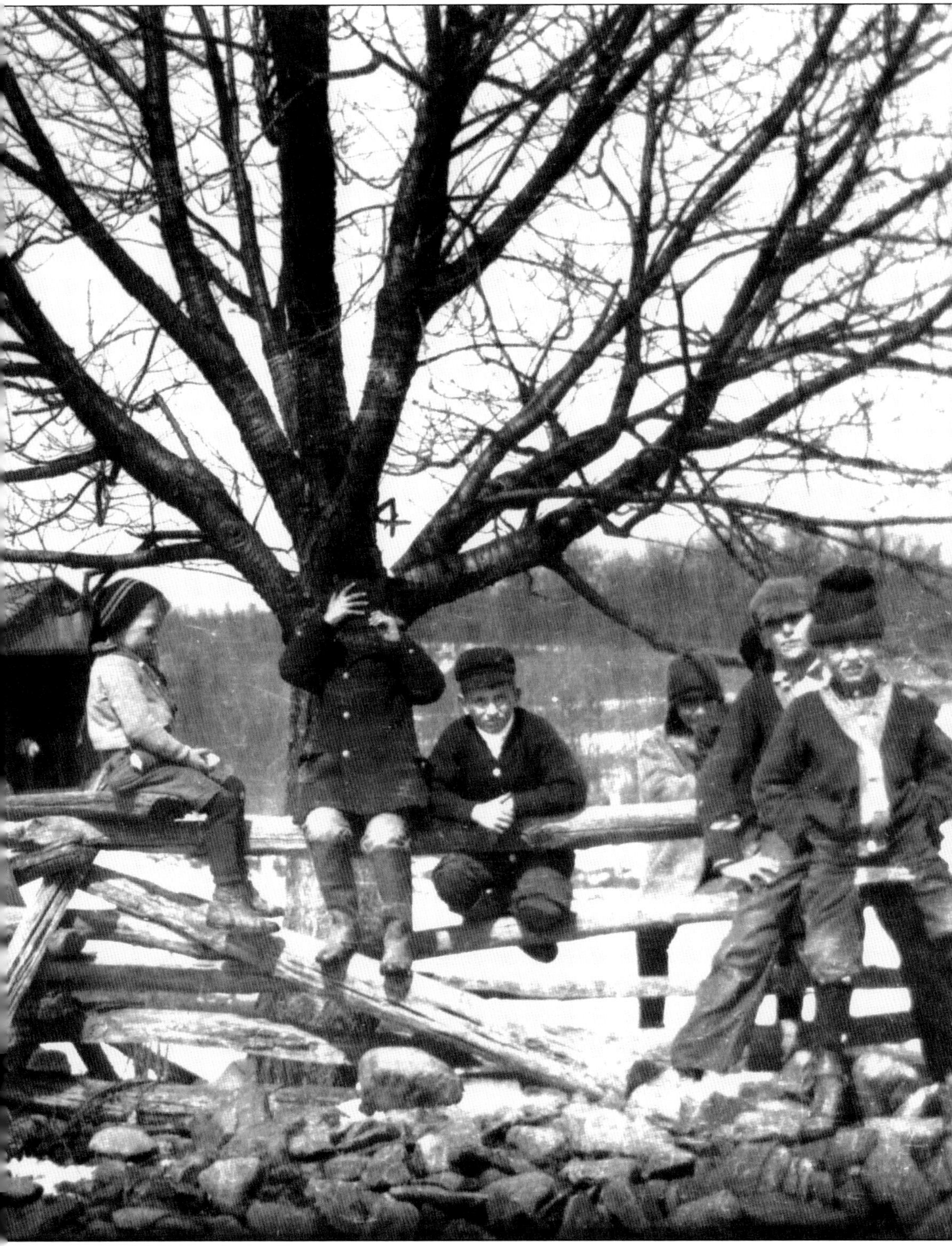

but it looks to be a clear, sunny day for the children to play outdoors at recess time. (Courtesy of Clyde Wallingford.)

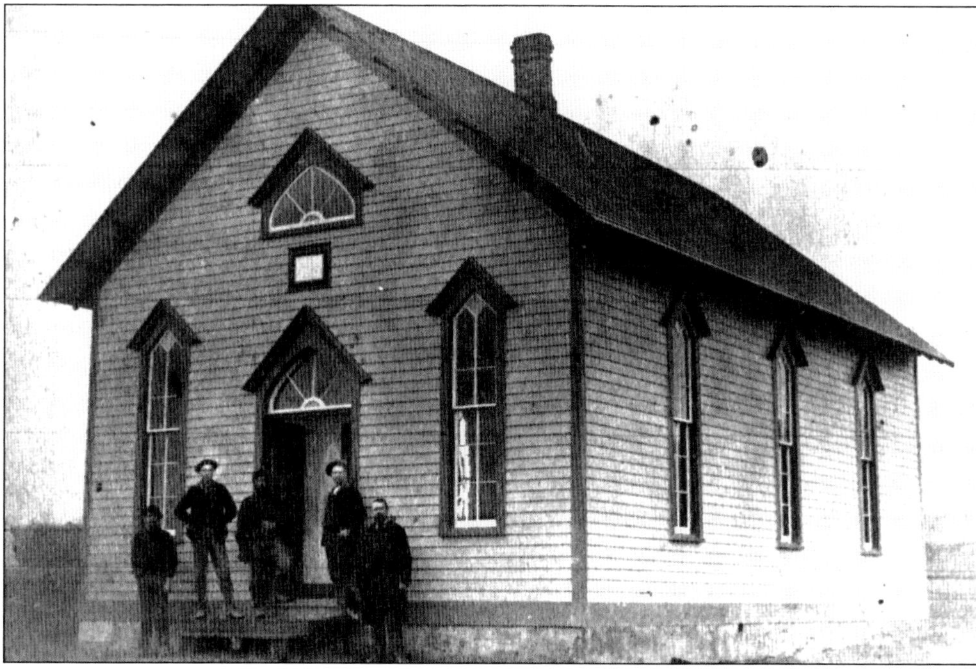

In 1883, Dungan's Chapel in Reeders was part of the Tannersville Circuit. The church was completed in December 1884 and dedicated on December 14, 1884. (Courtesy of the Pocono-Jackson Historical Society.)

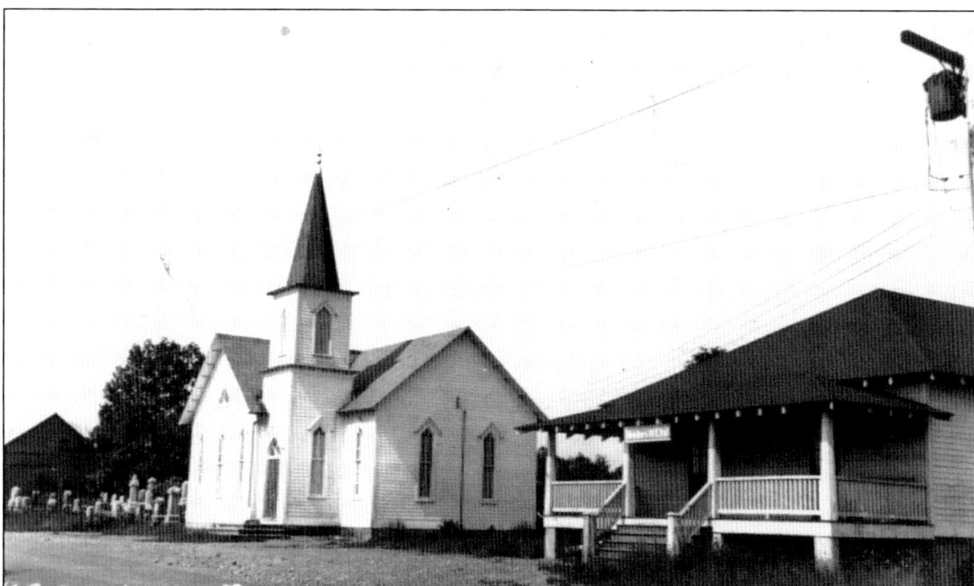

Records indicate the name of Dungan's Chapel was changed in 1891. In July 1927, the Reeders United Methodist Church social hall was built to accommodate church suppers and other social events. In the present day, an addition has joined the two structures. (Courtesy of Diane Davis Abeel.)

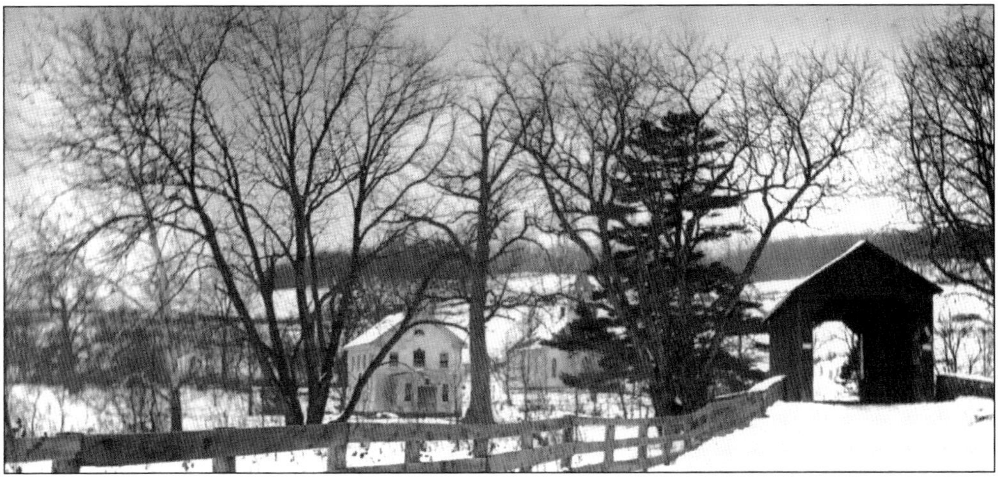

In the late 1800s, two churches stood at the intersection of Sullivan Trail and Route 715S. A log cabin on the site was built in 1834 to house the first church. The Lutheran Reformed church, built in 1834, is shown to the left, and Grace Evangelical and Reformed Church is on the hill. History has it that the churches were once housed in the Lutheran building, and the union congregation and the Grace congregation wished to build a new parish, so the Grace congregation constructed a new one on the hill. The Lutheran congregation then built its new church in the heart of Tannersville and abandoned the original union church building in 1910. All that remains at the site of the union church is the cornerstone near the roadside chapel. The lumber from the church was purchased in 1914 for $155 by George Werkheiser of Scotrun, who used it to erect a barn. (Courtesy of George Learn.)

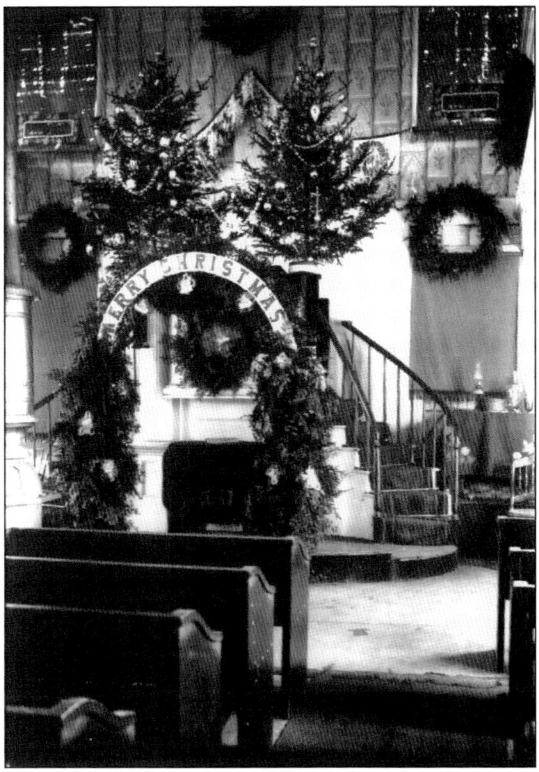

Very ornate decorations fill the sanctuary of the union church during the Christmas season. Note the raised pulpit at the front. (Courtesy of George Learn.)

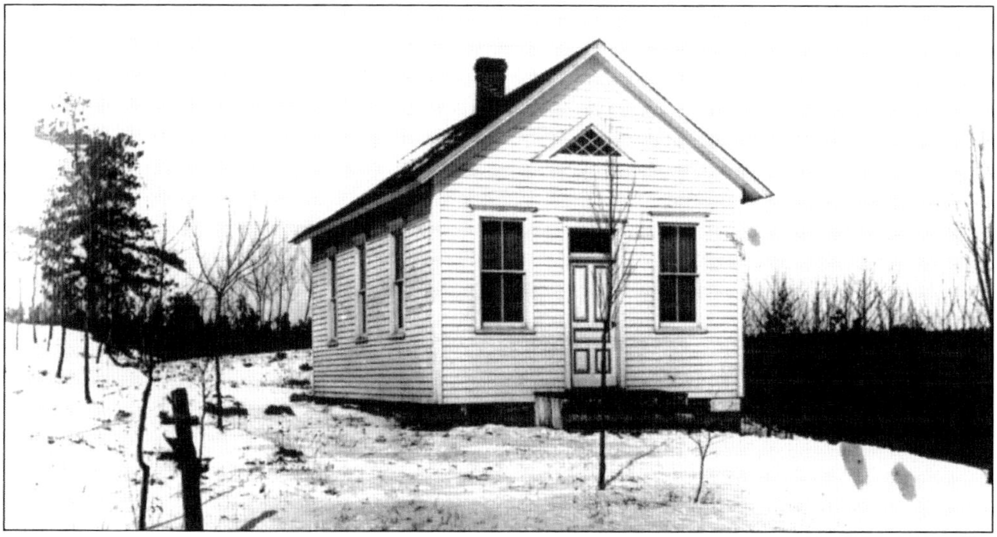

Late in the 1800s, Grace Reformed Chapel was built near Sullivan Trail in the area known as White Oak Run at the most northern reaches of Pocono Township. The one acre of land was bought from Elizabeth Ruehlman for $15. Grace Reformed Chapel is shown below as it was decorated for Christmas. The families from the immediate area included Turner, Ruehlman, and Widdoss. (Courtesy of Mike Iby.)

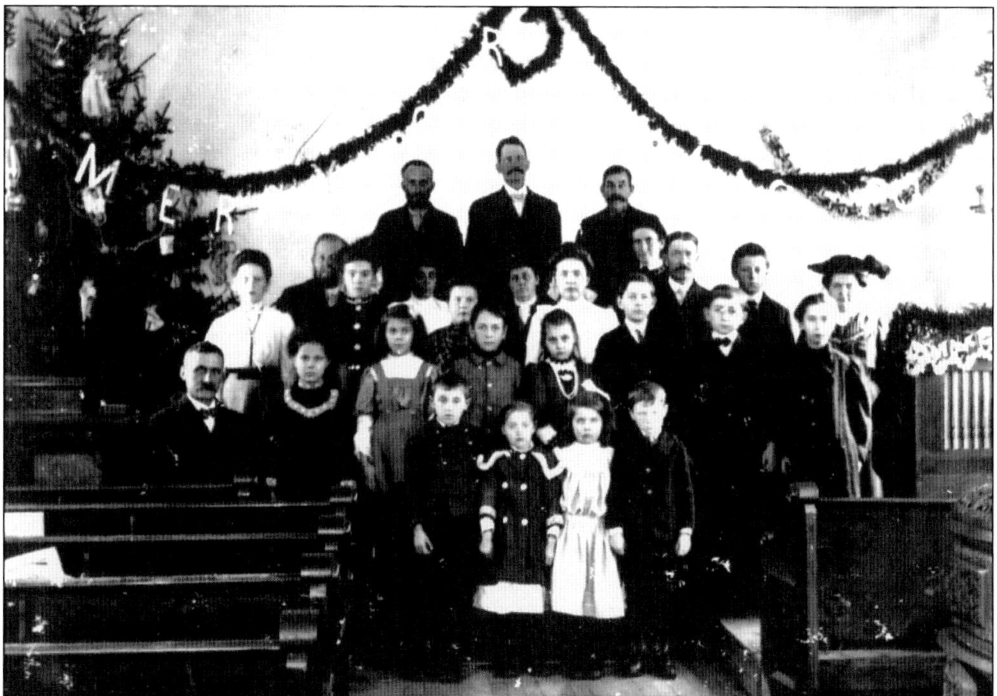

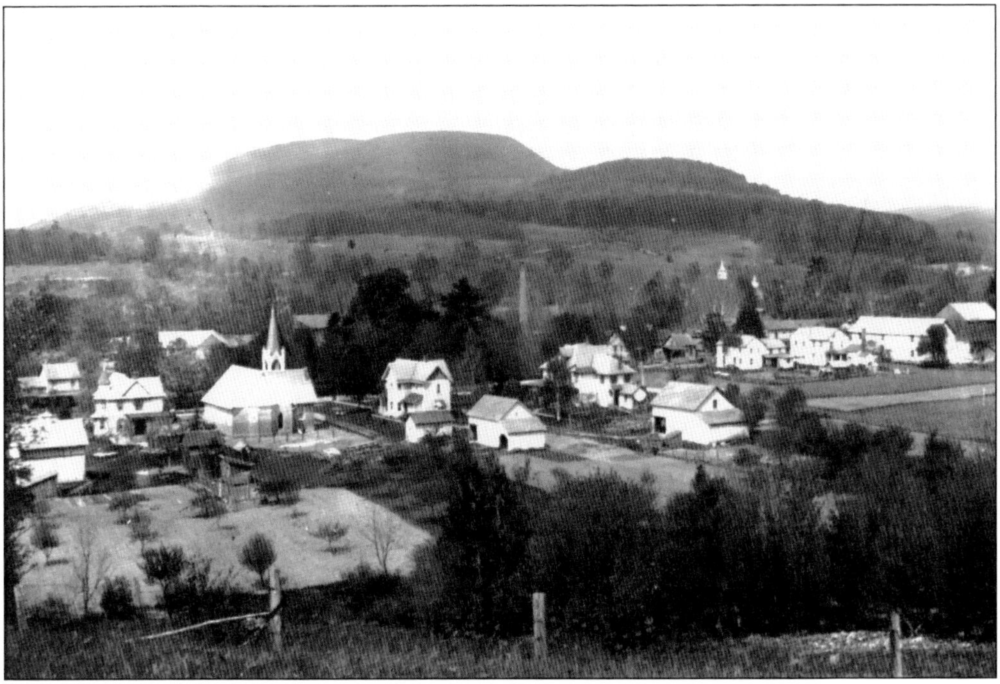

A bird's-eye view of Tannersville from atop Fish Hill shows St. Paul's Lutheran Church under construction, with a window at the rear of the church still waiting to be installed. In the distance at the base of Big Pocono, the steeples of Grace Evangelical and Reformed Church and the union church can be seen. The stack from the tannery still stands in the center of the photograph; it blew down during a storm in 1914. (Courtesy of George Learn.)

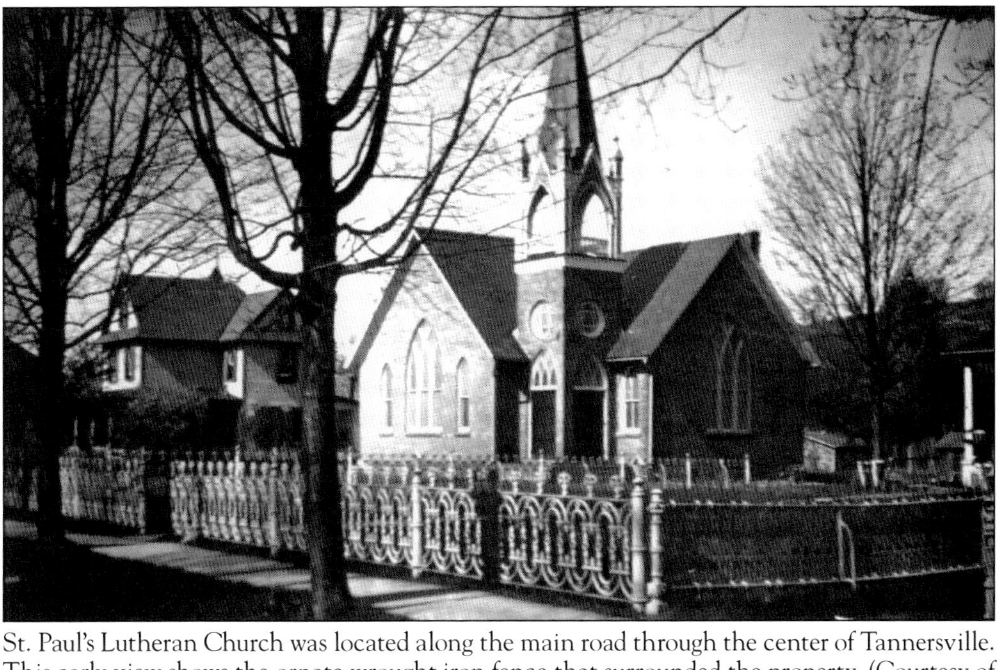

St. Paul's Lutheran Church was located along the main road through the center of Tannersville. This early view shows the ornate wrought-iron fence that surrounded the property. (Courtesy of George Learn.)

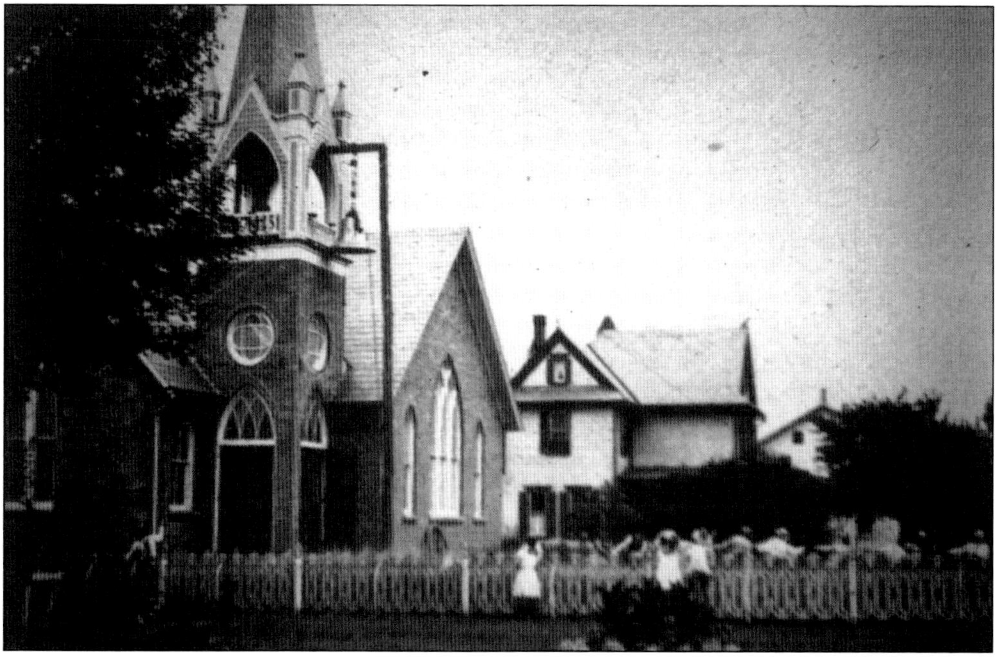

Here in 1910, the bell is placed in the steeple of St. Paul's Lutheran Church using a gin pole. It was removed by using a crane, taken to the new St. Paul's Lutheran Church on Fish Hill, and placed at the entrance by Neil Unternaher as his Eagle Scout project in 2002. (Courtesy of Olive Metzger Learn.)

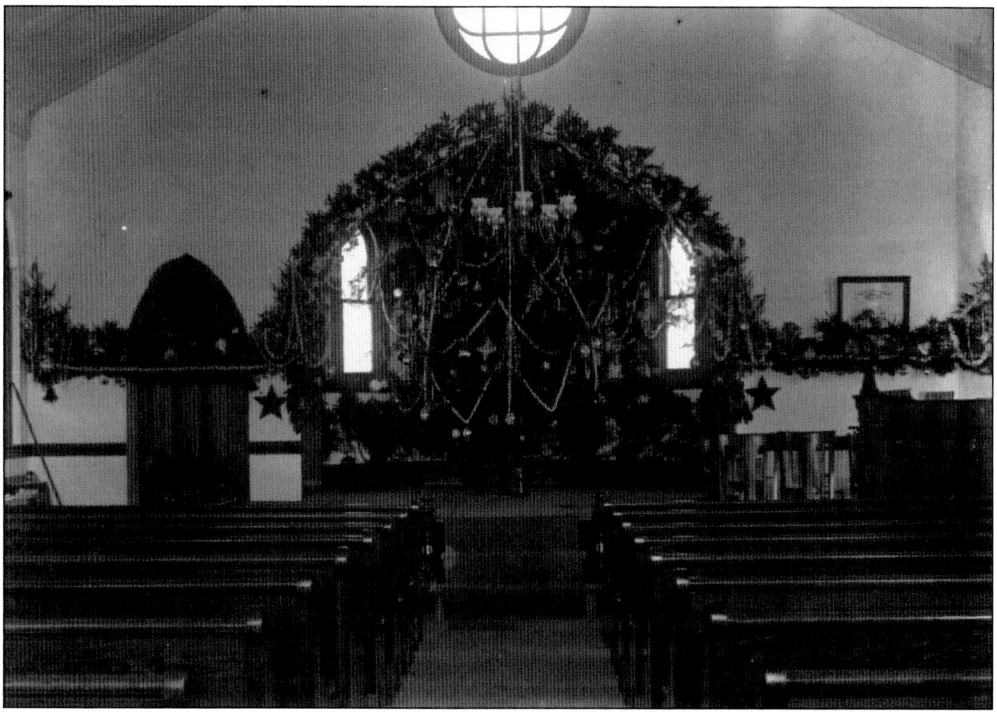

This early-1900s photograph shows the interior of St. Paul's Lutheran Church at Christmastime. (Courtesy of George Learn.)

Seven

HAVING FUN

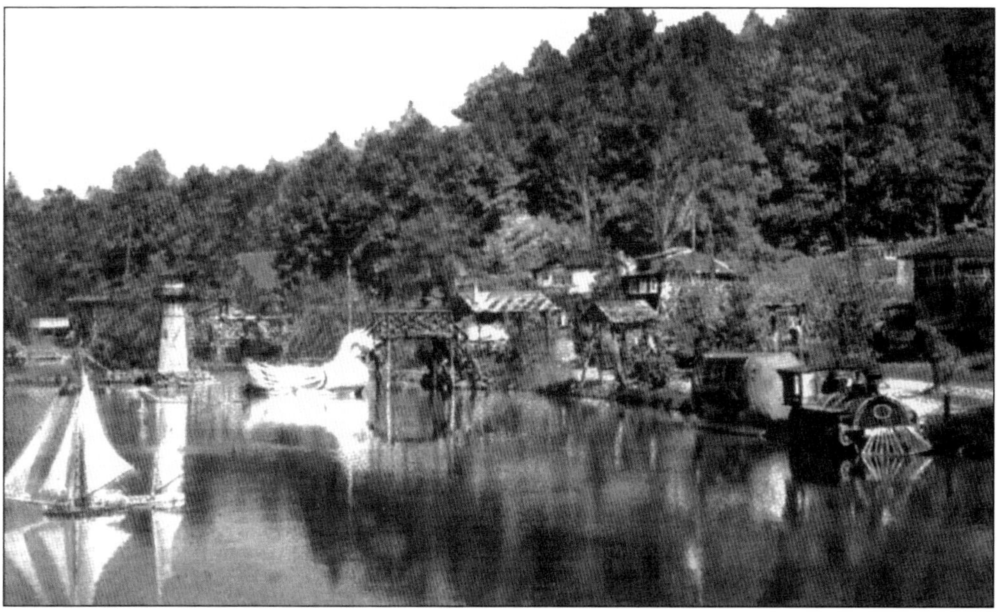

Redwood Amusement Center, built in 1932 by the Wunderly family, was located in Scotrun. It had a swan and a train boat ride, a penny arcade, picnic facilities, and a playground. It also had food stands and a restaurant, and during Prohibition, it had one tap that contained beer. It was destroyed by the flood of 1955 except for the stone house known as "the Castle." (Courtesy of Verdon Rustine.)

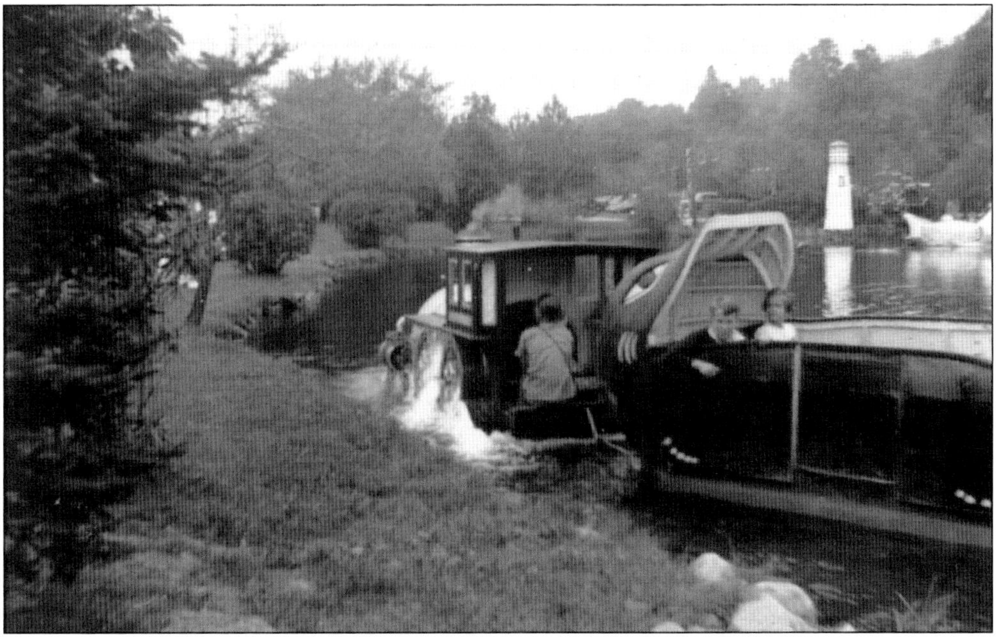

The Redwood Amusement Center train ride was built about 1930. A motorcycle engine powered the train with a chain drive that moved the paddles. It then ran on a track that moved it around the lake through the water. A nickel ride was one trip around the lake. (Courtesy of Verdon Rustine.)

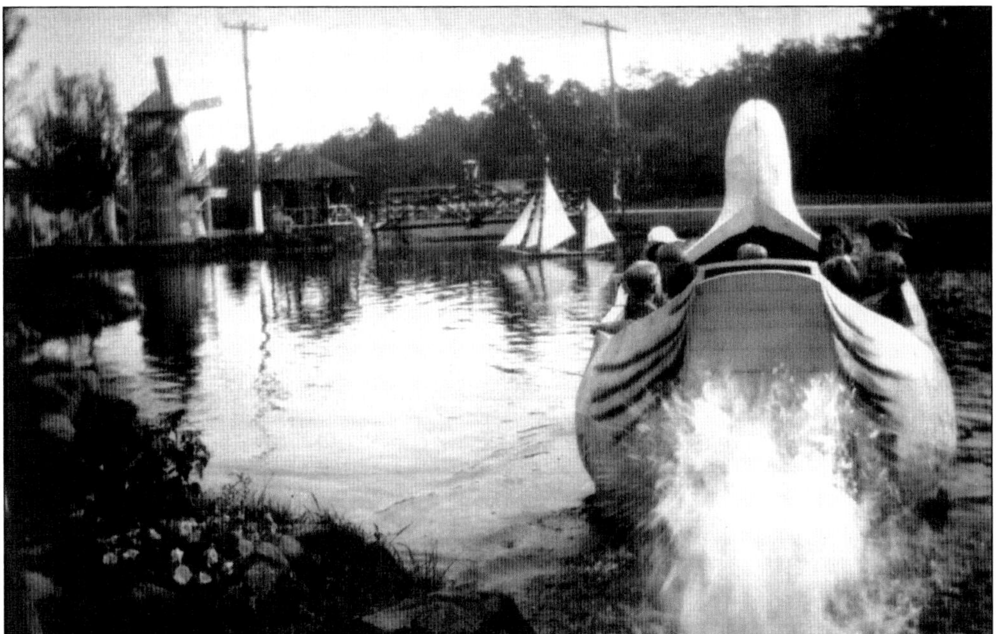

The swan boat was purchased from Saylors Lake and moved to Redwood. It was fixed to a rod that caused the boat to pivot in a circle with power from an electric motor. A ride was two circles around the lake, with 10 to 12 people sitting in the swan for the ride. (Courtesy of Verdon Rustine.)

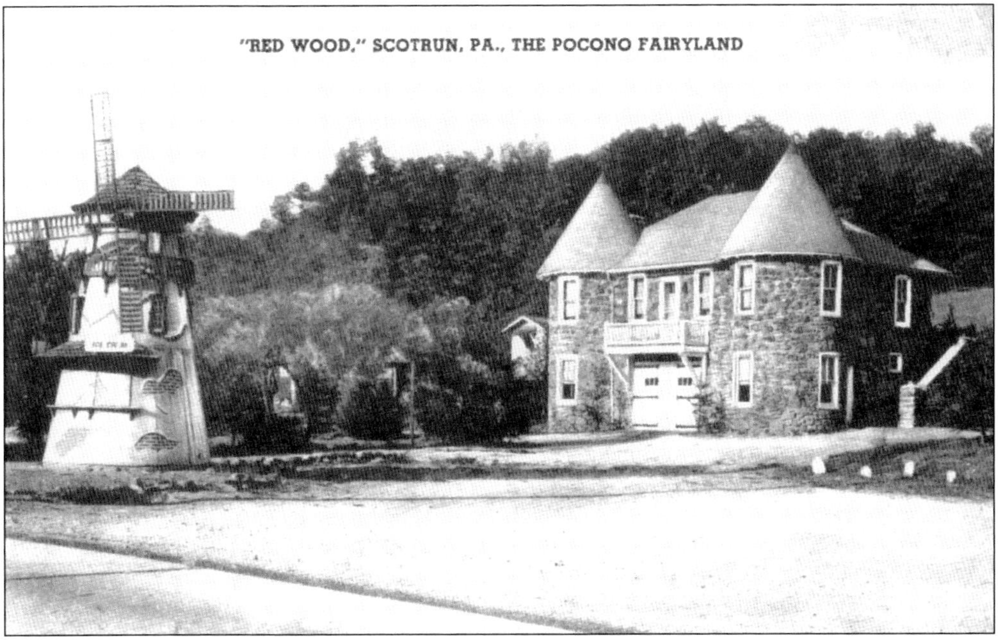

The windmill at Redwood stood on a little island in the lake and was a decorative attraction for the amusement park. The stone building, known as the Castle, was occupied by the park owners, the Wunderly family. In August 1955, everything at the amusement park was destroyed by the floodwaters, except the Castle. (Courtesy of Verdon Rustine.)

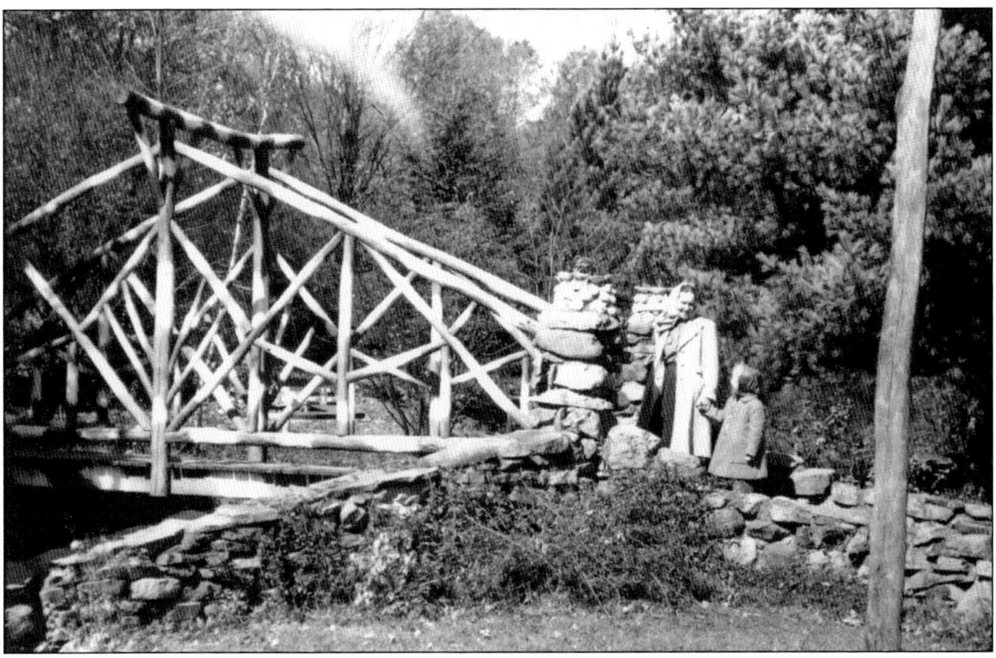

The log bridge at Redwood was used as an access way to other parts of the park. The penny arcade was one of the park attractions people could visit by crossing the log bridge. (Courtesy of Verdon Rustine.)

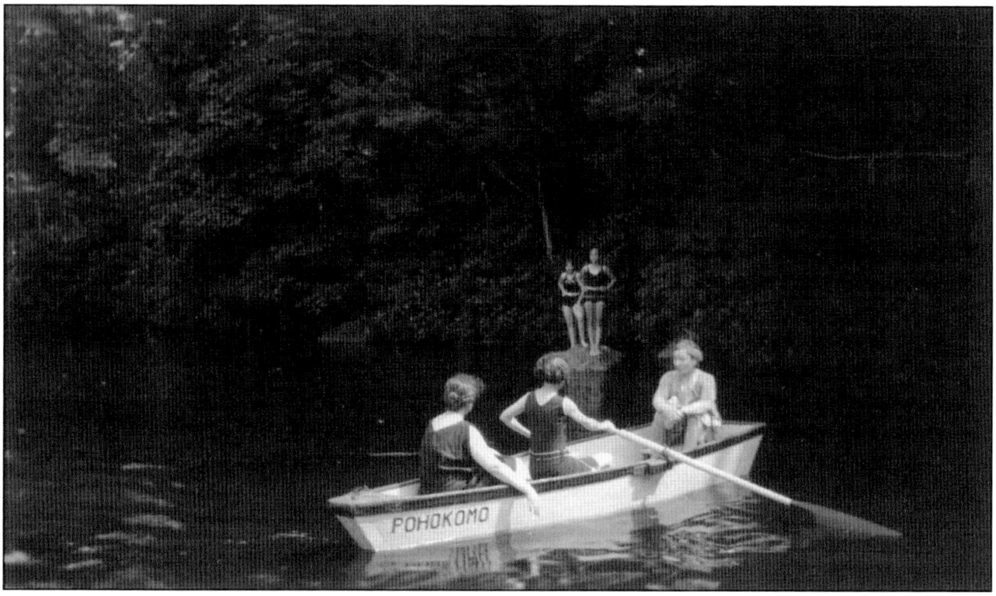

In 1907, the George Kerst family constructed a dam on the Scotrun Creek behind their Pohokomo home and boardinghouse. Swimmers seen here are ready to dive from the big rock toward the rowboat. The pond provided swimming, boating, and fishing in the summer and skating in the winter. Ice was cut in winter and stored in the icehouse beside the pond for later use. (Courtesy of Linford Werkheiser.)

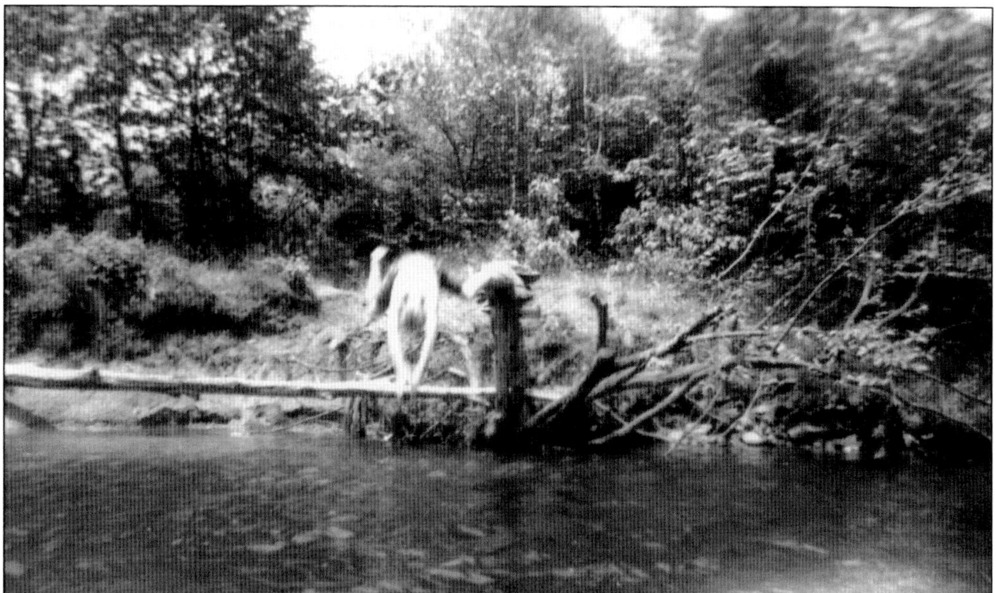

A favorite swimming hole was Stadden's, located on the Pocono Creek just south of Tannersville. Edward Price is shown here practicing his frog dive. Many local residents enjoyed swinging on a large rope hanging from an overhanging tree branch, letting go, and falling into the creek with a large splash. (Courtesy of James Price.)

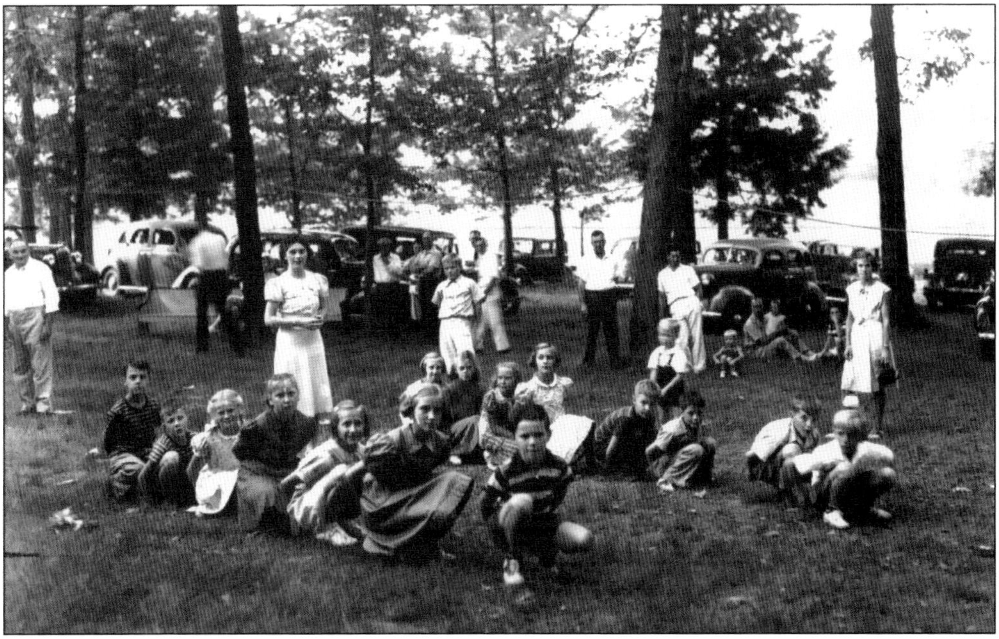

The Appenzell Picnic began at the end of the 1800s as a yearly family event for members of the Appenzell Lutheran and Reformed Church. The individual families built their own tables and benches. In later years, the picnic was open to the public. As a novel way of raising money, a cakewalk was started, which charged people for walking in the circle. More than 100 cakes are baked for the occasion. (Courtesy of Clyde Wallingford.)

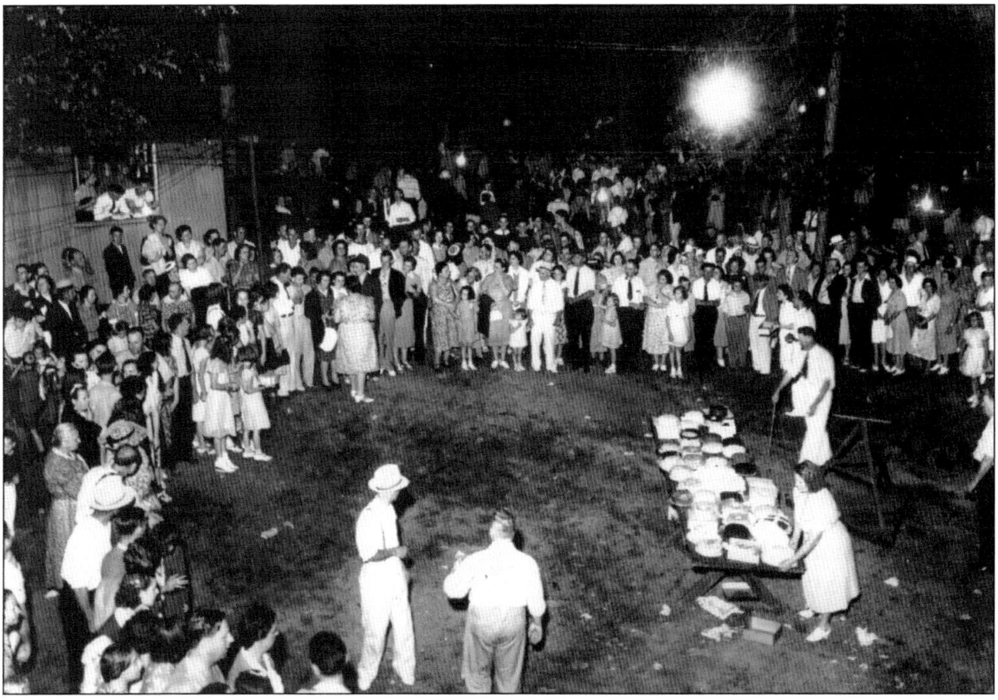

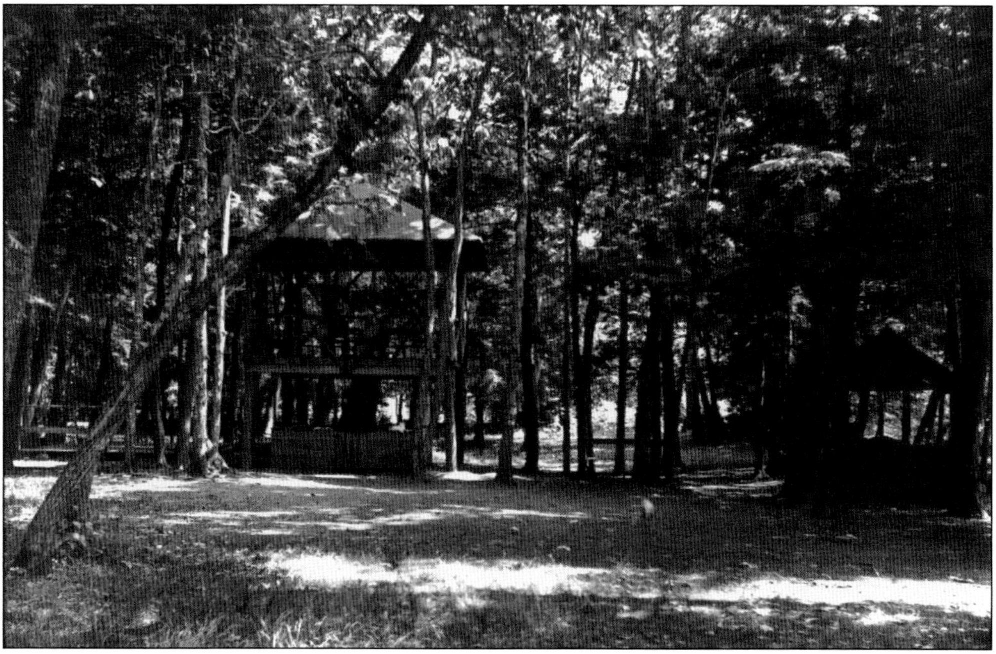

This two-tiered structure was located in Kistler's Picnic Grove along Route 611 above the Pocono Diner. The upper deck was the bandstand; the concession stand, which sold ice cream, was underneath. (Courtesy of John Frailey.)

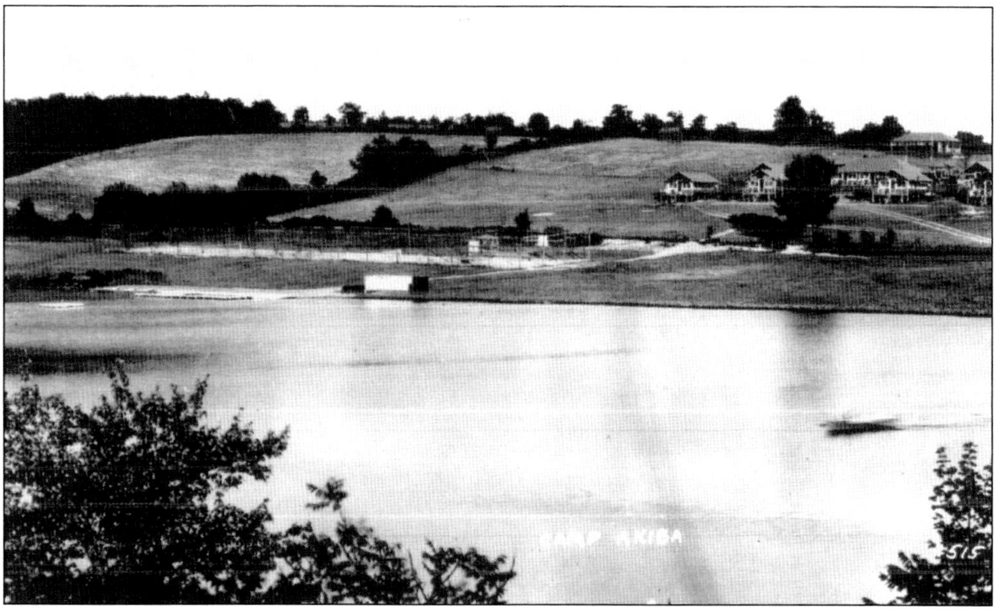

Camp Akiba was started in 1924 when the Ervin Miller farm and other surrounding farms were purchased to total several hundred acres. Miller was named caretaker and held that job for over 50 years. A large lake was built for swimming and boating. Both boys and girls attended the camp, which is still in operation today. (Courtesy of Verdon Rustine.)

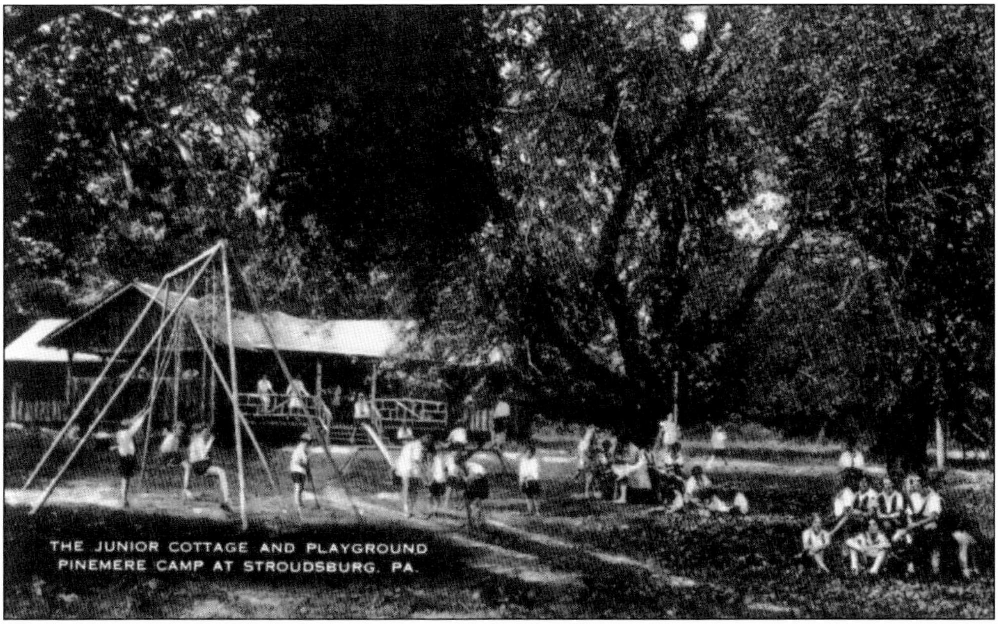

Located on Stoney Run, Pinemere Camp began operation in the 1930s. A Mrs. Cohen purchased property from the McClusky family and Joseph Nye. A lake was built for boating and swimming for the girls-only camp. It became coeducational when the Philadelphia Jewish Welfare Board bought it. The sleeping cabins pictured were built for those who were residential campers. Pinemere got its name from the reflection of pine trees on the lake. (Courtesy of Verdon Rustine.)

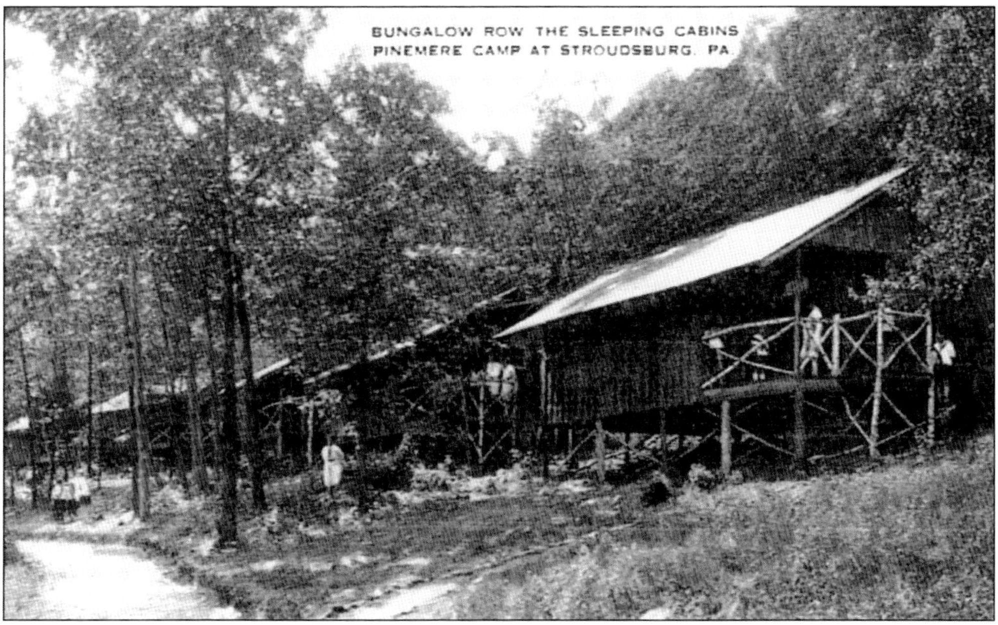

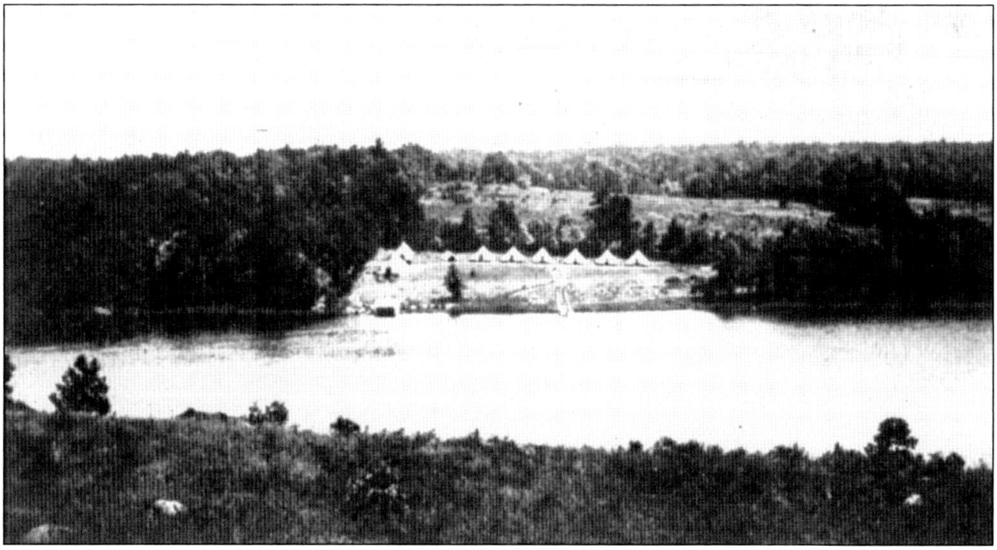

This camp was located on Hunter Lake in Jackson Township and began in the 1930s. This view is from a hill looking across the lake toward the Bartonsville Woods Road. The camp was later known as Golden Slipper Square Club Camp and is still in operation today. (Courtesy of Verdon Rustine.)

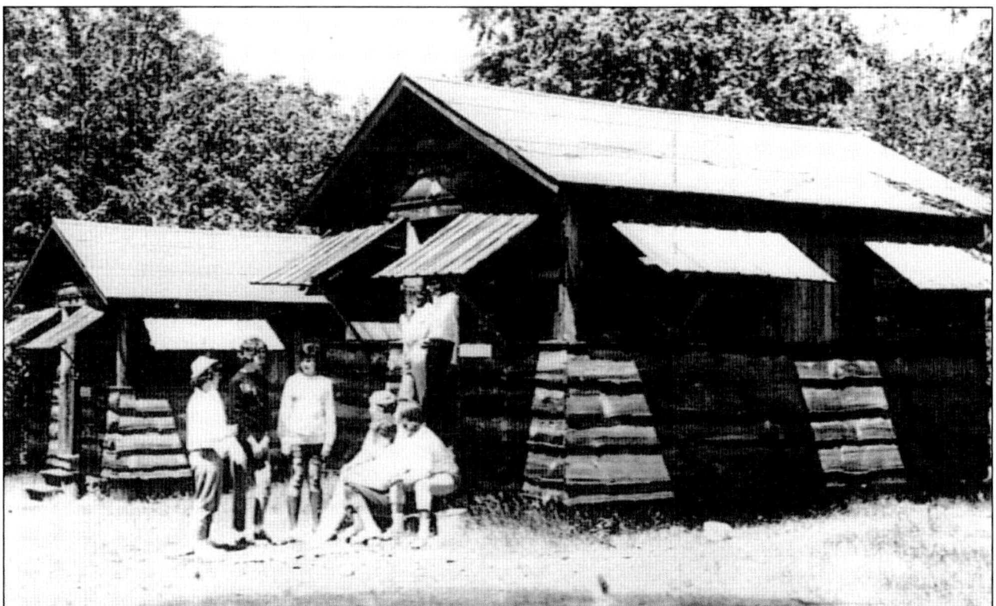

Camp Cherith was built in the 1950s at the base of Big Pocono on land formally owned by Frederick Doll. No lake was built, but numerous ever-flowing streams supplied excellent cold, refreshing drinking water. Camp Cherith was one of the smaller camps in the area; today it is known as Camp Gilead, a spiritual retreat. (Courtesy of Verdon Rustine.)

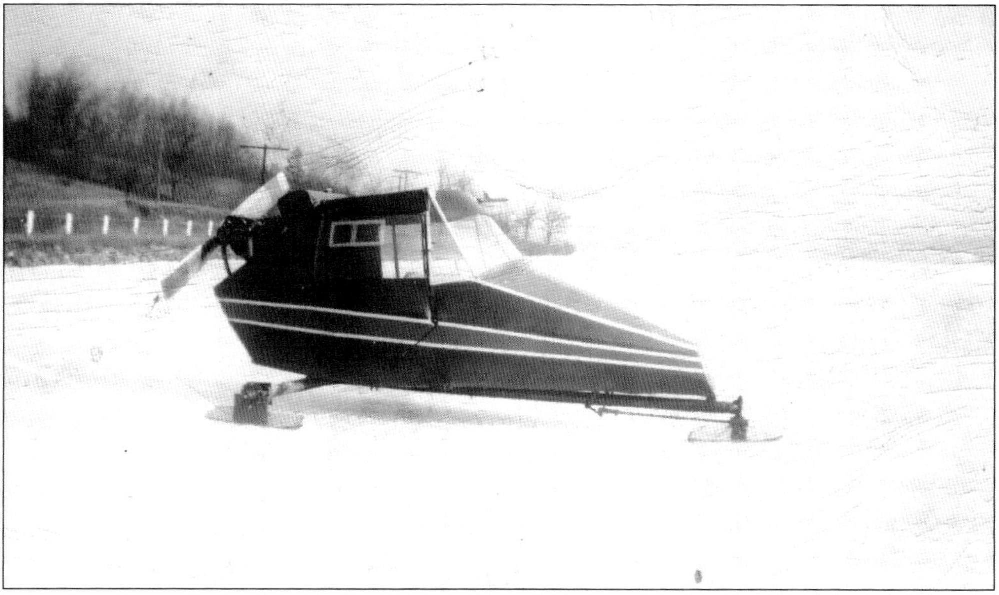

"You can always separate the men from the boys by the size of their toys." The iceboat shown here is one of three owned by Edward and John Belcher. They operated the boats on Trout and Saylors Lakes and other large bodies of water after World War II. The body of the boat was redesigned by Donald Nelson and built from wrecked airplanes with the engine mounted in the rear. (Courtesy of James Price.)

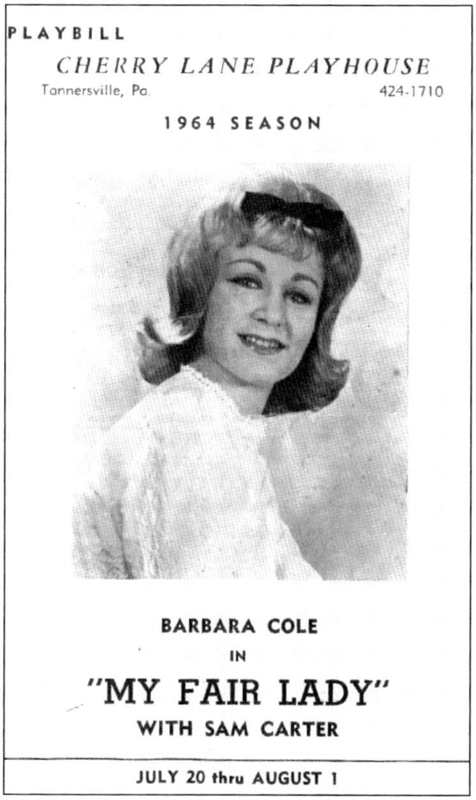

Cherry Lane Playhouse (1962–1967) brought a bit of Broadway to Pocono Township. The now-razed theater, created in a 100-year-old barn, was located on Birchwood Drive. Inside, the cozy arena-type theater had rows of steeply inclined seats on three walls, with the stage and scenery occupying the fourth. This photograph shows the program cover for the 1964 production of *My Fair Lady*. (Courtesy of John Alleger.)

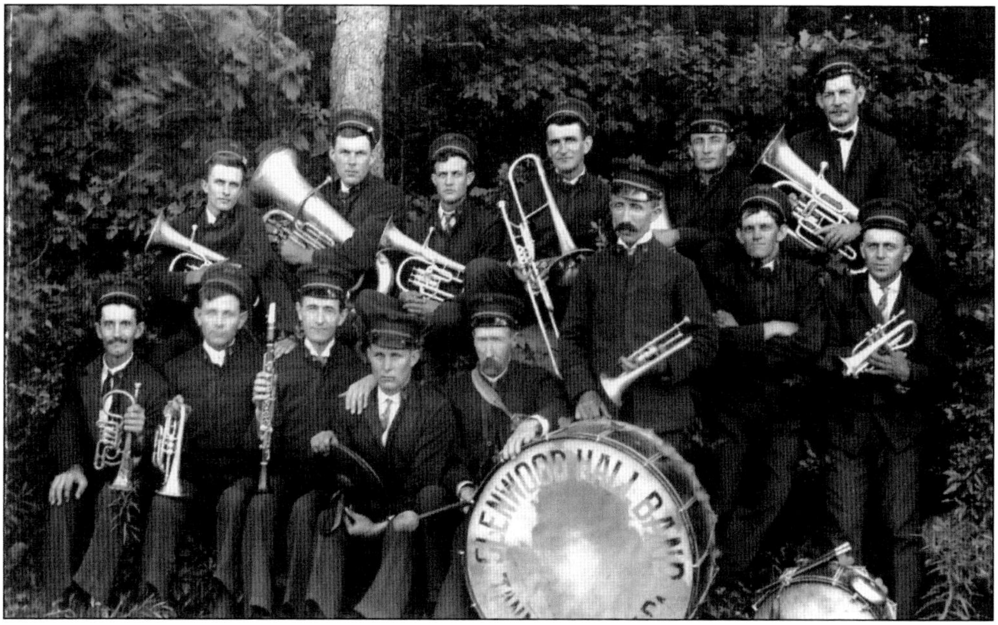

The Glenwood Hall Band was popular, playing for parades and socials. This photograph was taken in August 1909 at Appenzell. Pictured are, from left to right, (first row) Ben Granacher, Forest Warner, Charles Waas, Laverne Werkheiser, Adam Bellis, George Warner, Arthur Shively, and Arthur Post; (second row) George Warner, Allen Bryson, Milton Halstead, Harry Werkheiser, Earl Singer, and Samuel Werkheiser. (Courtesy of George Learn.)

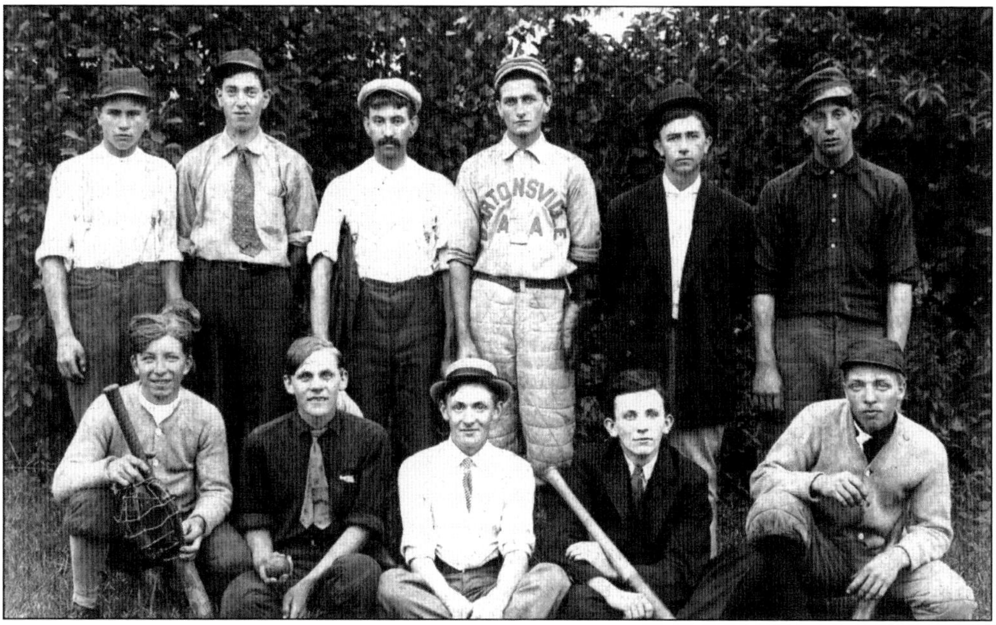

The Bartonsville baseball team is shown here around 1910, representing its village in the national pastime. Pictured are, from left to right, (first row) Lee Hartman (1889–1974), Richard Metzgar (1890–1965), Jesse Metzgar, Amzi Werkheiser, and Arthur Shiffer (1888–1970); (second row) Daniel Anglemyer, Robert Swink, John Alleger Sr. (1876–1946), Rodgers Shook (1889–1983), Joseph Shook (1890–1945), and Harry Neyhart. (Courtesy of John Alleger.)

Eight

Down on the Farm

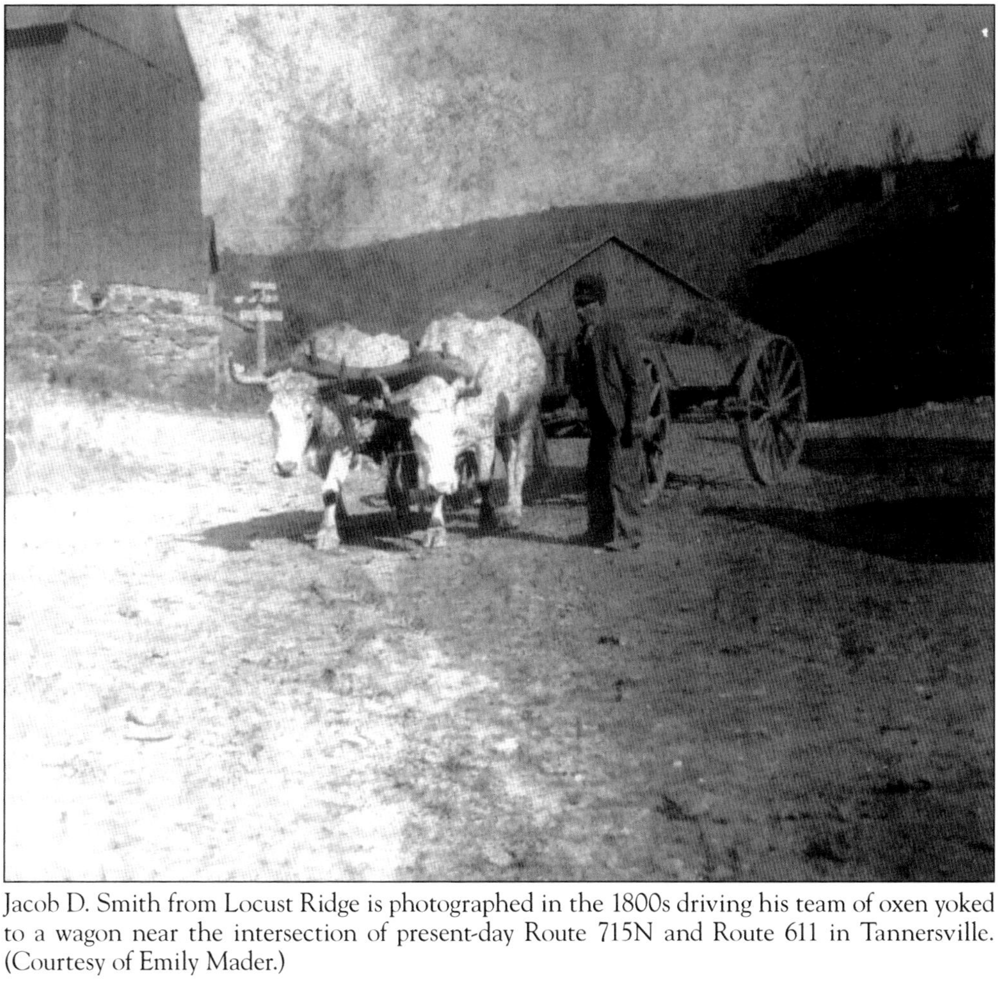

Jacob D. Smith from Locust Ridge is photographed in the 1800s driving his team of oxen yoked to a wagon near the intersection of present-day Route 715N and Route 611 in Tannersville. (Courtesy of Emily Mader.)

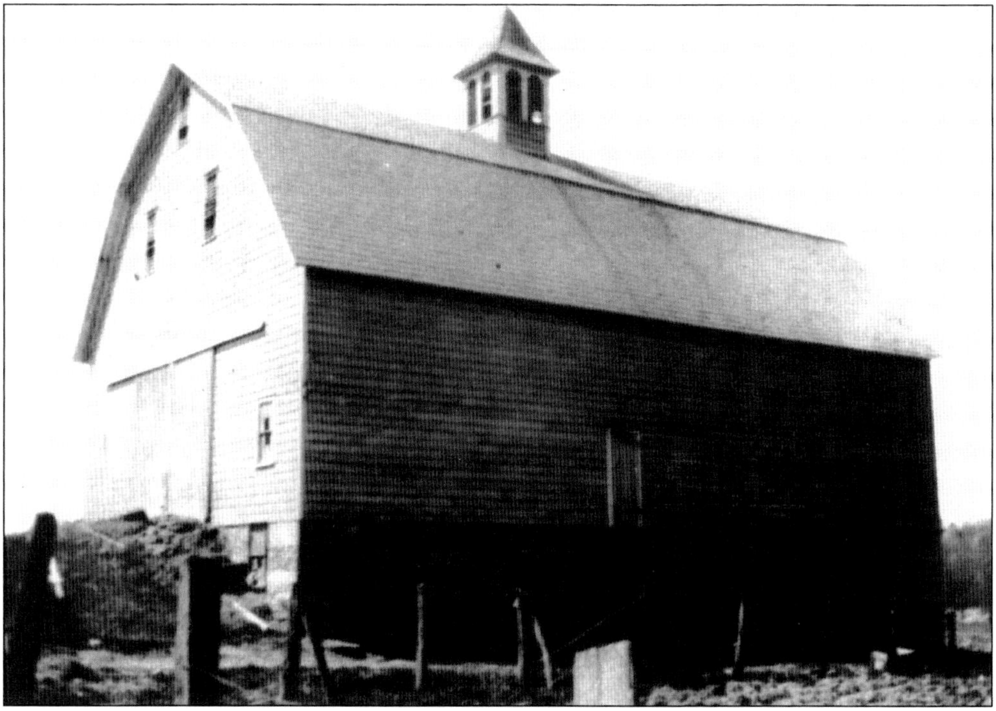

In 1941, the barn above was dismantled and relocated on the Learn farm away from its original location to allow for the construction of the new three-lane Route 611 in lower Tannersville. It still stands on the property that is now owned by Donald and Donna Schmoyer Simpson. Below is a photograph of an old Learn family homestead that later was used as a washhouse. (Courtesy of the Pocono-Jackson Historical Society.)

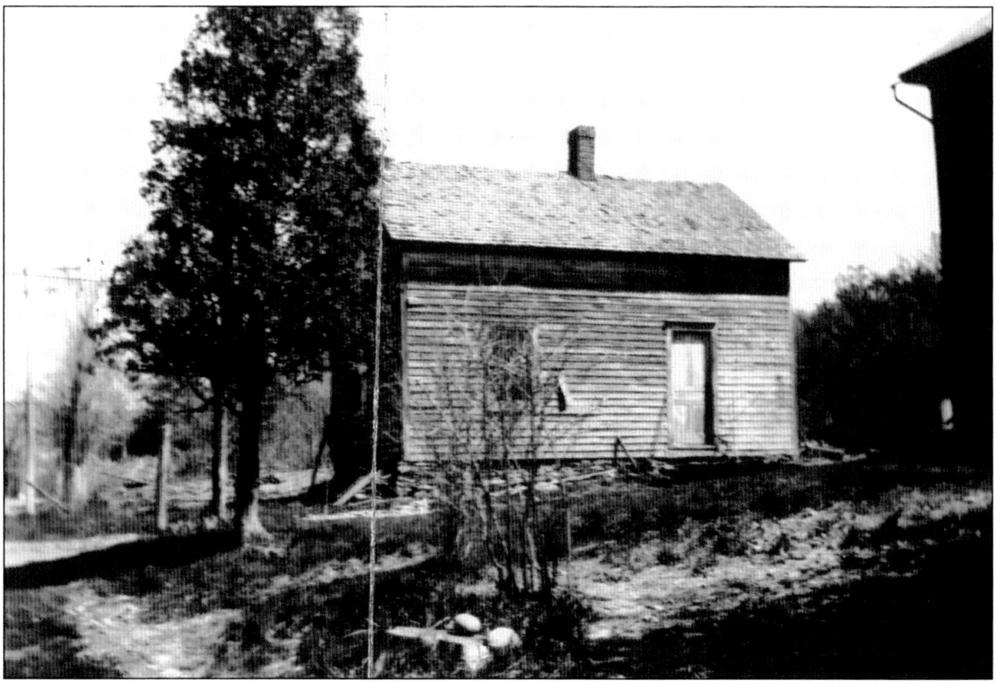

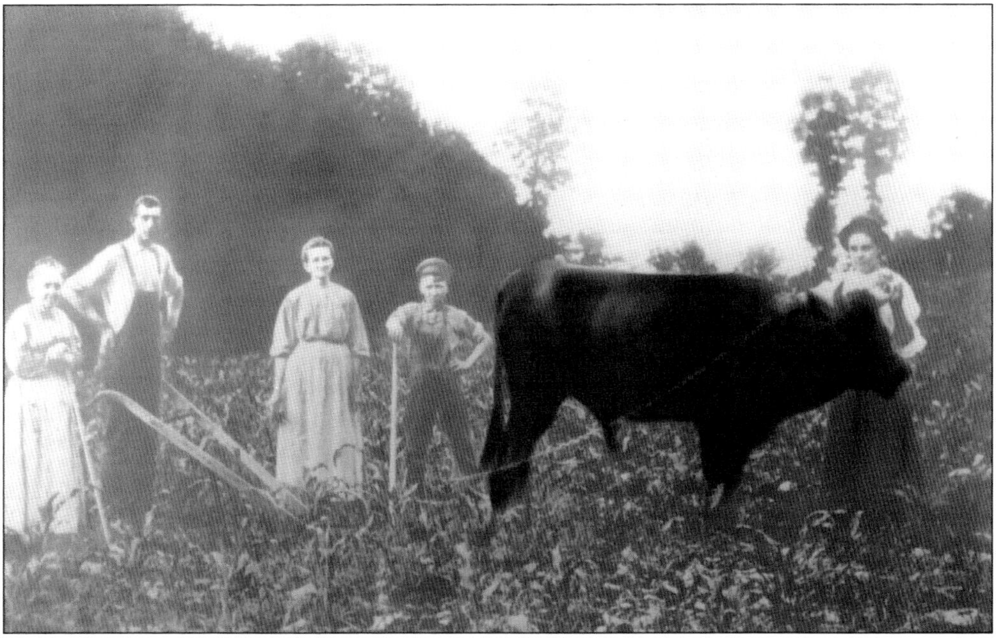

In this photograph, the Levi Miller family is shown with the ox used in plowing. (Courtesy of Lester Miller.)

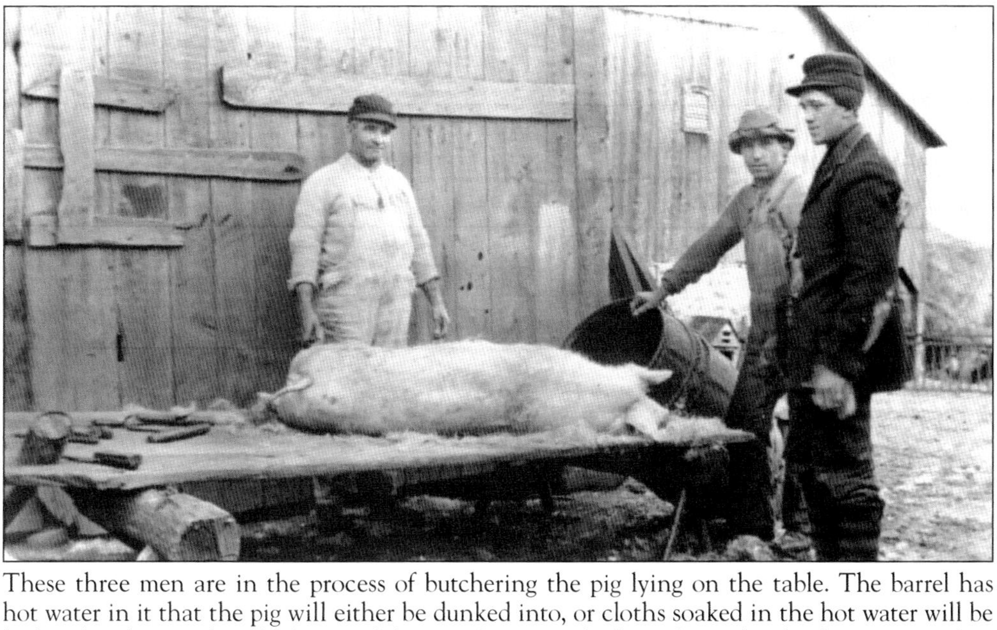

These three men are in the process of butchering the pig lying on the table. The barrel has hot water in it that the pig will either be dunked into, or cloths soaked in the hot water will be laid on his skin so that the hair and dirt can be scraped off. Looking closely, the man standing behind the pig has a scraper in his right hand. (Courtesy of Robert Wallingford.)

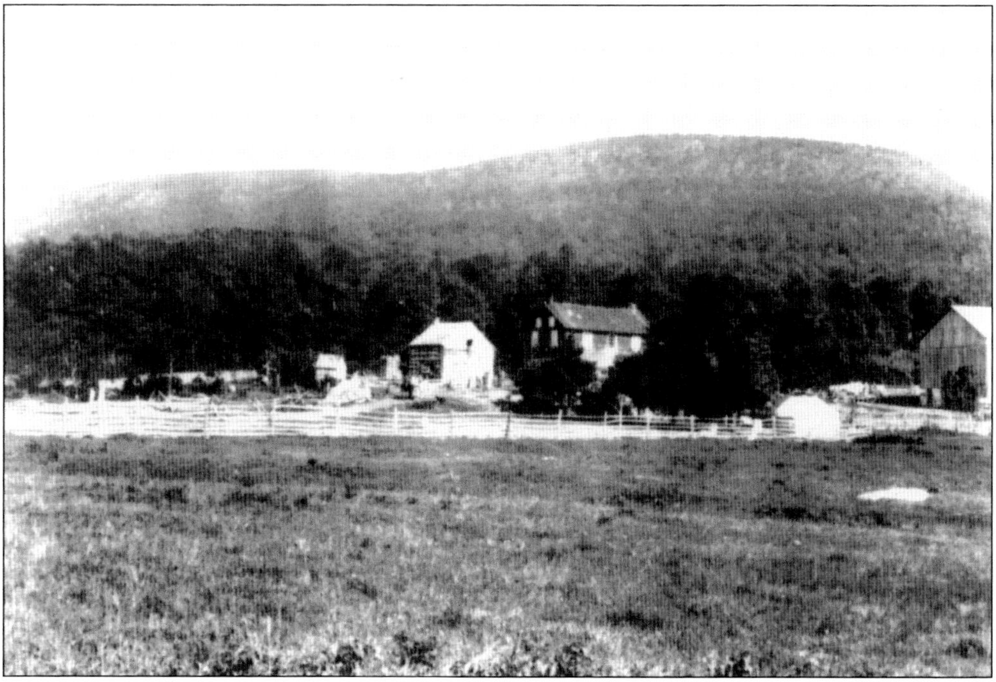

Situated at the base of Big Pocono, this 165-acre farm was purchased by John D. Gantzhorn in 1848 for $15. He and his wife had 13 children. His sixth child, John, built the house that still stands today. In 1998, approximately 95 acres were sold to John and Arlene Frailey, who established Mountain Shadow Farm on the site. (Courtesy of Emma Gantzhorn Arndt.)

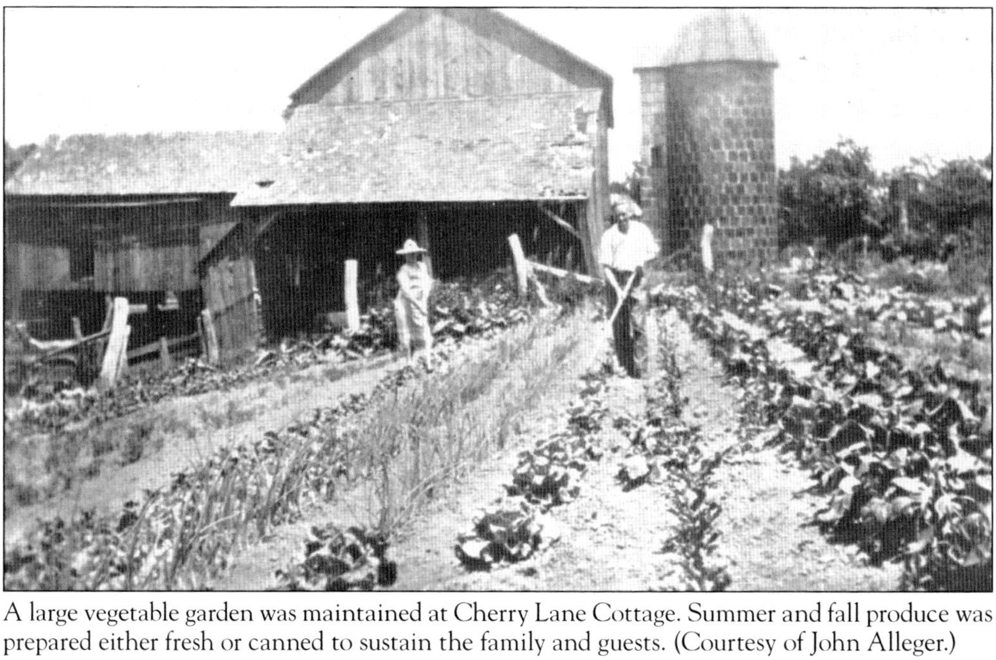

A large vegetable garden was maintained at Cherry Lane Cottage. Summer and fall produce was prepared either fresh or canned to sustain the family and guests. (Courtesy of John Alleger.)

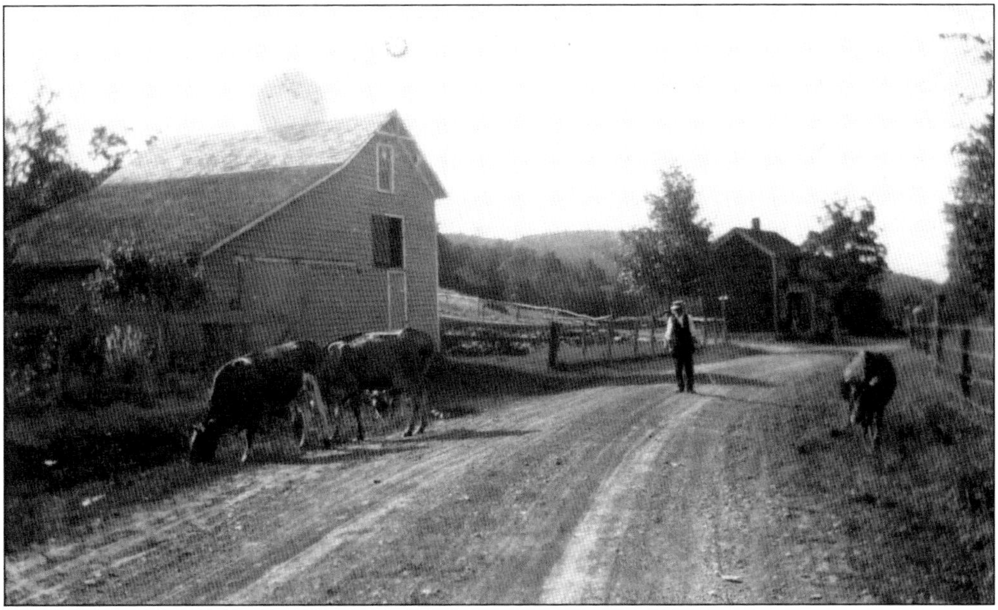

Mr. Werkheiser is shown in Scotrun driving the cows home at the end of the day. (Courtesy of Linford Werkheiser.)

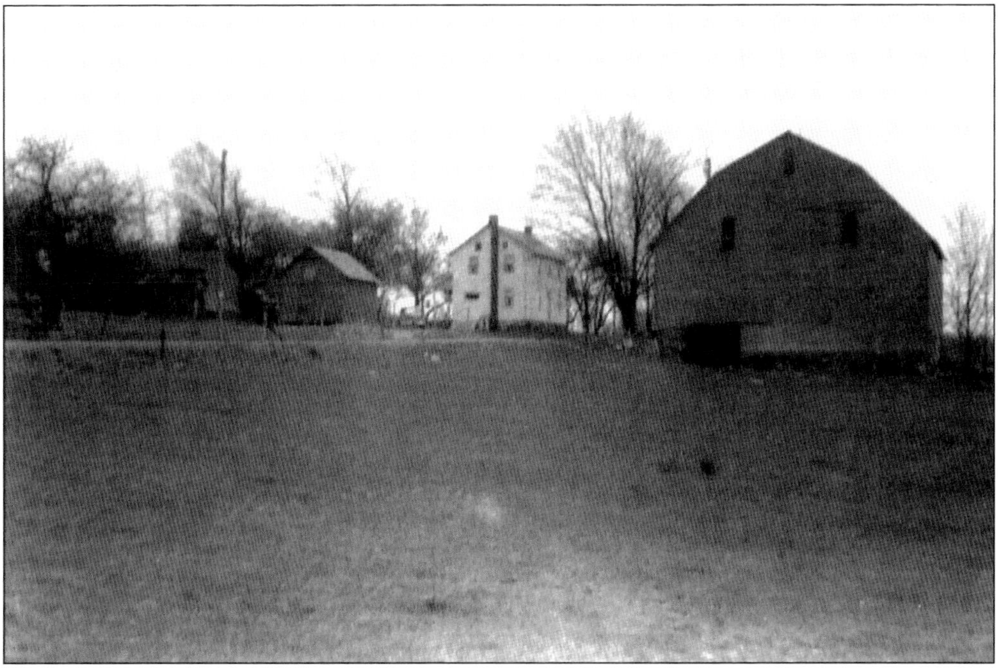

Located in Pocono Township and straddling Warner Road, the more than 48-acre farm is currently owned by James Price. Purchased from Henry Romberger in 1957, the farm was split in two by the construction of Interstate 80 in 1959. The barn on the property was originally painted yellow. (Courtesy of James Price.)

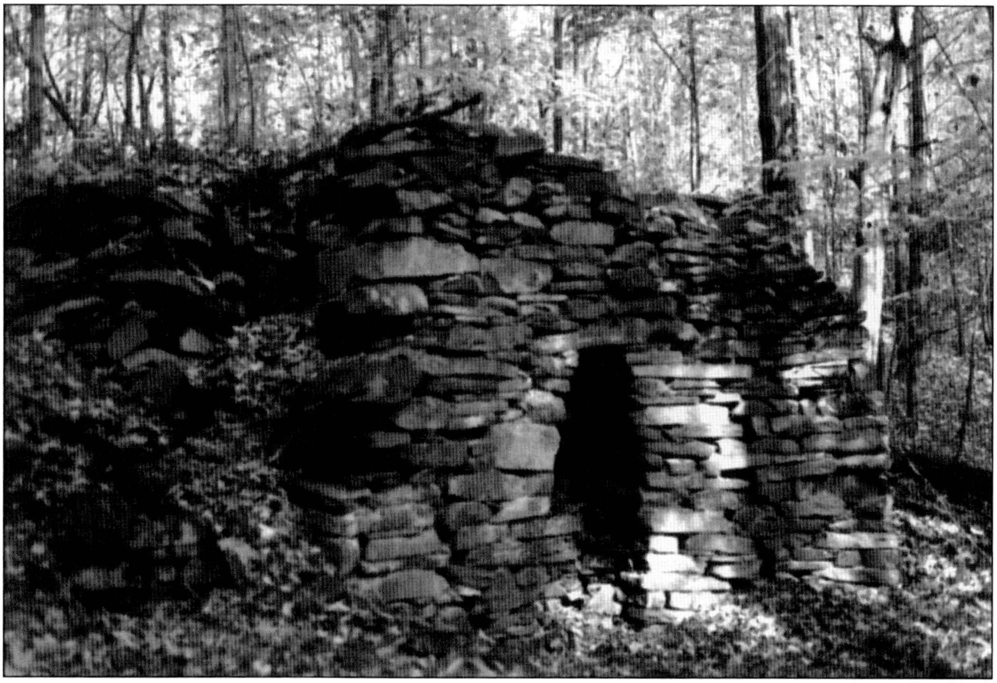

In these two photographs, two separate views are shown of a limekiln near the former Clyde Beehler home in Pocono Township. Limekilns were used to burn limestone with wood to obtain a powdered lime to put on the farm fields to increase the yield of crops. The hole in the top was used to unload the wood and limestone from the wagons. After the burning took place and the fire cooled, the lime was removed from the bottom. The small hole at the base was for draft. (Courtesy of Verdon Rustine.)

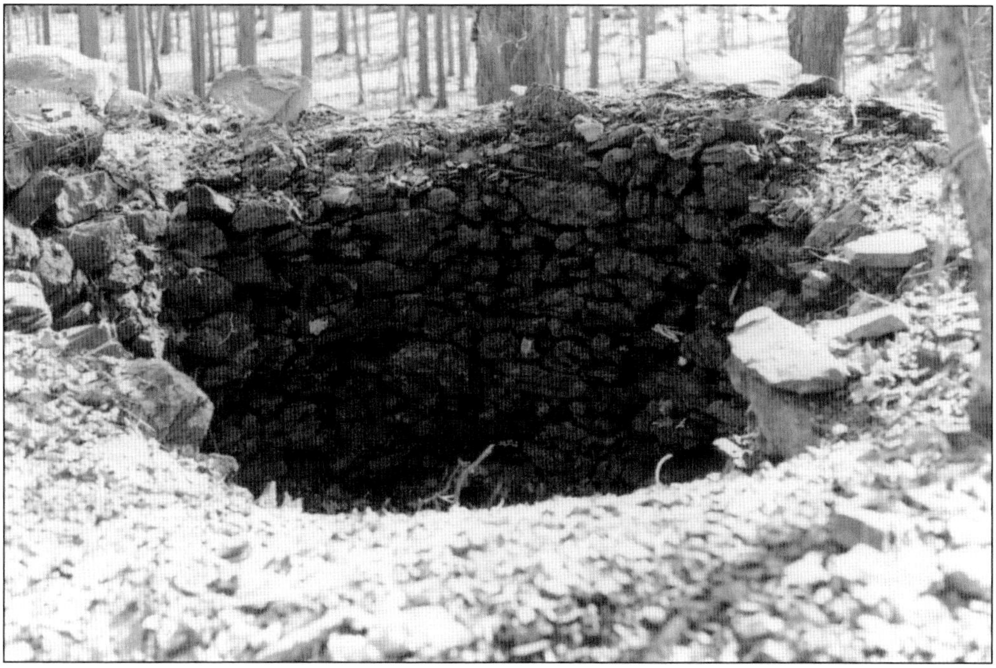

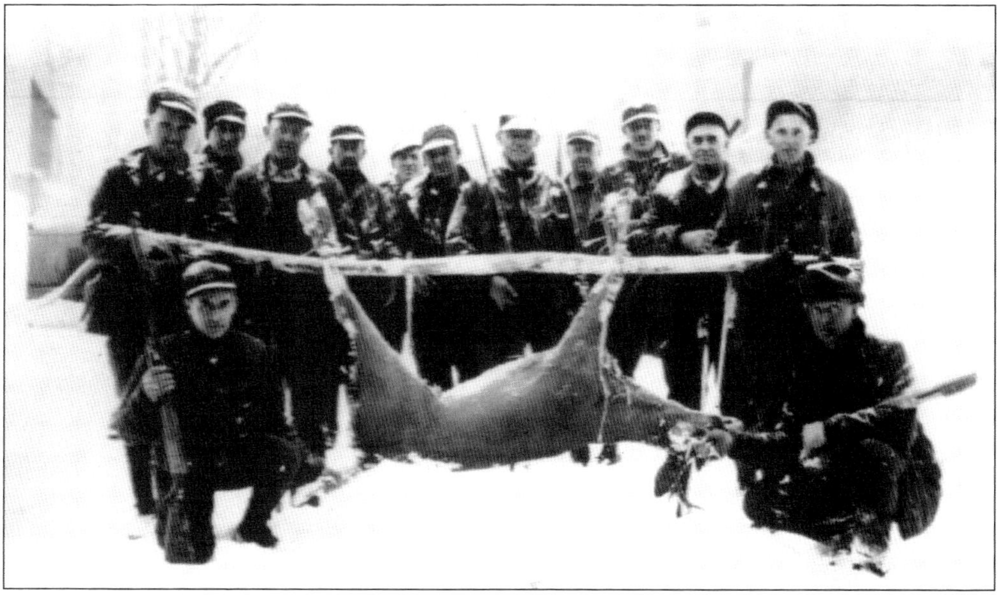

In December 1929, this Appenzell hunting party proudly posed for a photograph with its kill. Members of the hunting party included Morgan Butz, Norman Butz, Paul Hofford, Clyde Butz, James Wallingford, and Joe Rustine. (Courtesy of Robert Wallingford.)

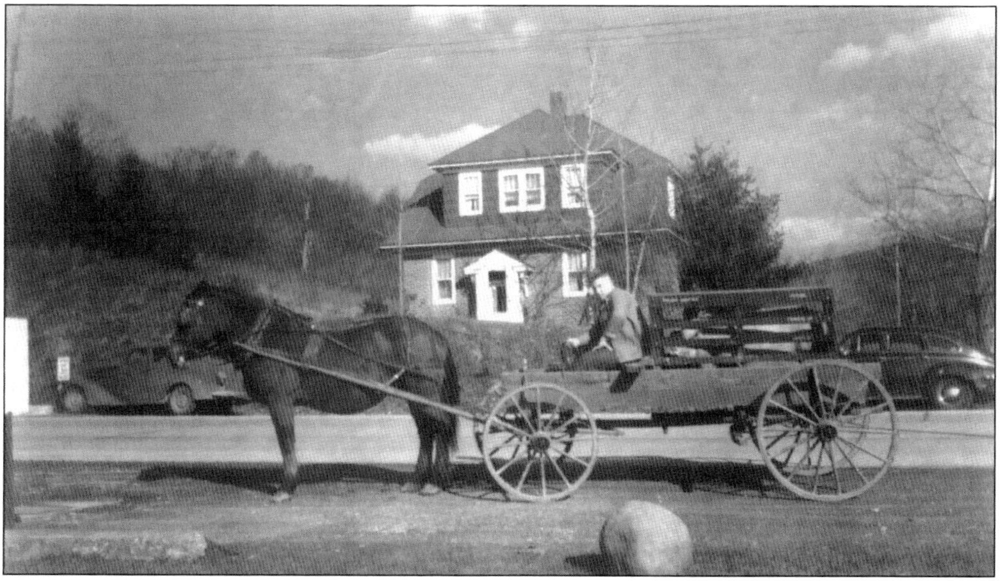

Harold Werkheiser is pictured with a sow in the crate that he is transporting for breeding. He was a member of the Future Farmers of America Club, which was offered at Pocono Township High School and mentored by John Montgomery. (Courtesy of James Price.)

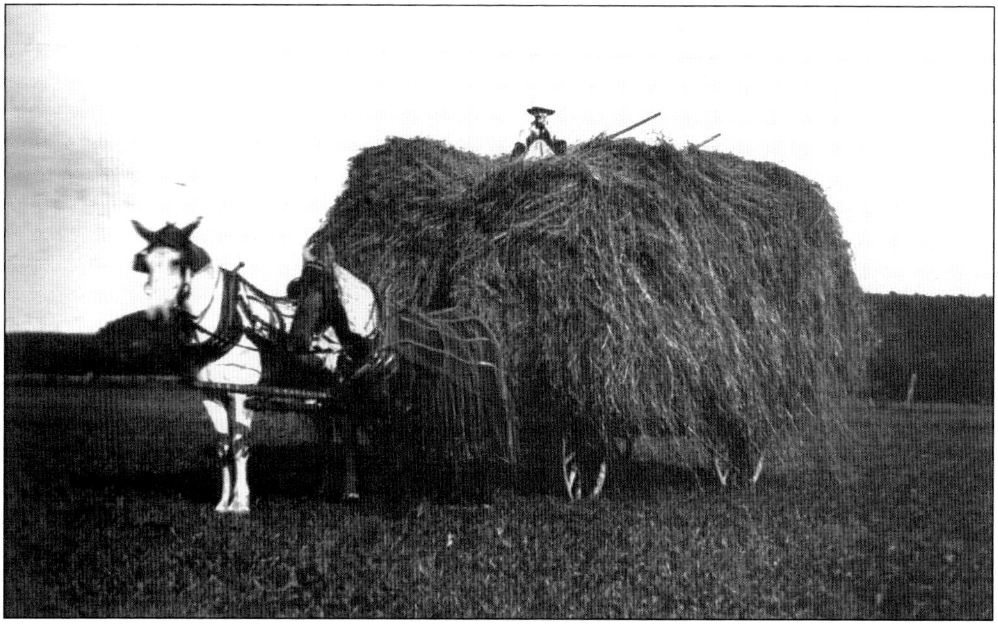

Before mechanical means were used to harvest hay, bale it, and transport it to the barn for storage, wagons such as this were loaded and the hay stored loosely in the barn. The horses are draped with fly nets. Evelyn Paul Wallingford is atop the hay wagon that is pulled by horses owned by her brother, Herman Paul. (Courtesy of Robert Wallingford.)

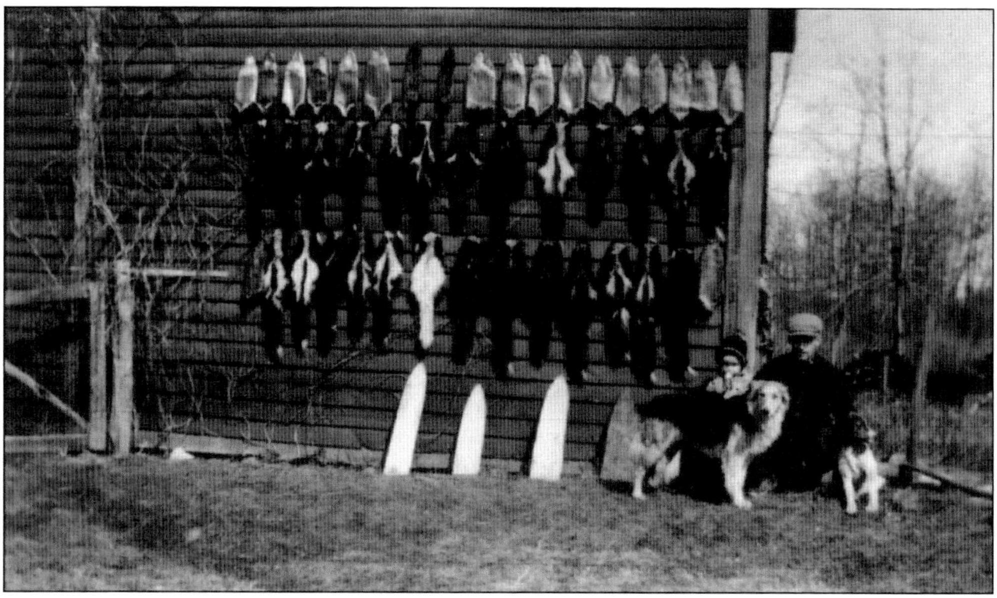

During the fall and winter, James Wallingford trapped fur-bearing animals, which he then sold. The skunks brought various prices. The pelts with the greatest amount of white fur brought the least amount of cash. (Courtesy of Robert Wallingford.)

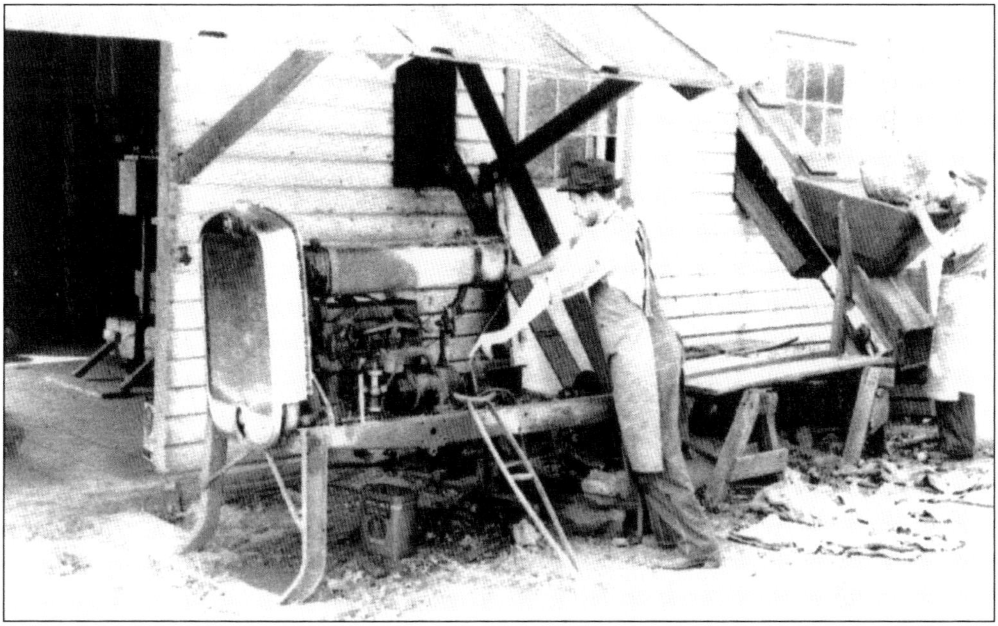

James Heller, operator of the cider mill in Appenzell, is adjusting the automobile engine that is used to crush the apples (above). His assistant is dumping apples into the hopper for transport to the grinder. In the photograph below, they are shown inside the mill, spreading apples on cloth pads in preparation for the squeezing of apple cider from the pulp. (Courtesy of Verdon Rustine.)

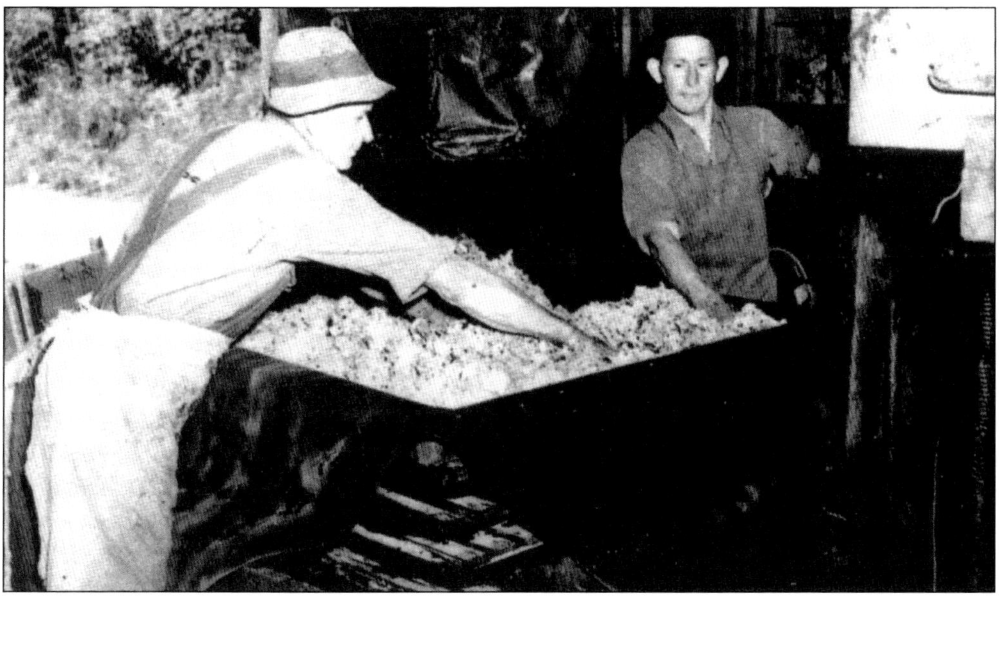

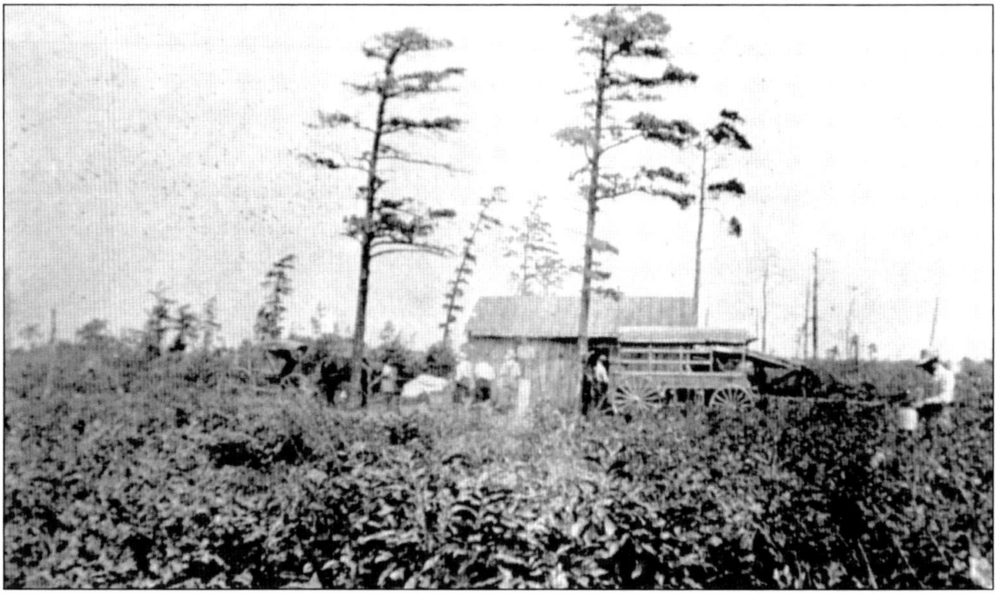

Blueberries were a valuable crop that was shipped by train to city markets. In this photograph are the harvesters picking the blueberries and a wagon used not only to transport the blueberries to market but also to carry the pickers back and forth to the location for the day. The mountain was deliberately burned every few years to promote growth of the blueberry bushes. (Courtesy of the Pocono-Jackson Historical Society.)

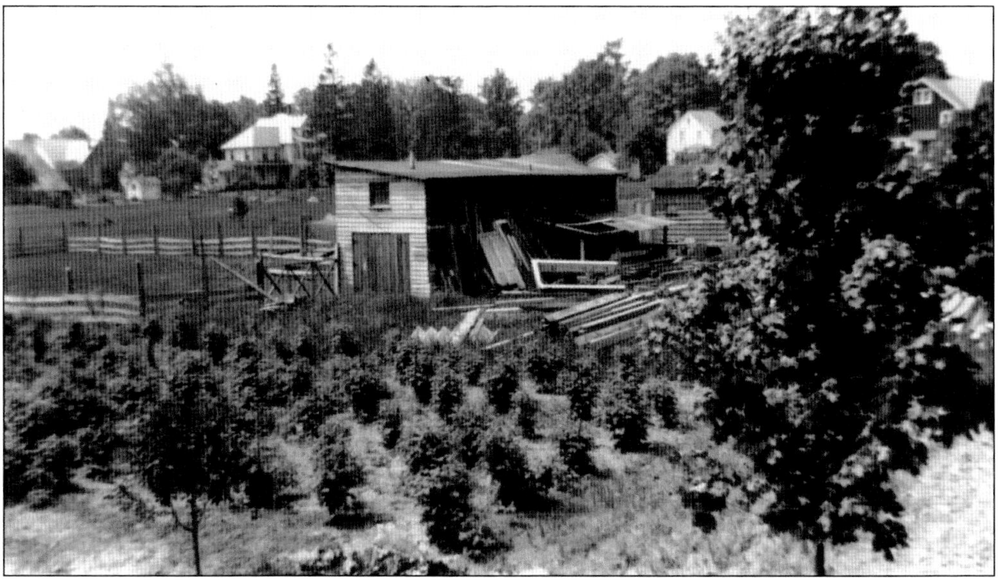

Richard Peechatka maintained a large raspberry patch on his father's property on present-day Route 715N. St. Paul's Lutheran Church can be seen to the far left in the photograph just south of the Wertman home. (Courtesy of Richard Peechatka.)

Nine

FAMILIES

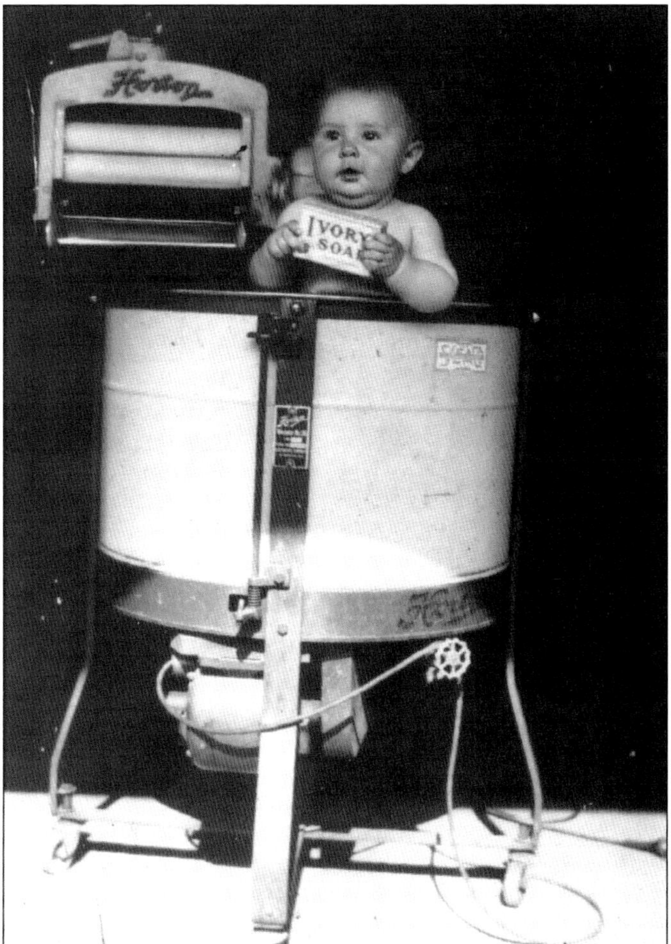

Clyde Wallingford is shown in this photograph taken in 1931. His family wanted to enter a contest for an advertisement for Ivory Soap. The photograph was taken in the washing machine at his father's store in Appenzell. (Courtesy of Robert Wallingford.)

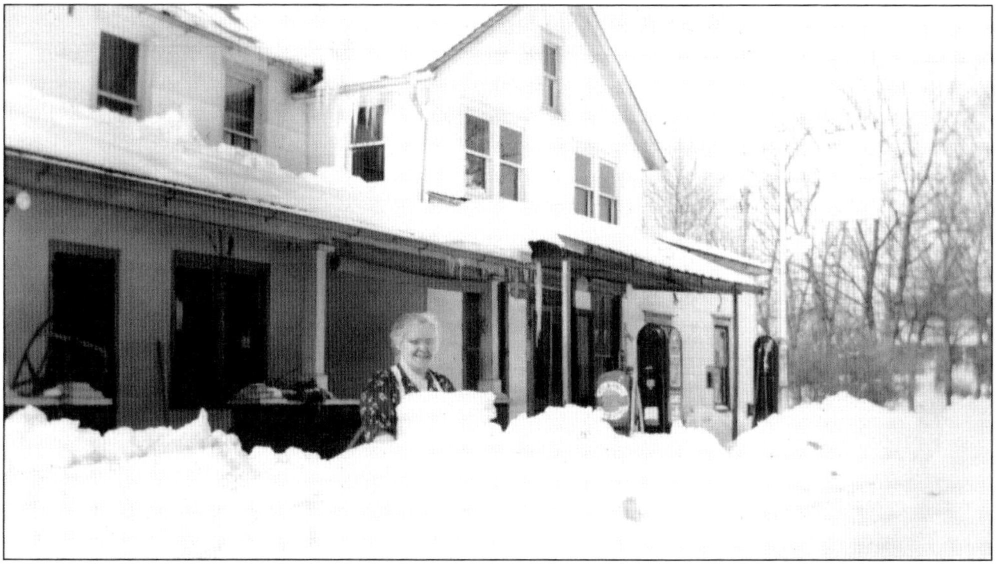

Evelyn Paul Wallingford is shown in this 1945 photograph standing in front of the Wallingford store. Wallingford was a "four-star mother," with four of her five sons serving in either the U.S. Army or U.S. Army Air Corps during World War II. (Courtesy of Robert Wallingford.)

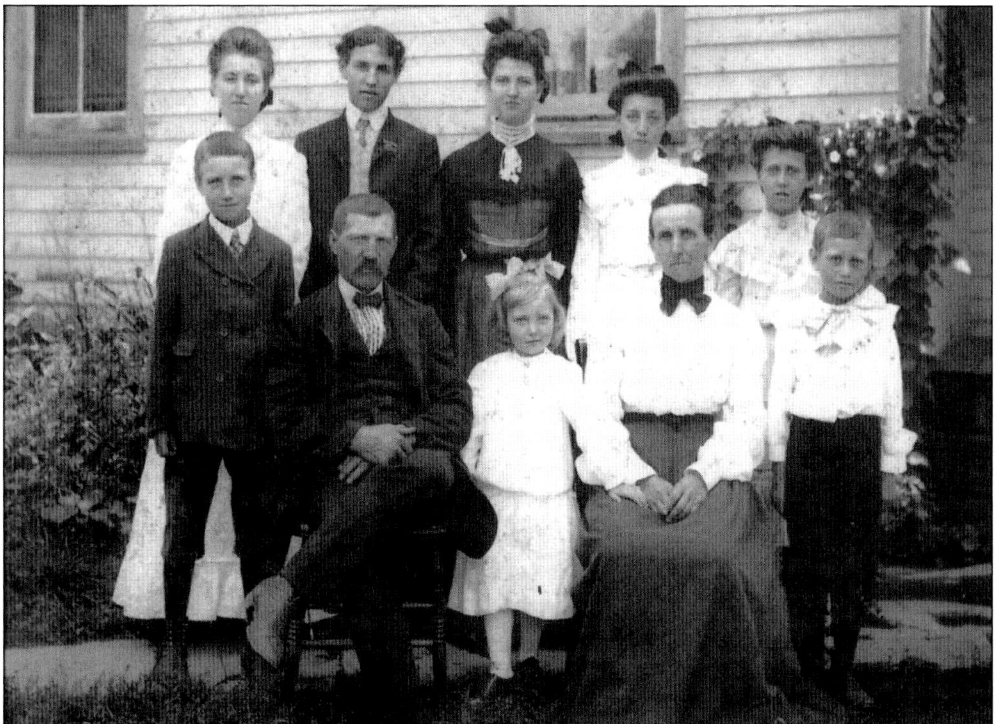

The family of Levi Miller is shown in this family portrait. Miller was an early store owner in Reeders as well as a farmer. (Courtesy of Lester Miller.)

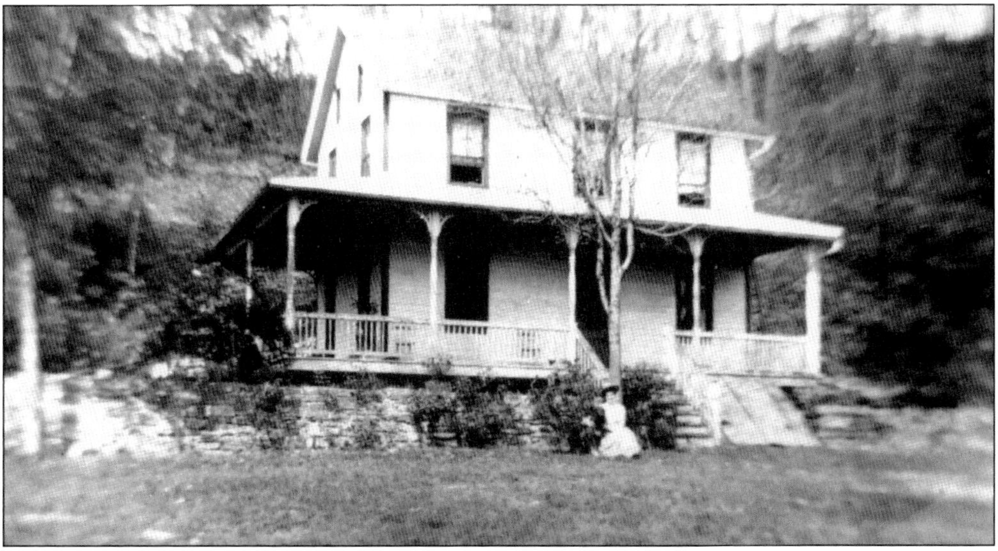

The Herman and Gesche Niering homestead was located at the base of Camelback Mountain, where Camelback Ski Resort now has its tubing park. Looking closely in front of the house, one can see a woman and boy seated on a bench. (Courtesy of Annabel Niering Peechatka.)

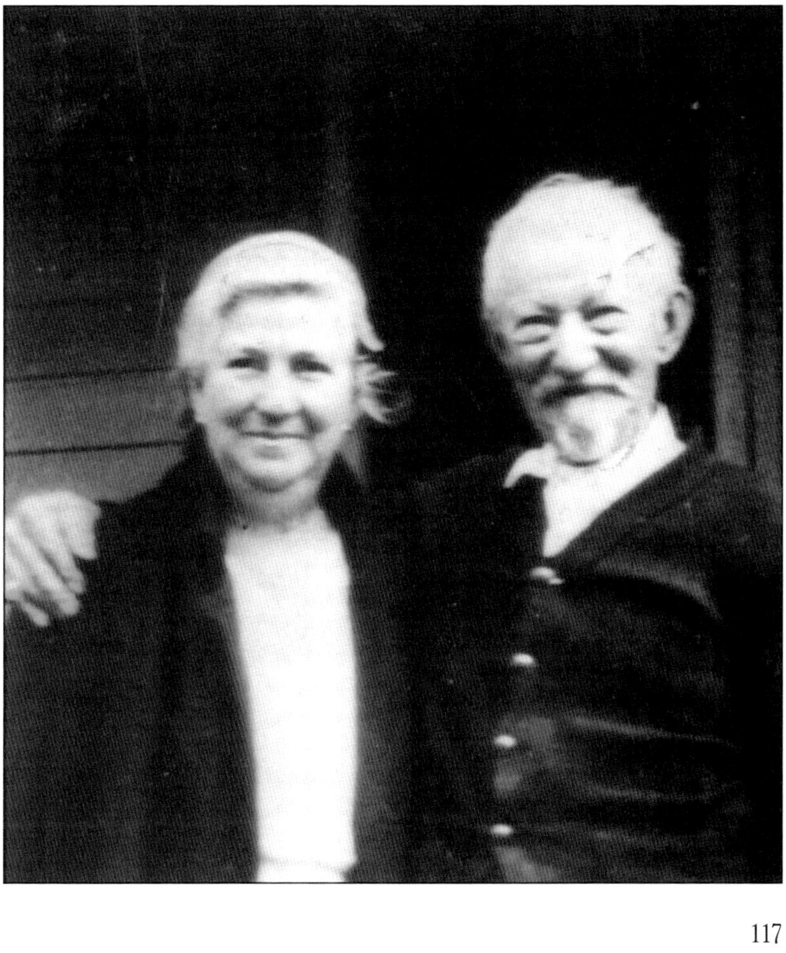

John and Anne Meiser emigrated from Germany and settled between Tannersville and Henryville, where the village Meisertown bears their family name. They raised seven daughters, each of whom operated an inn or hotel for tourists. Greenwa Lodge was one such inn. (Courtesy of Henry McCool.)

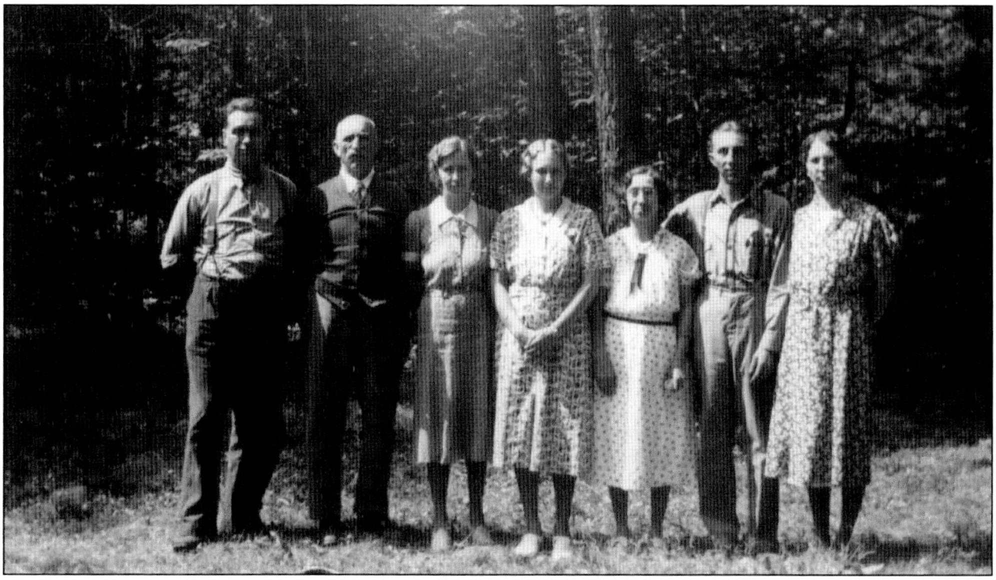

The Milton Metzger family of Reeders poses for a family photograph in 1939. Pictured are, from left to right, Edward Metzger, the first fire chief of the Pocono Township Fire Company who later became Monroe County sheriff; Milton Metzger, the father; Myra Metzger Possinger; Mabel Metzger Motz; Helen Metzger Pfeifer; Thomas Metzger, who was a partner with Edward in the Metzger Brothers Garage in Tannersville; and Alice Metzger Raitt. (Courtesy of Lois Metzger Gilbert.)

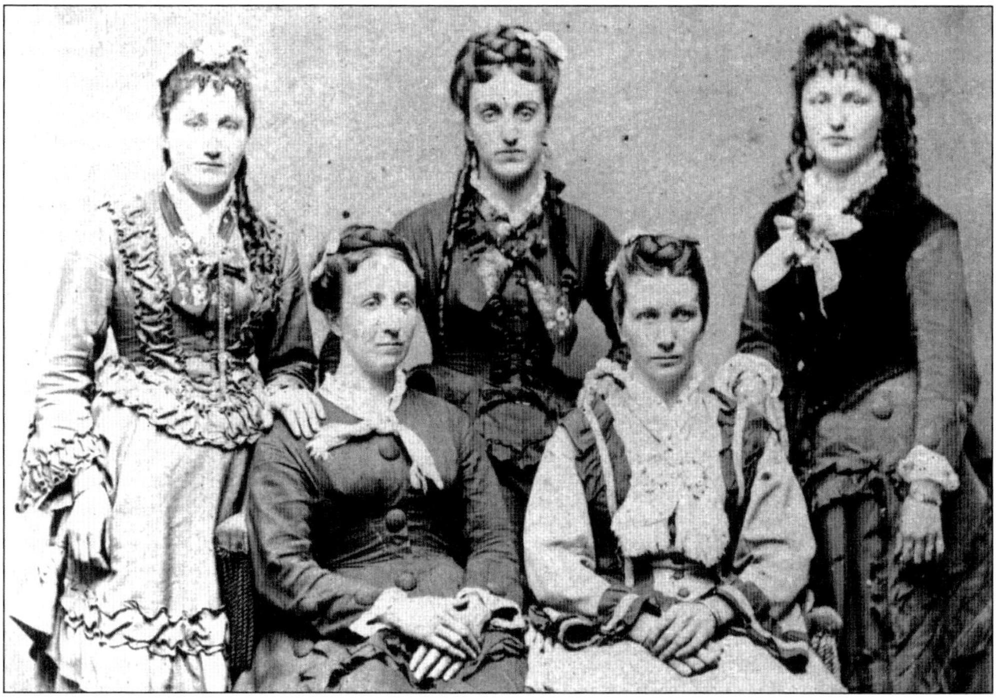

These five Reinhardt sisters posed in their finery with elaborate hairstyles. Pictured are, from left to right, (first row) Ella Schoch and Sara Wilson; (second row) Delilah Frailey, Martha Merwine, and Emma Smith. (Courtesy of Diane Davis Abeel.)

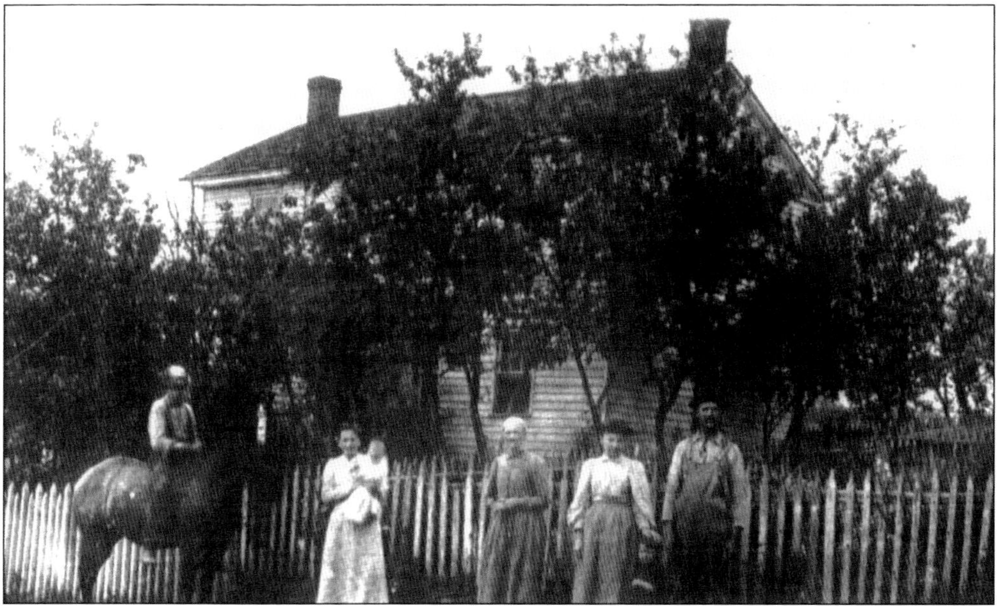

The family of Abraham Smith (on horseback) and Mary Jane Labar Smith is shown in this photograph, taken about 1895. Their daughter Emma Smith Starner, wife of John Denton Starner, is the woman holding baby Jessie. The man and woman flanking Emma's daughter Flossie are William and Margaret Smith Newhart. The house still stands on Post Hill Road in Pocono Township. (Courtesy of Marie Starner Guidry.)

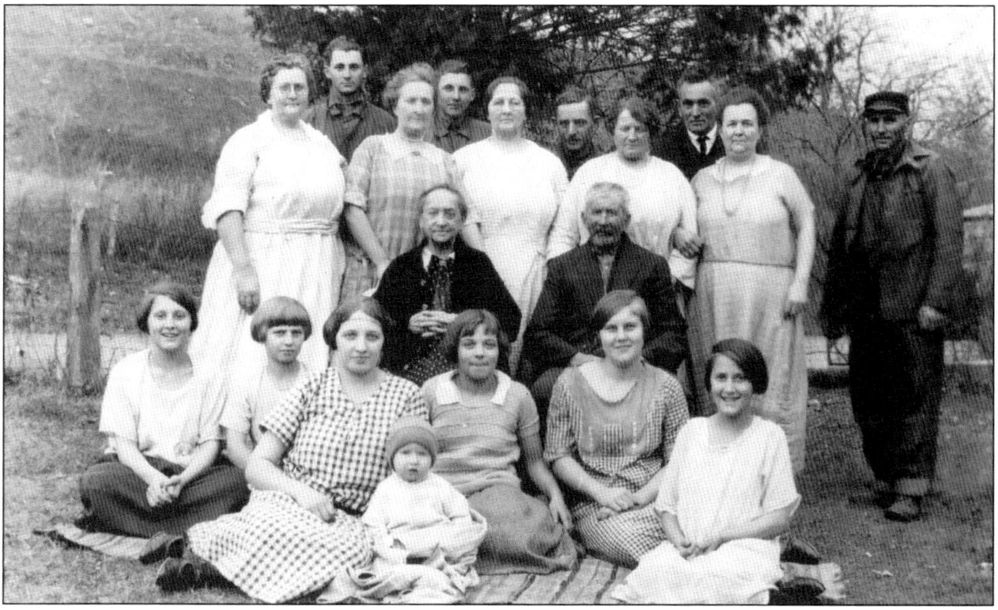

This 50th anniversary photograph captures the family of Jacob and Sarah Butz Felker. Pictured are, from left to right, (first row) Doris ?; (second row) Margaret Butz Williams, Pauline Nagle Stout, Mildred Nagle Everett, Louise Lambert, Sarah Felker Dyson, and Hazel Butz Custard; (third row) Jacob and Sarah Butz Felker; (fourth row) Nettie Felker Butz, Mary Felker Potter, Estella Felker Nagle, Nellie Felker Mosteller, Ida Felker Lambert, and Steward Butz; (fifth row) James Butz, Clyde Butz, Will Nagle, and Ora Lambert. (Courtesy of Leeanne Dyson.)

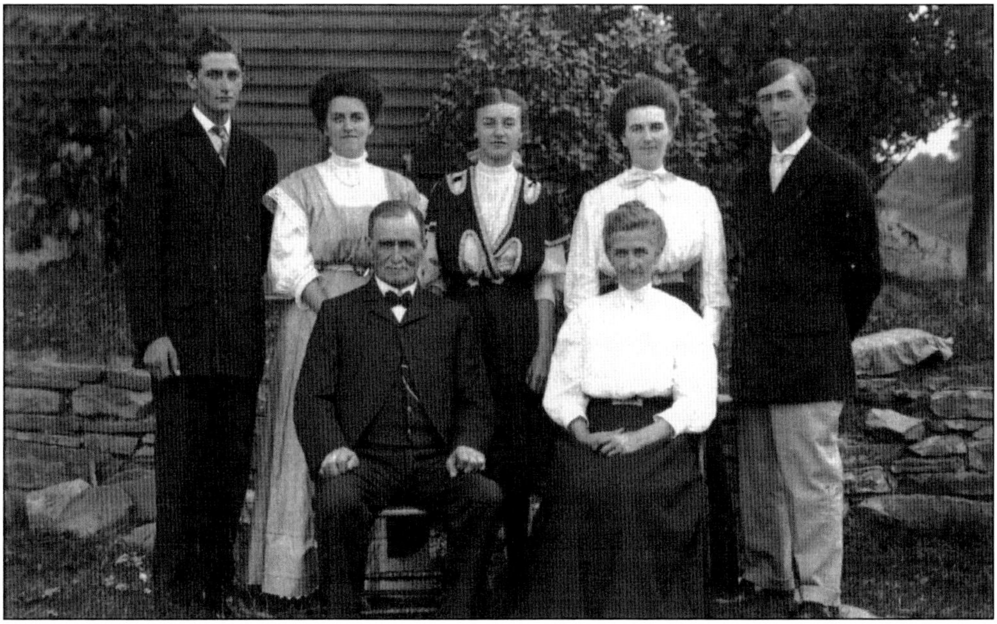

Seen in this photograph is the Samuel Shook family of Bartonsville. Shook purchased the 94-acre farm in 1892 for $1,850. Prior to taking up residence on the farm, the Shook family managed the hotel in Snydersville and the Pocono Hotel in Tannersville. Pictured are, from left to right, (first row) Samuel Shook (1847–1910) and his wife Martha (1856–1912); (second row) children Rodgers (1889–1983), Daisy (1883–1974), Anna (1895–1976), Mabel (1884–1974), and Joseph (1890–1945). (Courtesy of John Alleger.)

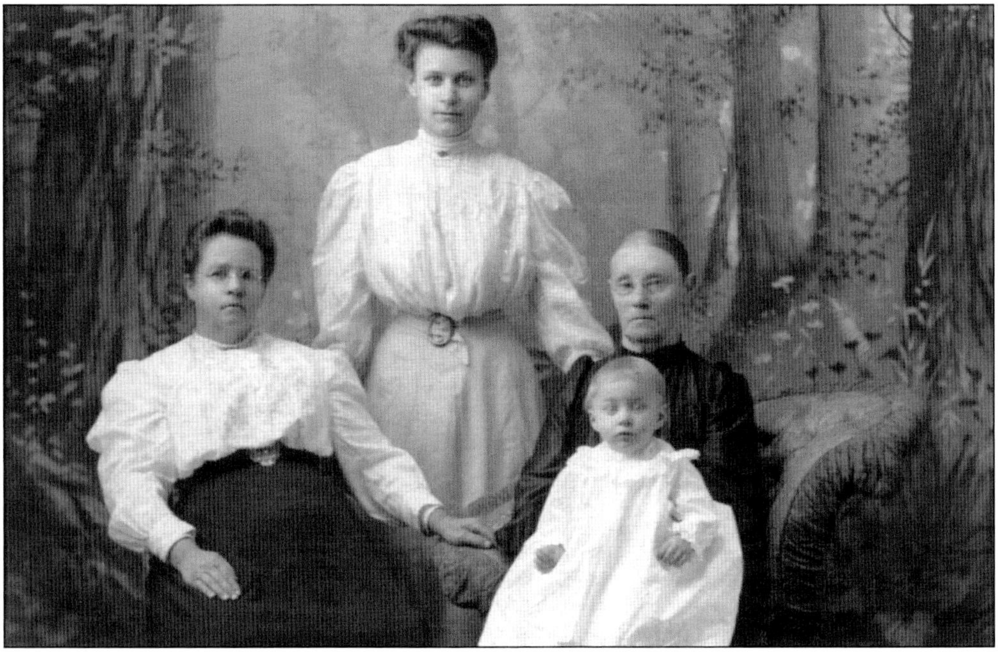

This photograph shows four generations. Lydia Kresge, age 78, is holding her great-granddaughter Emma Dunbar, age 1½. Kresge's daughter Emma Kresge Halstead, age 49, is the mother of Nettie Halstead Dunbar, age 21. (Courtesy of Leeanne Dyson.)

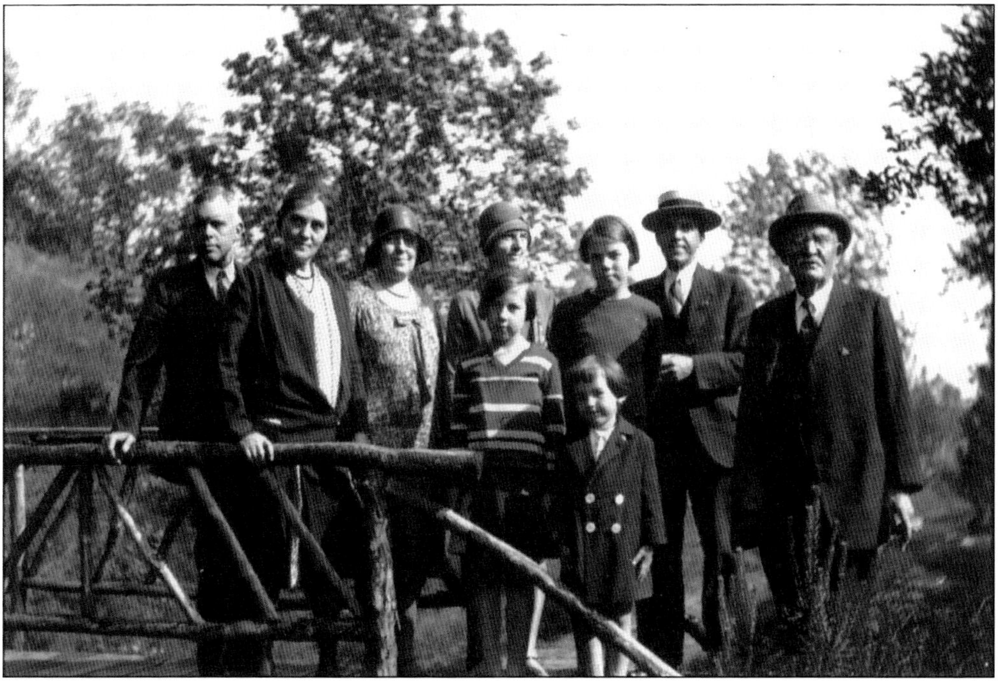

George Kerst and his descendants are pictured on the bridge across Scotrun Creek behind the Kerst/Heckman home in Scotrun. (Courtesy of Linford Werkheiser.)

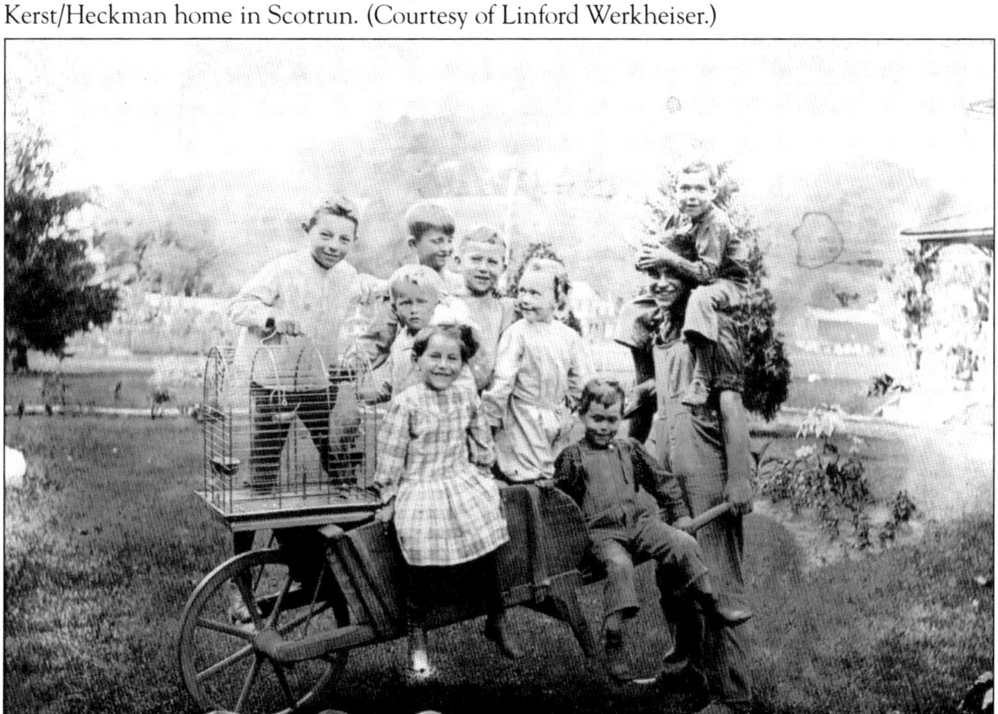

George Learn Sr. is holding the birdcage while the kids are having a wheelbarrow ride. Walt Sebring is trying to push while John Sebring is riding piggyback. Note the hats on the ground in the lower front of the picture. (Courtesy of George Learn.)

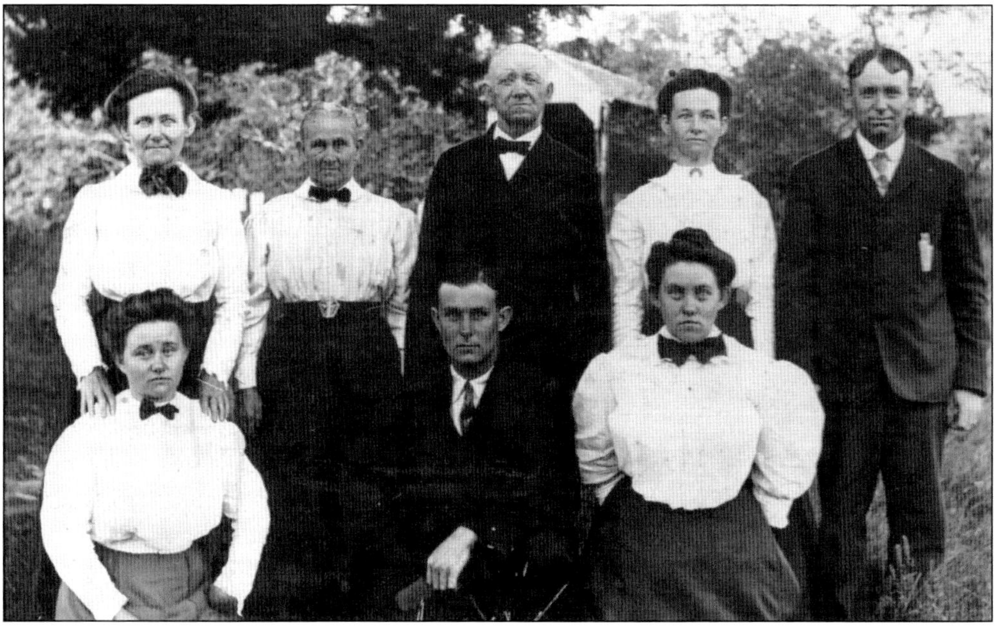

The Werkheiser family is shown in this photograph. From left to right are (first row) Hattie Werkheiser Hay, Lavere Werkheiser, and Bertha Werkheiser Felker; (second row) Emma Werkheiser Kulp, Lydia Werkheiser Werkheiser, Jacob Werkheiser, Mary Werkheiser Steen, and Peter Werkheiser. (Courtesy of Leeanne Dyson.)

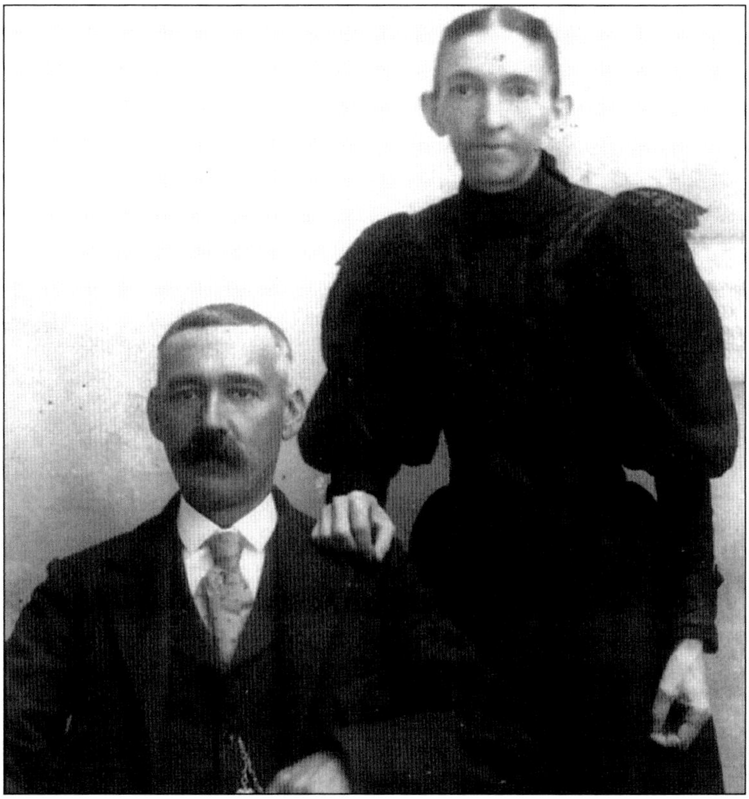

Emanuel Hay was an early landowner of several farms along the present-day Hay Road. He was a jack-of-all-trades who was able to fix waterwheels and musical instruments. He also dug water wells. He and his wife, Lydia, posed in their finery for this portrait. (Courtesy of Lester Miller.)

Ten

This and That

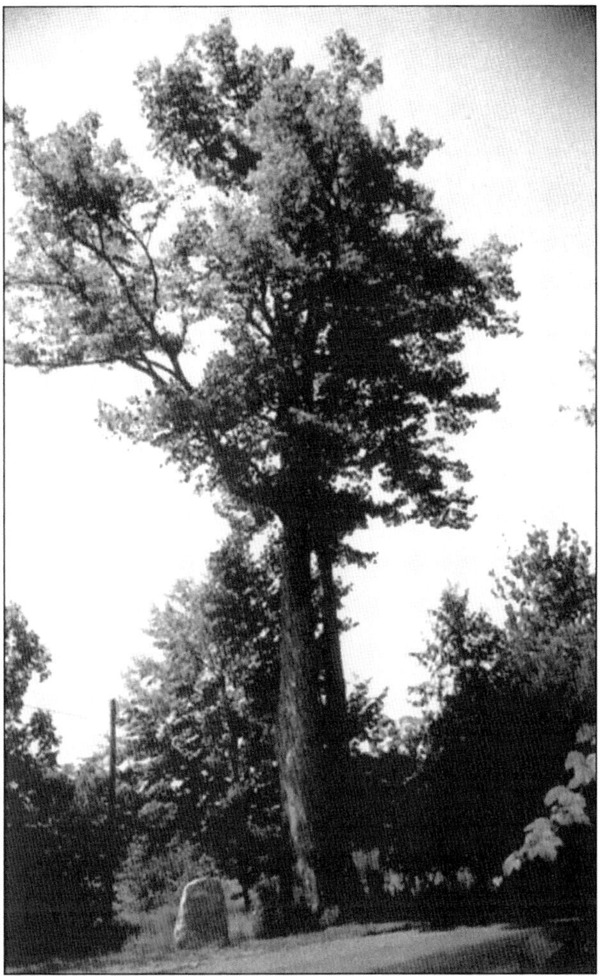

On April 25, 1947, this basswood tree, or American linden tree, was recorded in the American big trees report. Estimated to have started growing over 300 years ago, the tree recently succumbed to old age. (Courtesy of the Pocono-Jackson Historical Society.)

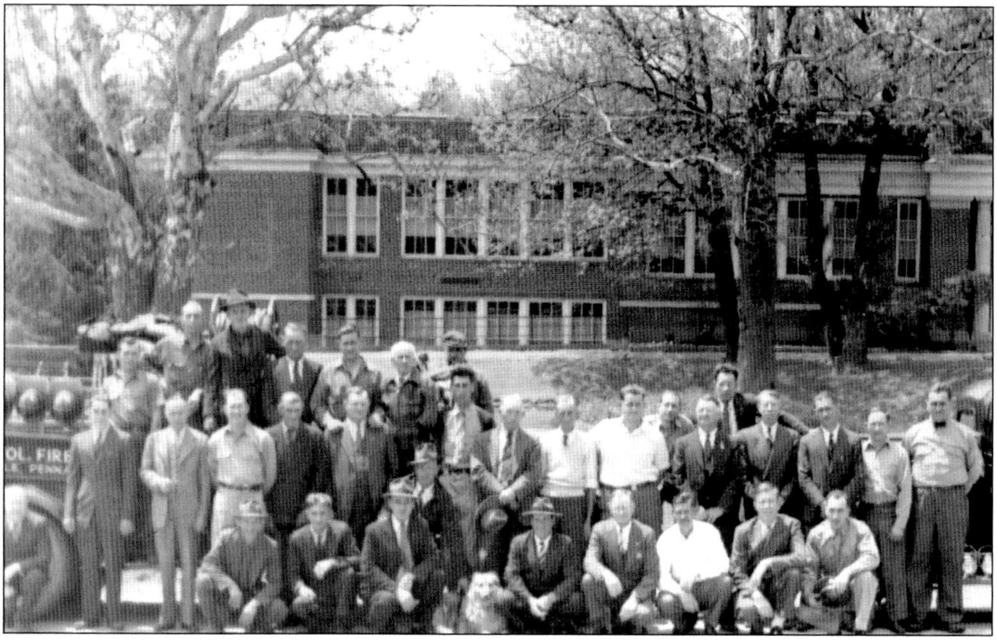

The Pocono Township Fire Company was founded in 1940. The photograph above was taken in front of the Pocono Township School. Pictured are Floyd Houck, Frank Turner, Raymond Butz, Lady the dog, Sterling Setzer, Rodgers Shook, Paul Shaffer, O. Richard Howell, Arlett Butz, Harold Bossard, Robert Setzer, Dr. George Zehner, Clifford Werkheiser, Herb Anglemyer, Layton Lambert, Russell DeHaven, Charles B. Hartman, Miles Dailey, John Smiley, Carl Miller, Harry Werkheiser, Lewis B. Sebring, Benjamin Howell, John Zugel, Kenneth Starner, Edward Metzger, Robert Starner, Thomas Metzger, George Raish, Russell Werkheiser, Ira Hay, and Herb Shick. In the photograph below, Edward Metzger (left), the fire chief, and George Raish, the president, stand next to the first fire truck. Luther Keller's restaurant is on the right, and the mill wheel to the left of Metzger was in his backyard for many years. (Above, courtesy of O. Richard Howell; below, courtesy of George Learn.)

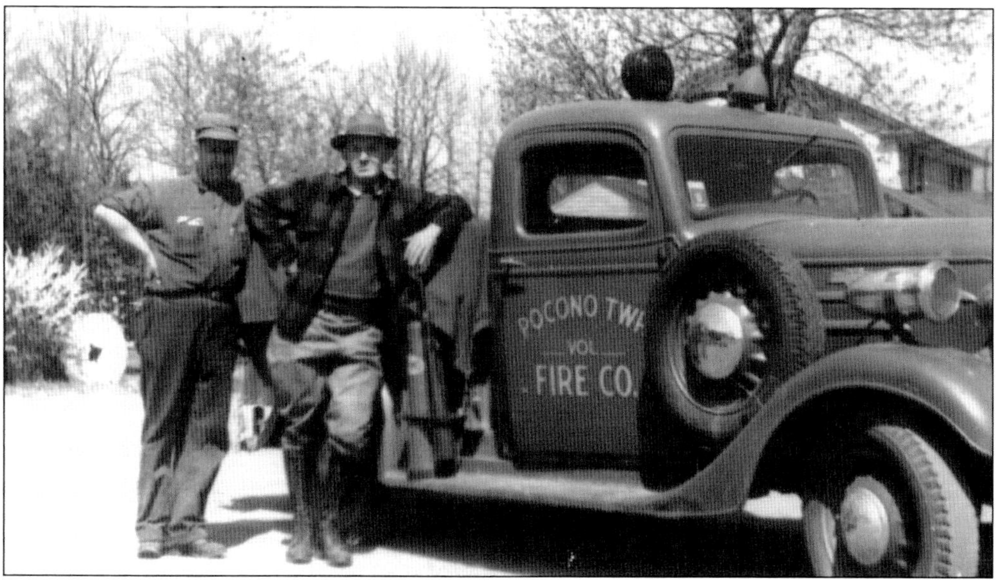

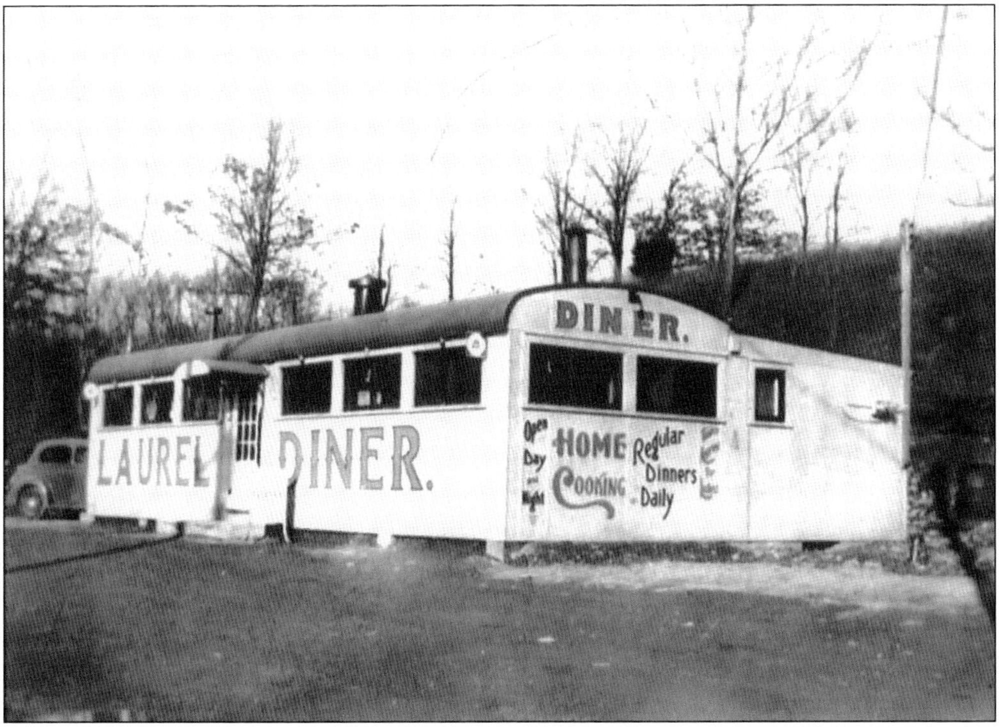

Bill and Effie Woodling Roberts owned the Laurel Diner, which was moved from old Route 611 opposite the Tannersville Graded School and the Methodist cemetery to a new location on the three-lane Route 611, where present-day Fountain Court is located. It was then operated by Walter and Cora Werkheiser Sebring and later by Grover Hay until it was torn down in the early 1970s. (Courtesy of James Price.)

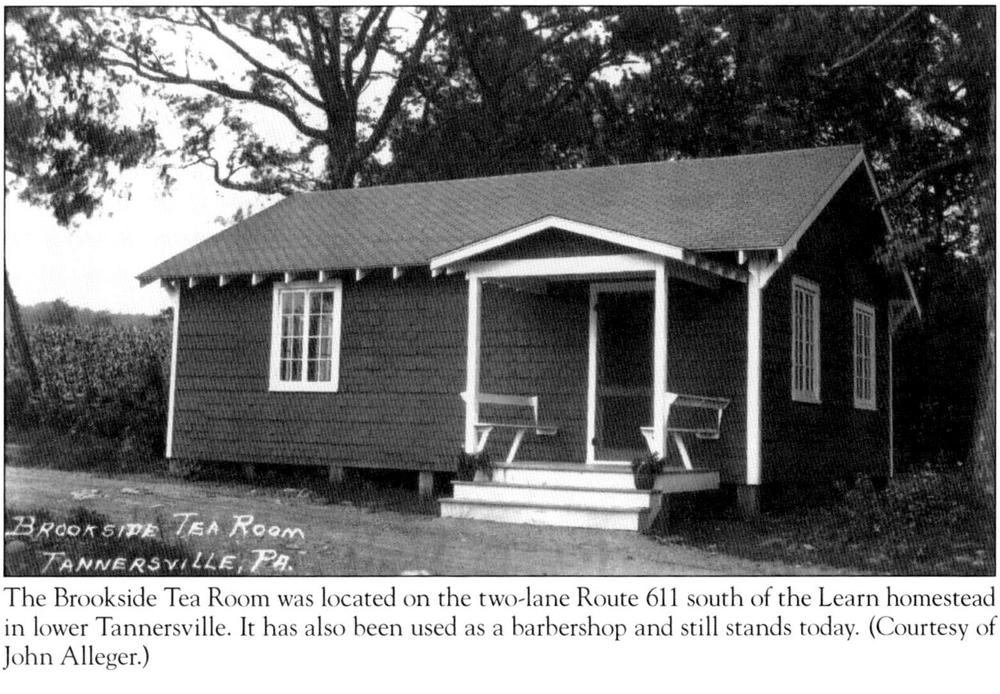

The Brookside Tea Room was located on the two-lane Route 611 south of the Learn homestead in lower Tannersville. It has also been used as a barbershop and still stands today. (Courtesy of John Alleger.)

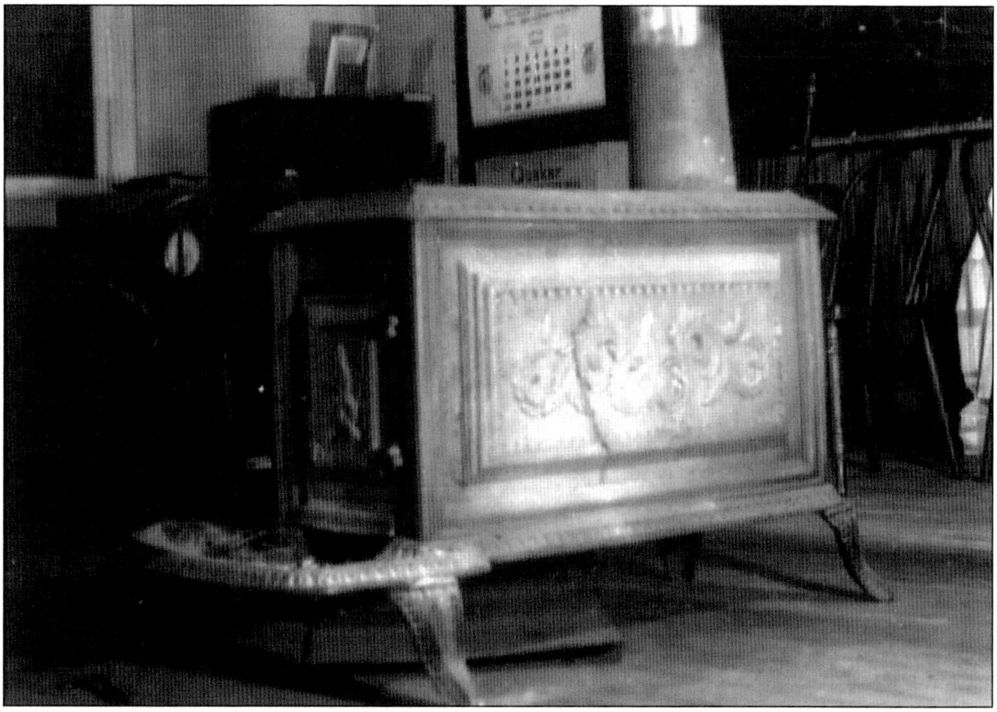

This stove was once used for heating the graded school located in Tannersville along old Route 611. The stove was removed from the building before it was demolished and now is in the restored Appenzell one-room schoolhouse. (Courtesy of O. Richard Howell.)

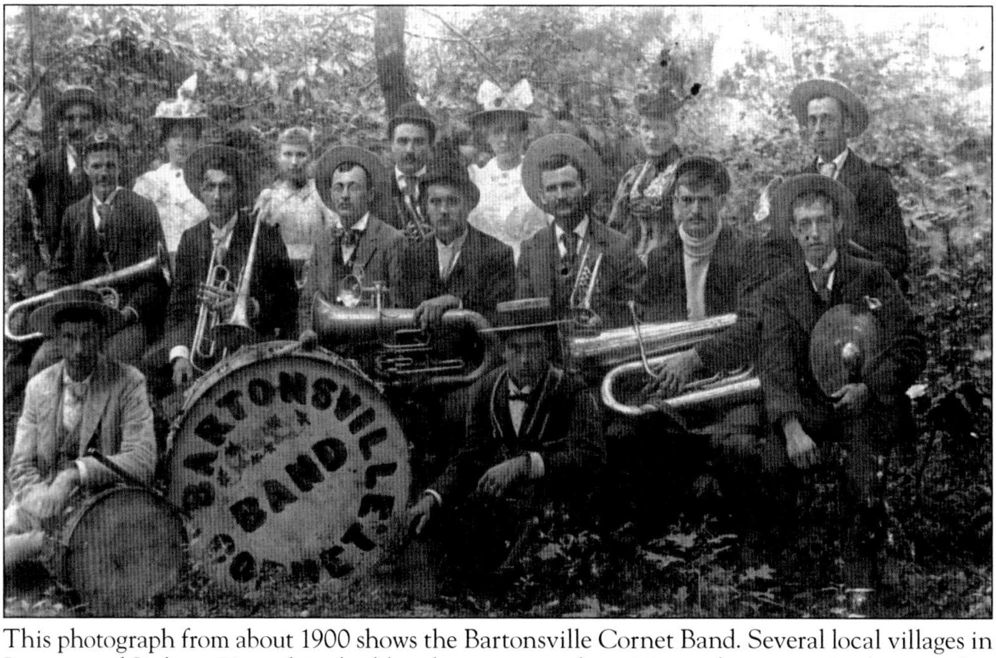

This photograph from about 1900 shows the Bartonsville Cornet Band. Several local villages in Pocono and Jackson Townships had bands or groups of musicians who entertained at parades, church functions, and community events. The most widely known and long lived of these musical organizations was Tannersville's Glenwood Hall Band. (Courtesy of John Alleger.)

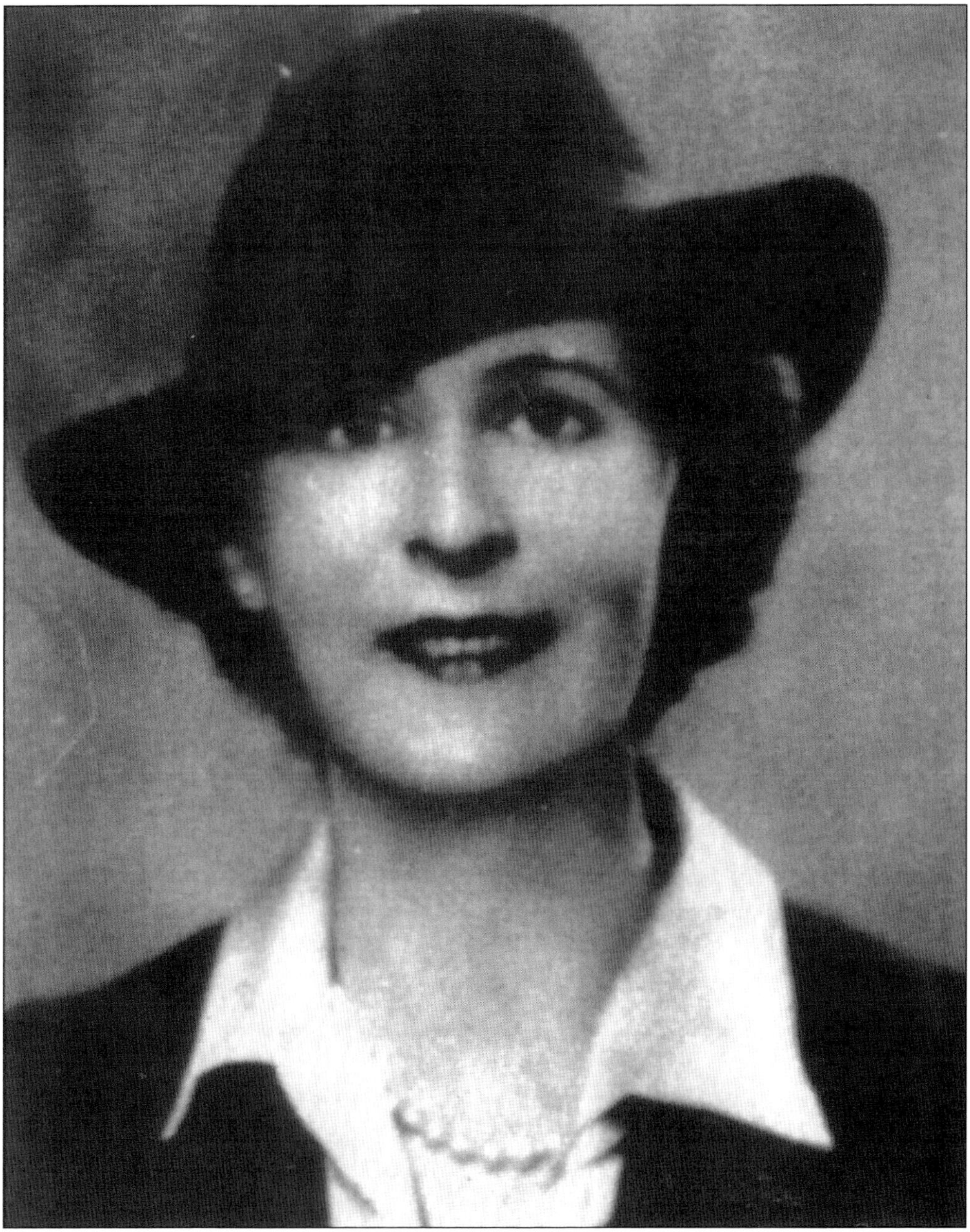

Clara Grabau Adams was the great-niece of former German president Paul von Hindenburg and a world-renowned air traveler. Her air travel firsts included the 1928 *Graf Zeppelin* transatlantic flight, the *Hindenburg* in 1935, and a Pan American around-the-world flight in 1939. In 1923, her husband, George Adams, built her the house known as Dr. Horn's. When her husband died in 1937, she moved to Long Island. She died in 1971. (Courtesy of James Werkheiser.)